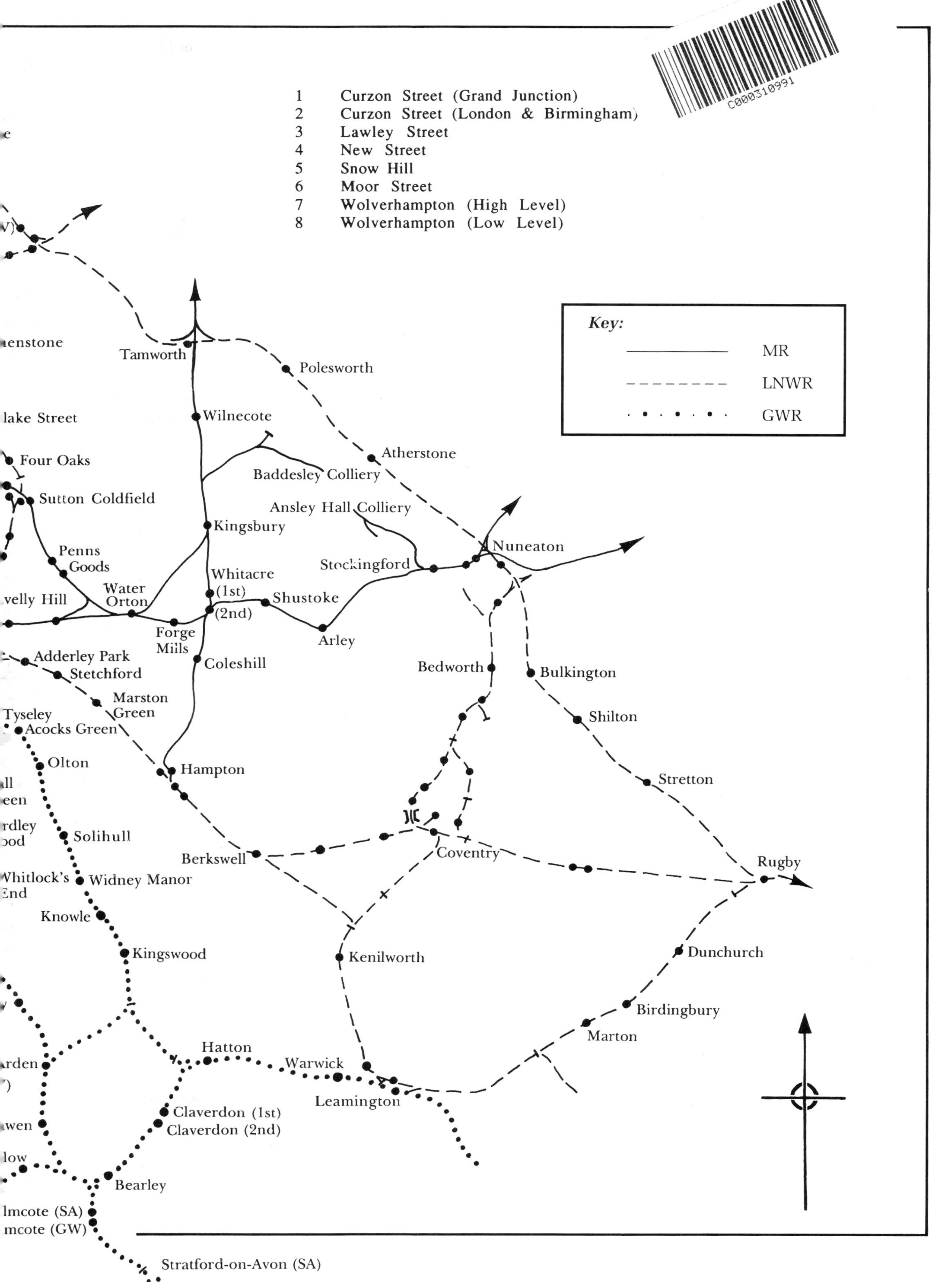

1 Curzon Street (Grand Junction)
2 Curzon Street (London & Birmingham)
3 Lawley Street
4 New Street
5 Snow Hill
6 Moor Street
7 Wolverhampton (High Level)
8 Wolverhampton (Low Level)
Key:
MR
LNWR
GWR
Tamworth
Polesworth
Wilnecote
lake Street
Four Oaks
Sutton Coldfield
Baddesley Colliery
Atherstone
Ansley Hall Colliery
Kingsbury
Nuneaton
Penns Goods
Stockingford
Whitacre (1st)
(2nd)
Water Orton
Shustoke
Arley
Forge Mills
Adderley Park
Stetchford
Coleshill
Bedworth
Bulkington
Marston Green
Tyseley
Acocks Green
Shilton
Olton
Hampton
Stretton
Solihull
Berkswell
Coventry
Rugby
Widney Manor
Knowle
Kingswood
Kenilworth
Dunchurch
Birdingbury
Marton
Hatton
Warwick
Leamington
Claverdon (1st)
Claverdon (2nd)
Bearley
Stratford-on-Avon (SA)

BRITAIN'S RAIL SUPER CENTRES

BIRMINGHAM

BRITAIN'S RAIL SUPER CENTRES

BIRMINGHAM

PAUL COLLINS

IAN ALLAN Publishing

First published 1992

ISBN 0 7110 2005 1

Published by Ian Allan Ltd, Shepperton, Surrey; and printed by Ian Allan Printing Ltd at their works at Coombelands in Runnymede, England.

Contents

Front cover:
Railfreight Class 90 No 90042 awaits its next duty at Birmingham New Street station on 7 July 1990. *Chris Morrison*

Front cover (inset):
The glory of the old Snow Hill station as a 'King' arrives with an up train in 1961. The last 'King' diagrams serving Snow Hill disappeared in September 1962.
Michael Mensing

Rear cover (top):
Centro liveried Class 150 Nos 150113/150116 depart from Birmingham New Street with the replacement 11.06 service to Reading on 29 June 1991. *Hugh Ballantyne*

Rear cover (bottom):
In 1960, prior to New Street's modernisation and electrification, Class 5 No 44716 awaits departure with an east-bound train. *Michael Mensing*

Previous page:
Few shots could emphasise the fact that InterCity 125s now run through New Street better than this posed publicity one taken in connection with their launch on the 'Heart Line of Britain' route on 17 May 1982.
British Rail

Right:
Stanier Pacific locomotive No 46235 was named *City of Birmingham*. Like certain others of its class this was built with full streamlining which was removed just after World War 2. Here the modified locomotive is seen having its nameplate replaced at Crewe Works on 25 April 1946. *City of Birmingham* now has pride of place in the locomotive hall at Birmingham Museum of Science & Industry. *LMS*

Introduction

Birmingham is 111 miles northwest of London, 81 miles southeast of Manchester and 110 miles south of Leeds. It is the country's second city in terms of population, and its centre with regard to industry and transport.

Birmingham's name is derived from Anglo-Saxon dialect, indicating that the area now occupied by the city was once the *ham* or 'home' of the 'followers' (or *inga*) of *Berm*: The *'Berm inga's ham'*. A 'Bermingeham' was recorded in Domesday in 1086, with a population of 60, and land and property worth just 20 shillings. Around 1166, Henry I granted the Lord of the Manor, Peter de Bermingham, the right to hold a weekly market. The de Bermingham's reigned over the town for four centuries, until 1529, when the young Edward de Bermingham was deprived of the Manor by his guardian, through involvement in a robbery from one of his tenants. During the Civil War the town sided with the Parliamentary cause. Much of its involvement centred around Aston Hall, where Charles I rested en route to the Battle of Edgehill in 1642, and which was besieged for three days in 1643.

Industrial activity fostered the coming of the canals and railways, bringing increased prosperity; enabling the Town Council to initiate a series of 'improvements', which led to the setting out of the Victorian city seen today. Birmingham was incorporated as a Borough on 1 November 1838. From that date the enterprise of the Town Council, most notably after Joseph Chamberlain entered public life in 1869, was remarkable. This was formally recognised on 14 January 1889, when Queen Victoria raised the town to the status of a city, and again in 1896, when Her Majesty granted the title of Lord Mayor to its Chief Magistrate. Outlying boroughs were soon added to the city boundaries: Saltley, Little Bromwich, Harborne and Balsall Heath joining in 1891; Quinton in 1909; Aston Manor, Erdington, King's Norton, Northfield and Yardley in 1911; Perry Barr in 1928; Castle Bromwich and Sheldon in 1929, and Sutton Coldfield in 1974.

Notable people with Birmingham connections include the famous members of the town's Lunar Society: John Baskerville, James Watt, Matthew Boulton, William Murdoch, Joseph Priestley; the politicians Joseph & Neville Chamberlain, and many of Britain's best loved entertainers, including the comedians Sid Field and Tony Hancock.

Following World War 2, Birmingham became notorious for the wholesale redevelopment it wrought upon itself. This began with the widening of Digbeth in 1954/55 and continued with the building of the Inner Ring Road (1959-71); Bull Ring Shopping Centre (1964); the rebuilding of New Street Station (1963-67) and the Newtown, Nechells, Lee Brook, Highgate and Ladywood housing schemes; all of which were symbolized by one building, a cylindrical office block called the Rotunda (1965). Some felt the city had entered the 1960s at the expense of its character, but 25 years on, both the Rotunda and Bull Ring Centre are themselves under threat from redevelopment, and the Council has belatedly woken-up to its heritage with the enhancement of the city's Jewellery Quarter. But the redevelopment continues apace, with the setting out of Centenary Square and the building of the International Convention Centre and its associated National Indoor Arena, which swept away many fine buildings in Broad Street.

Writing in the first edition of his history of Birmingham in 1780, William Hutton observed that: 'Birmingham may be considered as one vast and modern edifice, of which the ancient materials make but a very small part; the extensive new seems to surround the minute old, as if to protect it'. The intervening 200 years have made very little difference to this it would seem.

Acknowledgements

This book, indeed my whole interest in railways, stems from a rail journey into Birmingham. On 3 November 1978 I was travelling to the University there from Stourbridge Junction. The 09.06 train was late, and upon arrival was announced as being 'for Birmingham only'. It duly departed, setting off, not along the familiar route through Lye, Cradley, etc, but across Stambermill viaduct, through Dudley and Wednesbury to Walsall, where it reversed and worked into New Street via Aston. In two hours I had been carried on, over and through, lines, bridges and tunnels which previously had only been disconnected features of my local townscape; suddenly they were all united. I had to know more. Just how much more, you, the reader, can discover on the following pages. Before going on to name those who have helped me with the research for this book, I would once again like to place on record this writer's gratitude for the work of the late C. R. Clinker, whose numerous publications have proved so useful to me, and to couple these thanks with the name of the late George Dow, whose carefully annotated information files, preserved by British Rail, have been the source of many an obscure fact, which I had no hope of finding otherwise.

I am grateful to the following individuals, organizations, societies and journals without whose help this book would not have been possible: Apple (UK) Ltd; Birmingham Reference Library; Branch Line Society; Brierley Hill Library; Brierley Office Products Ltd; British Rail (London Midland Region) Public Affairs Department; Ray Bullock; Roger Carpenter; Celtip Computers Ltd; Centro; Tom Cockeram; June Collins; county record offices at Stafford, Warwick and Worcester; John Dawson; Dunns Photographic Services Ltd; Robin Etherington; John Fallon; Pete Glews; Mellanie Hartland; Keith Hodgkins; Ironbridge Gorge Museum; Ironbridge Institute; Stuart King; Michael Mensing; *Modern Railways*; National Railway Museum; Neil Pitts; Don Powell; John Powell; Public Record Office, Kew; *Railway Gazette*; *Railway Magazine*; *Railway Observer*; *Railway World*; *Trains Illustrated*; Barrie Trinder; University of Birmingham; Michael Vanns; Michael Walker; Shelley White; Margaret Wilson; WMPTE, and to any others I may have inadvertently failed to mention.

Paul Collins Wollaston, Stourbridge, West Midlands

1: Birmingham - Its Character and Development

Unlike many other centres, Birmingham does not possess any great natural advantages. Its rise must therefore largely be ascribed to the enterprise and initiative of its inhabitants, which, combined with their adaptability, made it one of the pre-eminent industrial cities in the world.

Birmingham's Industrial Development

At the time of Domesday, Birmingham was populated by tanners, millers and masons, whose homes congregated around the banks of the River Rea in Deritend. Surveying England for Henry VIII in 1538, John Leland recorded the foundations of Birmingham's industry: 'The beauty of Bermingham . . . is one street going up alonge almost from the left ripe of the brooke, up a meane hill, by the length of a quarter of a mile. . . . There be many smiths in the towne that use to make knives and all mannour of cutting tooles, and many lorimers that make bittes and a great many naylors. Soe that a great part of the towne is maintained by smithes, who have their iron and sea cole out of Staffordshire'. A century later, visitors to the town noted that it was: 'inhabited by blacksmiths and forging several kinds of iron utensils', and: 'swarming with inhabitants and echoing with the noise of anvils'.

During the Civil War these skills were put to use fashioning 15,000 sword blades for the Parliamentary forces. Following the Restoration there was a great diversification in the town's industries. Trade flourished, encouraging skilled craftsmen from neighbouring towns to migrate to Birmingham; something which was fostered by the freedom the town's inhabitants enjoyed from manorial control, and fuelled by the lack of any rigid system of trade guilds. Towards the end of the 17th century, the gun-trade became established, such that during the Napoleonic Wars 1,743,383 muskets were produced in Birmingham for the British Army.

Birmingham's early trades included the manufacture of steel toys, such as sword hilts, fancy buckles, cane heads, snuff boxes, chains and other personal ornaments. Their production arose from a refinement of the blacksmith's art and involved forging, grinding and polishing, skills which encouraged the manufacture of metal buttons and, ultimately, of jewellery and the ornate metal plated objects for which Birmingham was later to become renowned. Brass founding was introduced into the town around 1740, quickly followed by japanning. Pin manufacture began in 1750, at slitting and rolling mills in Digbeth, and elsewhere iron-foundries were established for the production of cooking utensils, fenders, fire-grates, fire-irons and furnace bars.

The town's prosperity increased throughout the 18th century; leading Edmund Burke, on 26 March 1777, to describe the town as 'the great toyshop of Europe'. Birmingham's most celebrated toy manufacturer was Matthew Boulton, who, upon inheriting his father's business in 1759, devised an ambitious scheme that was to have repercussions world-wide. Up to that time, Birmingham's industries were in the hands of 'Little Masters', who either worked alone or enlisted the assistance of their families. Skills and raw materials abounded, but they lacked that measure of organisation and training necessary to harness them to their greatest potential. Recognising this, Boulton established his Soho Works with the aim of building a great industrial college to train a highly skilled work force; the beginnings of the factory system. By 1774 Boulton was employing 1,000 people, and the following year he began a 25-year partnership with James Watt, the improver of the steam engine, and together they produced the machines which powered the Industrial Revolution, and founded the nation's wealth.

Business boomed, and on 15 July 1783 local traders established a Commercial Committee; the forerunner of a Chamber of Commerce. New industries, such as the manufacture of pens and jewellery, had become established, leading to the opening of an Assay Office in the town in 1773. The population also grew at an alarming rate. In 1700 this had stood at just 10,000, but by 1801 it had risen to 70,100. The 19th century saw an even faster growth, by 1851 233,000 people lived in the town, and the newly created city entered the 20th century with 523,000 citizens; a 50-fold increase in 200 years!

Birmingham's mastery of engineering and manufacture in metal made it well placed to become the hub of the nation's motor industry, with skilled engineers such as Herbert Austin and Frederick Lanchester developing the vehicles, whilst others produced the tools and components necessary to manufacture them. Until it was hit hard by the economic recession of the late 1970s, Birmingham was the home of numerous trades, with products as diverse as glass eyes and zip fasteners, but has since seen more and more of its economic activity directed towards service industries and tourism.

Transport in Birmingham before the Railway Age

1 - Roads

Road builders have been by-passing the centre of Birmingham for centuries. The nearest the Romans came was to build their Ryknield Street from Worcester to Perry Barr, and Hayden Way, which ran off the former near Selly Oak, to Alcester. Largely abandoned when the Romans left Britain, their roads were superseded by the pack horse and cart tracks which formed the basis of Birmingham's modern road system.

By 1800, 12 main routes had evolved, which were described thus in 1809: 'The way to Coleshill, which is ten miles, for want of a causeway, with an arch or two, every flood annoys the passenger and the road. . . . Upon the Lichfield road, sixteen miles, to the disgrace of the community, was a river without a bridge until 1792. . . . The road to Walsall, ten miles, is lately made good. That to Wolverhampton, thirteen miles, is much improved since the coal teams left it. The road to Dudley, ten miles, is despicable beyond description, the unwilling traveller is obliged to go two miles about, through a bad road, to avoid a worse. That to Hales-Owen, eight miles, like the life of man, is chequered with good and evil, mainly the latter. To Bromsgrove, twelve miles, made extremely commodious, under the patronage of John Kettle, Esq. To Alcester, about twenty, formed in 1767, on a tolerable plan, but is rather too narrow. . . . Those to Stratford and Warwick, about twenty miles each, are much used and neglected. That to Coventry, about the same distance, can only be equalled by the Dudley Road'.

Some improvements came with the creation of turnpike trusts, set up to gate and levy tolls upon roads to subsidize their repair. Establishment dates for Birmingham turnpikes include the roads to: Wednesbury (1727); Great Bridge (1727); Kidderminster (1753); Chester, via Castle Bromwich (1760); Wolverhampton, via Oldbury (1761); Shenstone, to the Lichfield Turnpike (1804) and Perry Barr (1831). But, when this last Act had been passed, some of the earlier turnpike trusts had already been dismantled; the gate in Deritend being removed in 1828, although one at Five Ways remained until 5 July 1841, and the Hagley Road gates beyond were last used in 1851.

Within the centre of Birmingham, new roads were made under improvement schemes in the late 1870s, which, amongst others, saw the driving of Corporation Street, and its later extension, through areas previously occupied by insanitary housing. In this century, an Outer Ring Road was planned as early as 1911, but not completed until 1939; whilst an ambitious Arterial Road Scheme of 1918 took about the same period to improve the major city approaches. This task was assisted by Government Unemployment Relief Schemes, which provided 50% grants for road building projects and were used to improve the Bristol Road and to build the Wolverhampton New Road, amongst others.

Since the war, the face of the city has been irrevocably altered by the building of the 2 1/4 mile Inner Ring Road. This was proposed in July 1944, but not authorized until 5 January 1954; the first section opening on 11 March 1960; its final link coming into use on 4 January 1971. Leading off this is the A38M Aston Expressway, opened on 1 May 1972, which joins up with the M6 near Erdington, at something its planners tried to term the Gravelly Hill Interchange, but which everyone calls Spaghetti Junction.

2 - Canals

At its greatest extent, Birmingham's canal system totalled about 130 miles within the city boundary, reaching 250 miles if the Black Country branches were included. This vast network was built up from six major schemes, plus numerous branches built to serve local industries. Birmingham's first canal, appropriately enough the Birmingham Canal, linked the town with the Staffordshire & Worcestershire Canal plus a number of collieries along its route. Authorized by an Act of 24 February 1768, a 10 mile section from Wednesbury opened to Paradise Street Wharf on 6 November 1769, immedi-

Below:
Christ Church, at the junction of Colmore Row and New Street, Birmingham, 1830. The demolition of this church, for the laying out of Victoria Square in the late 1890s, came to symbolise for many Birmingham's attitude towards its past and historic buildings. It is a spirit which is alive and well today. The illustration shows Birmingham's splendour growing up in between the huddled cottages and workshops of its many craftsmen.
Author's Collection

SUPERIOR TRAVELLING
TO NOTTINGHAM.

THE Public is respectfully informed, that a NEW COACH, called the MARQUIS of HASTINGS, leaves the ALBION HOTEL COACH OFFICE, Birmingham, every afternoon (except Sunday) at half past two, and arrives at the Black's Head, Nottingham, at nine the same evening; goes through Tamworth and Ashby.

N. VYSE and Co. Proprietors.
Albion Coach-office, Birmingham, July 7, 1825.

PARAGON TO KIDDERMINSTER.

THE Public is respectfully informed, that the PARAGON continues to leave the ALBION HOTEL Coach-office, for Kidderminster, every morning at a quarter before eight, and returns from Kidderminster at one o'clock.

A Report having been industriously circulated, that this Coach would be taken off the road, N. Vyse takes this opportunity of thanking the Public for the decided preference they have given the Paragon, and to assure them, that he has never had the least intention of discontinuing it, but is determined that no expence shall be spared to render it worthy the support it has received.

Albion Hotel Coach-office, Birmingham.

Above:
At the heart of Birmingham's canal system lay the many branches and wharfs in the town centre. The largest and most important of these was the Old Wharf of the Birmingham Canal Navigations, whose entrance was guarded by this distinctive office and gateway. This stood in Paradise Street until the wharf went out of use and the building was demolished in the mid-1920s. Its site became Birmingham's first off-street car park in June 1928, but is now occupied by Alpha Tower and the studios of Central Television.
Author's Collection

ately reducing coal prices from 11d/cwt to 6d (4.5p/cwt to 2.5p). The whole canal opened on 21 September 1772.

Next came the Birmingham & Fazeley Canal, authorized by an Act of 1783, from Riders Green, on the Birmingham Canal, to Broadwaters, en route to Walsall; with eight branches plus a line to the Coventry Canal at Fazeley, totalling just over 20 miles. The Birmingham Canal Company negotiated a merger with this rival, and in 1784 they combined as the Birmingham & Birmingham & Fazeley Canal Company. The main 'Fazeley' scheme was completed by August 1789, and, with the opening of Salford Aqueduct on 12 July 1790, Birmingham was now connected by water with London and Hull.

In tandem with the 'Fazeley' scheme, the Birmingham Company set about removing a major disadvantage of its original line: the summit level at Smethwick. This required 12 locks (six up and six down) to pass a 491ft summit, with consequent delays. To eliminate this, a new intermediate line was first cut, 12ft below the original, eliminating two locks at each end (opened on 2 July 1789), then a lower line was built, removing another pair of locks, this coming into use on 6 April 1790. Four years later, the company also trimmed its cumbersome name to become the Birmingham Canal Navigations (BCN).

The third major scheme was the 29 mile Worcester & Birmingham Canal, authorized by an Act of 1791, with connections to the Dudley Canal at Selly Oak, and the Stratford Canal at King's Norton. Its Birmingham end opened on 30 October 1795, but the line to Worcester did not open until 4 December 1815. A contemporary was the Warwick & Birmingham Canal, a 25 mile link from Digbeth, on the Birmingham & Fazeley Canal, to the Warwick & Napton Canal at Budbrook. Authorized by an Act of 1793, this opened on 19 December 1799.

New connections brought the BCN extra traffic, highlighting the deficiencies of the old main line to Wolverhampton. Thomas Telford was engaged to survey the canal, recommending three major improvements: a new reservoir at Rotten Park, and new lines between Bloomfield and Deepfields, and Tipton and Smethwick; the latter eliminating all locks by lowering the canal by up to 70ft! This scheme was approved, opening in stages: Birmingham-Smethwick, September 1827; Smethwick Cutting, 18 December 1829, and Bloomfield-Deepfields, 6 November 1837.

Completing Birmingham's canal system were two late schemes, conceived to relieve congestion at Farmer's Bridge locks, where BCN and Worcester & Birmingham Canal traffic met. The 8½ mile Tame Valley Canal joined the old BCN line at Ocker Hill, to the Birmingham & Fazeley line at Salford; the Birmingham & Warwick Junction Canal by-passed locks at Aston, linking the BCN with the Warwick & Birmingham Canal at Bordesley. Both schemes were authorised by acts in 1840 and opened on 14 February 1844.

Within Birmingham, the canals produced many basins and wharfs, three of which were on a grand scale: Worcester Wharf, on the Worcester & Birmingham Canal, and Old Wharf and Gas Street Basin on the BCN. Old Wharf was also where the BCN built its striking head office. Almost a century of canal building and improvement yielded an efficient transport system which, far from buckling under railway competition, complemented the youngster through its deft handling of the mass of short-haul movements which Birmingham's intricate industrial economy required. Gradual reductions were made though. Worcester Wharf became incorporated into the Midland Railway's massive Central Goods station, and Old Wharf fell into disuse during the late 1920s, suffering the ignominy of becoming Birmingham's first off-street car park in 1928. Other branches and sections declined with the industries they had once supported, but some were sustained by supplying coal to power stations, and the remainder of the city's canal system, centred on a restored Gas Street Basin, currently enjoys a revival of patronage by leisure and tourist boats.

3 - Public transport

Birmingham was a great converging point for coach services, the earliest recorded being 'The Fly' in 1673, which departed on Mondays, reaching London by Thursday. A popular destination, Birmingham's first regular coaching service to there began on 24 May 1731. Typical of these early services was the 'Flying Coach', which began on 28 May 1748, with 'children on the lap and footmen behind being charged half-price'. The fare was 25s (£1.25) and the journey took two days, but, in only 35 years, this was reduced to just 14 hours, showing the tremendous road improvements made.

A mail coach first passed through Birmingham on 23 August 1785, but a direct mail services from town did not begin until 25 May 1812. The growth in coach services was dramatic. In 1777 there were 52 to London and 16 to Bristol weekly, but by 1829, at least 100 departed or passed through Birmingham daily. Competition was fierce amongst operators, who were not above a little skullduggery to further their ambitions. At their zenith, around 1830, local directories listed almost 200 destinations, but railway competition gradually picked these off; some operators turned to running omnibuses, and by 1875, directory compilers could find no coach services to list.

Birmingham's first omnibus ran on 5 May 1834, through the town, from Snow

Left:
However tough competition may get between bus operators these days, it may come as some consolation to learn that this is nothing new. These notices appeared in *Aris's Birmingham Gazette* of 25 July 1825, and it would seem that Mr Vyse's 'Paragon' service to Kidderminster had been the victim of some nasty rumours put about by a rival operator! *Author's Collection*

Hill, to the turnpike gate on the Bristol Road, where it returned, to avoid paying the toll. Later that year services began to Edgbaston, Handsworth, Dudley and Wolverhampton, and within 10 years this list numbered 16, with rivals plying for trade on the popular routes. Horse trams arrived near the town when a standard gauge line opened between the city boundary, at Hockley Brook, and Dudley Port on 20 May 1872. A connecting line from Colmore Row, plus one to Bournbrook, were operating by June 1876, but no more tramways were built until a 3ft 6in gauge steam operated line opened between Aston Manor and Old Square on 26 December 1882. Six more steam operated routes (to Perry Barr, Moseley Road, Sparkbrook, Lozells, Saltley Road and Small Heath), and another horse drawn one (to Nechells), were added by January 1886; all on the narrower gauge. Experiments with cable haulage, between Colmore Row and Hockley Brook, began on 24 March 1888; and on 24 July 1890 a battery accumulator car began to operate along the Bristol Road.

The latter was also the route of the city's first overhead electric tramway, which first ran on 14 May 1901, operated by the City of Birmingham Tramways Co Ltd. The City Corporation had taken over all of the tramway companies within its boundaries by the end of 1903 and inaugurated its first electric route from Steelhouse Lane to Aston on 4 January 1904. Birmingham's last steam tram ran on 31 December 1906; and by the time that a new electric route was opened to Stetchford on 26 August 1928, the Corporation was operating 92 numbered services along 79.19 route miles of track. Six years earlier, on 27 November 1922, trolleybuses replaced trams on the Nechells service, the first such conversion in the country, and the start of a series of tramway route closures that would end 31 years later with the running of the last tram of all on 4 July 1953. On 7 January 1934, trolleybus operation began on the Yardley route, but a decision against their use, in favour of motorbuses, on the soon-to-be-closed Stratford Road tramway in 1936, turned opinion against their further spread; Birmingham's last trolleybus ran on 1 July 1951.

Birmingham Corporation ran its first motorbus service, between Selly Oak and Rednal, on 19 July 1913, just over a year after the Birmingham & Midland Motor Omnibus Co Ltd (established 26 November 1904), had begun its own. Better known as the 'Midland Red', the latter grew to become one of the country's largest bus and coach operators, having its headquarters in Reservoir Road, Edgbaston. From 1 October 1969, all of the Corporation bus services, and many of those provided by the Midland Red, came under the control of the West Midland Passenger Transport Executive, or WMPTE, who co-ordinated bus and rail services until bus deregulation on 26 October 1986, from when bus services have been provided by West Midlands Travel, amongst many others.

Below:
Birmingham Corporation operated a electric tramway service for precisely 49 years and 7 months; their service beginning on 4 January 1904 and ending on 4 July 1953. Here the last car, No 616, is seen about to depart from the Steelhouse Lane terminus. Virtually everything in this view has been demolished in subsequent years.
Birmingham Post & Mail

2: The 'North Western' Lines to 1962

Birmingham entered the railway age by virtue of being the meeting point of the country's first two trunk railroad schemes. Within 10 years of their opening, these railways had amalgamated to form the London & North Western Railway (LNWR), a company which was to have a major influence upon the development of the emerging city.

Early proposals 1806-1831

By 1800 the Birmingham area was already established as 'the workshop of England' and the want of a fast and efficient means of communication between it and other parts of the country, notably the capital and the northwest, was becoming acute. Railways were in their infancy, but had their advocates, like William James (1771-1837). He was a Warwickshire man, whose father, a solicitor, had lost a lot of money speculating on canal shares; it gave him a slight bias. In 1803 he proposed a railroad between Liverpool and Manchester, and in 1806 he put forward a plan for a line of engine railroad extending northwest from Birmingham, passing through Wednesbury en route to the Staffordshire coalfields. Two years later James developed the idea of a railroad from Walsall to Erdington.

These were early days still for railways; they had more detractors, who saw the technology involved as unproven, than promotors, and William James's schemes were not implemented. Others followed though, underlining a growing dissatisfaction with the capacity of the roads and canals in the Birmingham area. Elsewhere, notably in the northeast, a succession of colliery railways had opened from 1812 onwards, demonstrating the potential of both railways and the steam locomotives that worked them. Patient and persistent, around 1821 William James surveyed a railroad line linking Birmingham with Wolverhampton. This was to terminate at Newhall Hill in Birmingham, on land for which James held the lease. By 1822 interest had been rekindled in a West Midlands/Northwest railway link. Much rumoured in the past, the proponents of such a link now had much more experience upon which to draw.

Quite independently, groups of businessmen in Birmingham and Liverpool began to plan the construction of a railway to link the two places; and, hearing of each other sometime in 1823, formed a joint committee for 'making a railroad from the town of Birmingham, through the Staffordshire collieries and ironworks, by Wolverhampton, Nantwich and Chester to the River Mersey at Birkenhead, opposite Liverpool; the line to be known as the Birmingham & Liverpool Railroad Co' (B&L). A Bill to authorise the construction of the line was heard in the 1824 Parliamentary Session, but was heavily defeated by the combined opposition of canal proprietors and landowners, who had also woken up to railways' potential.

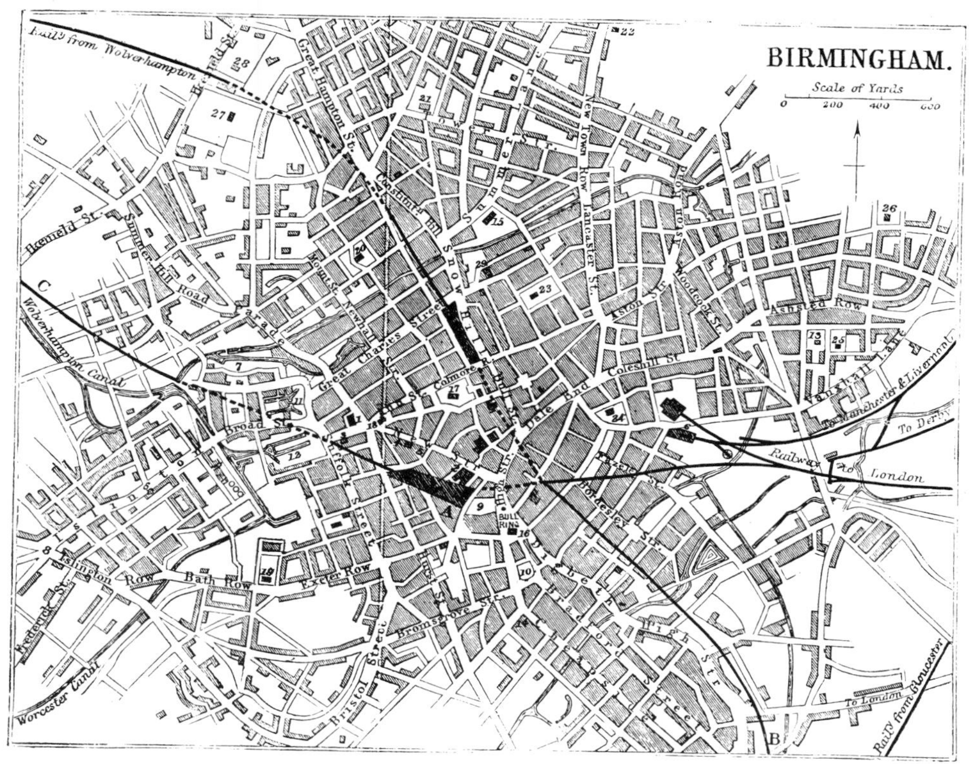

Above:
Birmingham caught at a unique point in time. This little map is actual size and comes from *Birmingham in Miniature*, a guide to the town published in 1851. Both A (New Street) and B (Snow Hill) are yet to be built, and the Stour Valley Railway terminus is shown at Monument Lane. Curzon Street is undistinguished at No 6, and something very odd appears to have happened to the trackwork around Lawley Street, shown left of the 'to' in 'Railway to London' at right.
Author's Collection

Other groups had similar ideas. The rates of tonnage on the Black Country canals were exceedingly high and the South Staffordshire ironmasters had long tried to get them reduced. Negotiations with the Staffordshire & Worcestershire Canal Co. resulted in a 5d (2p) per ton reduction in rates from 25 December 1823, but this was revoked by the company with effect from 25 March 1824. Notice of this decision angered the ironmasters and at their Lady Day quarterly meeting, held in Wolverhampton on 7 April 1824, they drew up a resolution which stated: 'We the undersigned propose . . . forming and carrying into effect a railroad from Birmingham and the Staffordshire and Shropshire Ironworks to Liverpool and Manchester for the conveyance of iron and other goods . . .'. Twenty-four of those present signed, including some of the most famous names and companies in the Black Country iron industry, John Bagnall & Sons, William Sparrow, James Foster and John Bradley & Co, the latter, with 50 shares, being the largest subscriber. In all, 307 shares were subscribed, raising £30,700. The full document is reproduced in Appendix 1.

A deputation of four was appointed to travel to Liverpool and Manchester to see what assistance might be expected from those places, and a public meeting was held at the Swan Inn, Wolverhampton, on 26 April 1824, to outline the scheme and to form a company 'for the purpose of affecting this great national communication under the denomination of the Birmingham, Manchester & Liverpool Rail Road Company'. Contact was made with the other groups who had made the earlier attempt to build such a line, but the ironmasters scheme also came to nought, partly through the obstinacy and arrogance of the landowners affected by it. Many of them refused to see let alone settle with the line's promoters: 'When he heard our business he had not even the courtesy to ask us to sit down, for two hours he kept us standing before the fireplace', one confided to his journal.

The Birmingham and Liverpool camps also fell out, the former wanting to keep the line's eventual charges as low as possible to assist their businesses; the latter wanting them to be as high as possible, to maximise the dividends to their investors. Such bickering delayed the submission of a Bill to Parliament by over a year. By the time that they got around to this, in 1826, most were somewhat invigorated by the opening of the Stockton & Darlington Railway in September 1825, but they were, if anything, even more heavily defeated at this attempt. Having twice failed, some gave up; prematurely. Others, like William Sparrow, persisted; forming a lasting friendship with George Stephenson, which was to be of great assistance to the project the next time around.

Four years were to elapse before the success of the Liverpool & Manchester Railway gave the public perception of railways a much needed fillip. The revenue returns weren't bad either. The Birmingham and Liverpool committees were both revived, each working on half the line. Three engineers were appointed, with George Stephenson, hero of the Liverpool & Manchester line, in overall charge; Joseph Locke, a Stephenson prodigy, tackling the Northern section, and John Urpeth Rastrick, designer of the *Stourbridge Lion*, the first steam locomtive to run in the USA, responsible for the Southern section. A new survey was undertaken and two Bills, one for each section, were presented to the 1830 Parliamentary Session; the Southern one being rejected out of hand, the Northern one being lost through the dissolution of Parliament following the rejection of the Reform Bill.

The Grand Junction Railway

At the turn of 1831, prospects for the B&L scheme were poor; but the tide of public opinion was turning in favour of railways. A southward spur off the Liverpool & Manchester line, the Warrington & Newton Railway, opened that year, and elsewhere a scheme for another trunk railroad, to link Birmingham with London, later to become the London & Birmingham Railway (L&B), was also revived. It therefore occurred to someone that should the Warrington & Newton line be extended south, it could join up with the proposed B&L line, linking all three regions. And, if the Birmingham to London line was also built, then the B&L would unite the nation's most important industrial areas and port, with its capital. These ideas were embodied in new plans and expressed in a fresh title for the line: the Grand Junction Railway (GJR).

Planning and construction

Behind the scenes of the newly styled GJR, engineering duties were still shared between Messrs Stephenson, Locke and Rastrick. On 9 February 1831, the latter completed a survey and estimate for the line's southern portion, which he calculated would cost £1 million, or £20,000 per mile. The Royal Assent was granted to the 219 clause Grand Junction Bill on 6 May 1833, the same day as an Act authorising L&B line. Construction work began straightaway, but soon a series of disagreements grew up between the three Engineers, and first Rastrick resigned, in September 1833, followed by Stephenson precisely two years later; leaving Joseph Locke alone to finish the work. The greatest engineering difficulties lay at the southern end of the line; which were exacerbated by a number of route changes. One involved the approach to Birmingham, through Perry Barr and Handsworth, to which James Watt's son, the resident of Aston Hall, objected; resulting in a costly deviation, sanctioned by an Act of 12 June 1835.

Unforeseen engineering difficulties were also confronted. At Wednesfield Heath, the site of the Wolverhampton station, a 186yd tunnel and a deep approach cutting were needed, with a series of shallow cuttings and embankments to the north of this. These difficulties were reflected in progress on the line, which was patchy. All of the contracts were let for the northern section by November 1834, but none of those for the southern section; and despite progress throughout 1835, it was not until 9 March 1836 that any rails or chairs were ordered, or 31 August that year before orders were placed for locomotives.

The Opening of the Grand Junction Railway

By the end of May 1837, the GJ had been completed between Liverpool and Wolverhampton, and on 1 June a Directors' train made this 83 mile journey in three and a half hours. Completion of the line to a temporary Birmingham terminus at Vauxhall was achieved later that month, and a second run, including this portion, was made on 24 June. A third Directors' train covered the whole line on 1 July, three days before the public opening.

Being the first trunk railway to open in the country, suitable ceremony would have been expected, but its Directors decided that the GJ's opening, on 4 July 1837, would be very subdued affair. There were two reasons for this. Firstly, the nation was in official mourning for King William IV, who had died on 20 June and would not be buried until 8 July; and secondly, some of the Directors had witnessed the death of William Huskisson, past whose birthplace, Oxley Hall, the line passed, at the opening of the Liverpool & Manchester Railway on 15 September 1830. Wishing to avoid seeing such scenes repeated, the GJ company just opened their doors for business. Luckily the public appreciated the significance of the occasion. From Birmingham, the first train departed at 07.00, and the prospect of the town's first ever early morning departure deterred few. By 06.00 the station approach at Vauxhall was choking with people, and crowds lined the route to Wolverhampton. The first train achieved a speed of 40mph between these towns, but later ones were delayed by the masses of people who had strayed on to the line.

Vauxhall and Curzon Street stations

Under powers contained in its 1834 Act, the GJ company was authorised to build an extension of their main line to Nova Scotia Gardens in Birmingham, a site which adjoined the proposed terminus of the L&B Railway in Curzon Street and where the GJ intended to build its own station. Three years later, as the opening date of the line drew nearer, work on completing this final section of the line, and the terminal station, was behind schedule. A viaduct carrying the railway over the River Rea and Lawley Street was finished but this was of little practical use as the line had nowhere to go once it crossed it. Therefore, to allow the line to open, a temporary station was required. A site for this was chosen at Vauxhall, about one mile from the incomplete terminus. It consisted of a small building which housed the booking office and waiting rooms. There were two platforms, one for arrivals, the other for departures, both of which were covered by a roof. Contemporary engravings of this roof suggest that it was far from an insubstantial structure, possibly having cast-iron columns supporting a heavy timber frame. The remainder of the facilities befitted the temporary nature of the station; but it was a terminus, and therefore had to be provided with an engine shed, a goods depot, plus means of replenishing the locomotives and turning them for their return journeys.

A service of cabs and omnibuses conveyed passengers to and from the centre of Birmingham; a practice which continued for 16 months. In his *Road Book of the Grand Junction Railway*, published on 1 September 1838, Drake notes that: 'until the completion of the permanent buildings, those at Vauxhall have been temporarily used', which they were until 19 November that year, when the Curzon Street ones were finally ready. Curzon Street was the GJ's only terminus, the line utilising former Liverpool & Manchester buildings at its other end; so the Directors were determined to make their presence felt in Birmingham. They engaged

Right:
Vauxhall served as the GJ line's terminus for 16 months, until the company's permanent station, alongside that of the L&B Railway at Curzon Street, came into use on 19 November 1838. The frontage of this station is shown here, but all was not as it seemed. This elegant front is all that it was, a screen to hide somewhat more modest premises behind.
Ironbridge Gorge Museum Trust

Left:
With their station at Curzon Street unfinished, the Grand Junction Railway opened to this temporary station at Vauxhall on 4 July 1837. As shown in this illustration, the frontispiece to *Drake's Road Book* of the line, this was a fairly substantial affair, with the booking office and waiting rooms to the left and an iron and timber train shed. A coach service, seen loading at left, conveyed passengers on the the centre of Birmingham.
Ironbridge Gorge Museum Trust

Joseph Franklin, the Liverpool based architect of Lime Street station, to design a station for them. He produced an unusual design which made the best of the station's somewhat awkward site. A high 700ft long frontage, decorated in the Italianate style, ran along one side of Curzon Street. It contained four large arched doorways, a pair each for the entry and exit of passengers and carriages to the departure and arrival platforms, and the booking office; but it was essentially a curtain wall to screen the rather more modest premises which stood behind.

Following the opening of the GJ's Curzon Street station, the temporary buildings at Vauxhall were utilised for goods traffic, the locomotive accommodation there being expanded. The latter were used for over 30 years, until the opening of running sheds at Aston.

Early train services

There were no fewer than five intermediate stations, at Perry Barr; Newton Road; Bescot Bridge; James Bridge and Willenhall, along the 14½ miles of the GJR between Birmingham and Wolverhampton; more than on any other stretch of the line between two first-class stations. Six trains per day ran in each direction from the line's opening; leaving Birmingham at 07.00; 08.30; 11.30; 14.30; 16.30 and 19.00. All of these carried first-class coaches only, with just the second and fifth having any second-class accommodation. On the GJ, first-class trains only stopped at first-class stations, locally these were Birmingham and Wolverhampton only; whilst mixed trains stopped at every station. An additional train left Wolverhampton at 08.00 and returned from Birmingham at 19.00. Only first-class trains ran on Sundays, they carried second-class accommodation, but only stopped at first-class stations! The fares between Birmingham and Wolverhampton were: First-class 2/6 (12.5p); Second-class 1/6 (7.5p) (journeys of 40 and 56min respectively); Birmingham to Liverpool or Manchester, First-class £1 1s 0d (£1.05); Second-class 14/- (70p) (4 ½hr and 5hr 24min respectively). This timetable was recast for the opening of the London & Birmingham Railway, to offer some connecting services but, with a few minor alterations, the basic service on the GJ line was as described.

London & Birmingham Railway

In the early years of the 19th century, when trunk railways existed only in the minds of visionaries like William James; the probability that someone would propose such a link between the nation's centre of commerce, London, and its centre of industry, Birmingham, was very high. James and his ilk had little on their side; the technology was unproven, and the interests lined up against them: landowners, canal companies and Turnpike Trusts, formidable. The balance between these was first upset and then turned in favour of railways by the success of the Stockton & Darlington and the Liverpool & Manchester railways in 1825 and 1830 respectively.

Pity then those involved in promoting railways before these successes; people like Sir John Rennie (1794-1878), who, around 1820, proposed one such line linking London with Birmingham and following the Thames Valley through Oxford and Banbury. Not surprisingly, Rennie's idea remained such, but in 1823 groups were formed to promote the building of two major trunk railways, one of which would become the GJ Railway, the other of which would become the London & Birmingham Railway (L&B). The fortunes of both lines were inextricably linked from the beginning and the fact that the GJ was the first to open is more a reflection of its shorter length and comparative ease of construction than it is a comment upon any lack of zeal behind the L&B's promoters.

Aware of Rennie's proposal, in January 1824 the Provisional Committee of the London & Birmingham Railroad commissioned him to survey a 'practicable route'. Rennie in turn hired John and Edward Grantham to take levels over a wide area so that he could thread a line along the most advantageous route between London and Birmingham. His deliberations took two years and his final report, presented to the Provisional Committee on 1 April 1826, recommended a route from a London terminus at Islington, via Harrow, Rickmandsworth, Watford. Hemel Hempstead, Cheddington, Quainton, Brackley and Southam, by-passing Coventry and terminating in Birmingham. Some familiar place-names there, but the Rennie route was not proceeded with.

Indecision, procrastination, or otherwise, wasted the next three years and in 1829 the Provisional Committee, somehow still going, commissioned two further surveys. For some strange reason, Sir John Rennie was requested to re-survey his original proposal of 1820, via Oxford and Banbury, and Francis Giles was asked to survey Rennie's more recent proposal of 1826, eventually coming to modify the route to pass through Coventry and to go via Rugby. Emerging as rival proposals, each scheme had its adherents and served only to shatter whatever vestiges of unity had existed amongst the Provisional Committee. Two committees emerged, the Giles camp seeking the advice of George Stephenson, but as 1830 wore on, each saw the sense of promoting one line only and reunited at a meeting held on 11 September 1830.

Consider this date. Four days later the Liverpool & Manchester Railway opened to great public tumult and acclaim. The name of George Stephenson was everywhere. Move to the first meeting of the reunited Provisional Committee of the London & Birmingham Railroad a week or so later. Now, if someone was to suggest that the recommendations of one George Stephenson were to be rejected out of hand, the motion would receive a lot of support; hardly! George and Robert Stephenson were duly appointed joint engineers of the L&B, and from October 1830 they began to modify details of the line to produce the one that was eventually built.

A Bill was presented before the Parliamentary Session of 1832. This passed through all of its stages in the Commons by 19 June 1832 but was opposed in the Lords by landowning interests and duly rejected. The next three months were spent placating said landowners and in making further adjustments to the Bill ready for it to be re-submitted to Parliament that November. Second time lucky; the L&B Bill passed all of its stages and received the Royal Assent on 6 May 1833, the same day as the GJ Bill, authorising a line between London and Birmingham, with a terminus adjoining Curzon Street in the town.

On 7 September 1833, Robert Stephenson was appointed Engineer-in-Chief of the newly incorporated company; his father being fully engaged on a number of projects, not the least of which was the GJ line. Father and son were therefore heading towards Birmingham in opposite directions. It took six months to secure the land required for building the L&B and tenders were accepted for work on the first 21 miles in late May 1834; the first sod being ceremonially cut at Chalk Farm on 1 June that year.

Construction took just over four years. An Act of 3 July 1835 extended the London terminus to Euston, adding to the work. A number of the engineering tasks were impressive: a deep cutting at Tring, and three of the tunnels, one of 3,493ft through Primrose Hill, another of 5,374ft at Watford and the massive 7,326ft one at Kilsby. Much of this activity was recorded by the artist John Cooke Bourne, his book of drawings, published in 1839, providing probably the finest record of railway construction of that period. Sadly, many lives were lost in building the line, espe-

Right:
London & Birmingham Railway 2-2-0 locomotive No 28, built by Edward Bury & Co of Liverpool in 1838. Bury was also the company's Locomotive Superintendent (useful), for the whole of its separate existence. He developed the light bar-framing seen to good advantage in this view, but although excellently made, his locomotives were a little short on power, some L&B expresses requiring four of these, and the heaviest goods trains were often septuple-headed!
Locomotive Publishing Co/IAL

Below right:
A three-car Metro-Cammell DMU set is just arriving at Hampton-in-Arden station on the L&B line with the 14.50 New Street to Leamington service on 15 June 1958. This replaced the original Hampton station, which was ½-mile to the south east, on 1 September 1884, and assumed its present name in July 1886.
Michael Mensing

cially in the tunnelling and notably at Kilsby, where flooding and quick-sand contributed to drawing out its construction over two and a half years, causing it to exceed its estimated budget of £99,000 by a staggering £221,000 (223%)!

The Opening of the London & Birmingham Railway

By June 1837 a partial opening of the line was in the offing and on 27 June a Directors' party travelled the 49 miles from Euston to Boxmoor and back. A formal opening took place on 13 July when the same trip was repeated; the line opening to the public a week later on 20 July. The remainder opened in sections: Boxmoor-Tring, 19 October 1837; Rugby-Birmingham to goods, 12 November 1837; Tring-Denbigh Hall, and Rugby-Birmingham to passengers, 9 April 1838, the latter having intermediate stations at Brandon, Coventry and Hampton. This left a 36 mile long gap between Denbigh Hall and Rugby, where work continued on Kilsby tunnel. For five months this was 'bridged' by a coach service, which took 8½ hr for the combined road/rail journey. But on 20 July 1838, a record was set. The French Ambassador had to be in Birmingham fast, and so a special service was laid on for him. A train left Euston at 04.20, arriving at Denbigh Hall by 05.55 where a coach departed at 06.00, arriving at Rugby by 09.20. There, 50min was spent on breakfast, before the final leg was completed, by rail, in just an hour, arriving at Birmingham at 11.10. Only six hours had been spent in transit; a (soon to be broken) record for travel between London and Birmingham.

Kilsby tunnel was completed in mid-August 1838, a Directors' special inspecting it on the 20th of that month. The L&B was therefore able to open throughout at last, which it did on 17 September 1838. Although not directly linked by rail with the GJ line at that time, the latter were hurredly completing the continuation of their line, from their temporary station at Vauxhall, to their new permanent one at Curzon Street. A short coach journey therefore linked the two lines, but by the end of September 1838 the GJ had opened a temporary track between Vauxhall and Curzon Street; sufficient to enable them to announce that from 1 October 1838 their timetable would be entirely revised to run their services in connection with the L&B company.

The coach link continued until 19 November when the GJ brought their Curzon Street station into use, from which date stock was transferred between the two companies' lines by being hauled out of one station, passed over connecting points and being reversed into the other. This proved a practical if not very efficient solution, but one which soon proved inconvenient as these stock movements got in the way of arrivals and departures. Then, common sense suddenly prevailed, both companies starting to work through trains into the other's station: northbound L&B trains working into the GJ station; southbound GJ ones working into the L&B station.

Curzon Street Station

The vestige of the L&B's station that we know as Curzon Street station today is but a part of the railway establishment built in Birmingham by that company; it also fronts to New Canal Street. Both termini of the L&B were designed by the London architect, Philip Hardwick. The company's grander edifice was Euston, with its famous portico or Doric Arch, the demolition of which in 1962 has come to symbolise the destruction of the old for the new. Of course this very understandable view ignores the demolition that preceded it several generations earlier, over which our forebears had equal right to be miffed. Two of them certainly were, but for less noble reasons; the landowners whose properties were required by the L&B in order that construction of their station might begin. They held out until 25 July 1837, endangering the completion of the building in time for the line's opening.

Hardwick's design for Curzon Street was elegant, simple and symmetrical. A central block housed a hotel, which would be named the 'Victoria' after the new Queen. This was fronted by four massive columns, 45ft high, aping the design of the Euston propylæum, topped off by a parapet and pediment. Either side of the hotel was adorned by open gated arches, again aping the lodges at Euston, with a planned further series of pillared gateways beyond each. Unfortunately, between quarrelsome landowners, and the usual lack of funds, the whole of Hardwick's design was not executed; with just some part of the peripheral gateways, on the left-hand side, being built.

The main station lay, slightly off-centre, behind the hotel, separated, as at Euston, by a courtyard. It had arrival and departure platforms, the latter bearing a range of buildings which housed the station offices, booking offices and waiting rooms, etc. There were six lines of rails, covered by an overall roof, which Wrightson & Webb's *Railway Guide* (1840) described as: 'being one of the finest in the world. It covers a space of 217 feet long and 113 feet wide. It is formed of wrought iron, in two spans of 56 feet 6 inches each and the length is divided into 33 bays, or spaces between each principal rafter, making 34 double or 68 single sets of principals, a double one going across the whole width of 113 feet, and a single one going across the 56 feet only. These principal rafters are supported by three tiers of open ornamented arched girders of cast iron, each tier running the whole length of the roof, the girders being supported by two rows of cast iron columns, one at each side of the roof and one in the middle. The weight of this immense roof may be taken as 326 tons'.

Also included on the station site was a goods depot and a roundhouse style locomotive shed of distinctive design, being 124ft in diameter and having 16 sides. This was capable of holding 16 locomotives plus their tenders or 32 locomotives without. At its centre was a 15ft diameter turntable; the shed also having stores and shops to permit running repairs to be made. Unfortunately, the modern generation did not have a chance to fight for this roundhouse's survival, as it was demolished by the LNWR in 1859 to make way for

Below:
Philip Hardwick's design for the L&B's terminus at Curzon Street was simple and symmetrical, aping his at Euston. The central block housed the 'Victoria' Hotel, but the pattern of gateways to the left was supposed to be copied on the right, only the owners of the buildings seen there in this view wouldn't sell up! The main station can be glimpsed through the gateway.
John Cooke Bourne / Ironbridge Gorge Museum Trust

Bottom:
On the other side of Hardwick's elegant Curzon Street frontage was a pair of rather more utilitarian train sheds. Coaches and passengers appear to have become separated in this view. Note the locomotive tender in the foreground and the carriage loaded on to a flat-bedded wagon on the extreme left.
Ironbridge Gorge Museum Trust

Above:
The locomotive engine house at Curzon Street station (L&B) in 1839. This engraving, from *Groombridge's Handbook* to the L&B of 1839, obscures the fact that the round house was 16-sided; and also 124 ft in diameter. Up to 32 locomotives could be accommodated within and at its centre was a 15 ft diameter turntable. It must have looked magnificent, but did not survive to be preserved, being demolished in 1859 to expand the goods facilities at Curzon Street.
Ironbridge Gorge Museum Trust

expanded goods facilities at Curzon Street.

Quite soon after opening, it became apparent that the Victoria Hotel was too small; its situation, remote from the centre of Birmingham, being to its advantage for those of its patrons who wished to avoid the town's rougher quarters. An extension was therefore needed, and was planned in 1839. This was built on the left-hand side of Hardwick's central block; the arched and pillared gateways being swept away, destroying the frontage's albeit skewed symmetry for ever. The hotel extension opened in 1840.

Curzon Street station was also used by the B&G Railway from 17 August 1841. It was closed to regular passenger traffic on 1 July 1854, when the Midland Railway, heirs to the B&G's rights to use the station, transferred its regular passenger services to New Street; but it was retained for use by holiday Monday trains to and from Sutton Coldfield by both the LNWR and Midland companies until 22 May 1893, from which date this excursion traffic was handled at the respective company's stations at Vauxhall & Duddeston and Saltley.

Early train services

From the L&B's opening a basic service of nine trains in each direction (two first-class; six mixed; one mail), was operated on weekdays, being reduced to four on Sundays. The first departure was at 06.00, the last at 18.00, save for a midnight mail train. Mixed (first and second-class) trains were the slowest, calling at all stations and taking six hours for the 113 miles between Birmingham and London. First-class trains only called at first-class stations (Birmingham, Coventry, Rugby, Blisworth, Wolverton, Tring, Watford and Euston), taking five hours; the first-class fares being £1 10s (£1.50) by day, £1 12s (£1.60) by night; second-class being £1 and £1 5s (£1.25), respectively. This basic service was retained throughout the L&B's independent existence. Like the majority of the railways of the time, the L&B also worked to local time; Birmingham being seven and a quarter minutes behind London; further confusion arising from the company's habit of setting its clocks three minutes fast, in a vain attempt to hurry passengers along. This practice outlived the company, being abolished by its successor the LNWR, which adopted Greenwich Mean Time as the standard throughout its system from 1 December 1847.

The Coventry to Warwick line

In 1836, as part of the main L&B scheme, Robert Stephenson surveyed a branch to Leamington and Warwick via Kenilworth, but this was rejected following strong objections from local landowners. The opening of the L&B main line changed a few minds on this matter, and moves began to build a line of the kind proposed by Stephenson. A new survey was undertaken by Thomas Woodhouse, who produced his plans on 28 February 1839. These were not proceeded with immediately, and soon rumours, then surveyors, of a Birmingham & Derby Junction Railway branch between Warwick and Leamington threw matters into confusion. When calm returned, some local people felt sufficiently galvanized to promote the line themselves, which they did, under the title of the Warwick & Leamington Union Railway (W&LU).

Meanwhile, in early 1840s, as the GWR backed Oxford & Rugby line threatened to bring that company's broad gauge into its West Midland heartland, the L&B proposed a line linking their main line at Coventry with Rugby. It was fortuitous therefore that the promoters of the W&LU should turn to the L&B for help with their line. Discussions ensued, and on 1 July 1842 the L&B agreed to take over the scheme; a move sanctioned by an Act of 3 April 1843. The W&LU became the first stage in the L&B's proposed Coventry-Rugby line, opening on 9 December 1844. The Warwick station was named Leamington, but underwent no fewer than nine changes of name in the ensuing 110 years! The line was extensively remodelled in connection with the construction of the LNWR's Kenilworth-Berkswell line, including new stations at Kenilworth and Milverton. These opened to passengers with the new line on 2 June 1884, both surviving until passenger services were withdrawn along the line, although Kenilworth was considerably damaged in a fire, which destroyed the booking and parcels offices there on 30 April 1923.

The formation of the London & North Western Railway

The spate of railway promotion in 1844 that marked the beginning of the period known as the 'Railway Mania',

Left:
Stetchford station on the L&B line, with a two-car Derby-built DMU set calling with the 12.40 Coventry to Birmingham local on 19 September 1959. The former L&B station here was called Stetchford Gates and opened on 9 October 1844. This was replaced by the station shown, which is west of the original, on 1 February 1882, built in conjunction with the new cut-off line to Aston.
Michael Mensing

Above:
The L&B's Coventry-Warwick line leaves the main line just west of Coventry station, where, sometime in 1960, ex-LMS 8F No 48312 takes a freight on to the line down to Leamington. In the background, the new Coventry station is emerging.
R. C. Riley

forced both the GJ and L&B companies to accept that they could not reasonably expect to retain their monopolies of lines serving London, Birmingham and the northwest for much longer. Accordingly, early in that year they concluded an agreement which stated that they would 'remain separate and distinct as at present, but shall unite for mutual protection'; followed by a number of clearly worded examples stating instances of conflicting interest, and what each company would do or not do in return for corresponding action from the other. Unfortunately, in a matter of weeks, both parties were accusing the other of breaching these agreements.

Many parties involved in these disputes grew weary of them. Matters came to a head at the summer half-yearly meetings of both companies, held in early August 1845; at which the shareholders, many of whom held shares in each company, pressed for the disputes between the two to cease. Talks began, and by the end of October an agreement to amalgamate had been finalised. Pending the passing of an Act of Parliament to sanction formally their amalgamation, the two companies began to function as one from 1 January 1846. All previous agreements made by one or the other with regard to supporting new lines were cancelled. On 16 July 1846, the Royal Assent was given to the Act of amalgamation, formally constituting the two companies as one: the London & North Western Railway (LNWR).

Left:
Leamington (Avenue) station on 13 June 1959, the last day of passenger services along the line to Rugby, with ex-LMS Ivatt designed 2-6-2T No 41228 arriving with the 15.05 from the latter. The line had opened on 1 March 1851 and was part of an L&B Railway scheme to combat the GWR's proposed Oxford & Rugby Railway.
E. J. Dew/IAL

South Staffordshire Railway

Until the mid-1840s, none of the railways planned to serve the Birmingham area had made any inroads into the Black Country. Centred around the south Staffordshire coalfield, this area, with its abundance of mineral extracting and manufacturing industries, offered rich returns for any railway company prepared to build lines to serve it. Around 1845, two groups were promoting complementary railway schemes, focussed upon Walsall, which did just this. The South Staffordshire Junction Railway proposed to build a line from a junction with the planned OWW at Dudley, to Walsall, also connecting with the GJ line, via a spur line from Pleck to James Bridge and a curve at Bescot. The Trent Valley, Midlands & Grand Junction Railway (TVM&GJ) proposed a line from Walsall, to a junction with the B&DJ at Wichnor, also connecting with the planned Trent Valley line at Lichfield via a spur line there. Both groups presented bills to Parliament in November 1845 and succeeded in obtaining authority to proceed with their lines in Acts which received the Royal Assent on the same day: 3 August 1846.

Amongst the other powers contained in each act was that for the two companies to amalgamate, which they did with effect from 6 October 1846, adopting the simpler name of the South Staffordshire Railway (SS); a move confirmed by an Act of 9 July 1847. Construction began at once and proceeded fastest at the Walsall end; the 1¾ mile line between Bescot and a temporary station in Bridgman Place Walsall opening on 1 November 1847. The initial service was operated by the LNWR and consisted of four trains, between Walsall and Birmingham (Curzon Street) via the GJ line, each day. Next to open was the 17¼ mile line between Walsall and Wichnor Junction, which opened on 9 April 1849, with stations at Rushall, Pelsall, Brownhills (renamed Brownhills High Street from 2 June 1924, reverting back to Brownhills from 1 August 1930), Hammerwich and Lichfield; although timetables do not show any services using Rushall, Pelsall or Hammerwich until that June. On the same date, the SS opened a new station at Walsall, simultaneously closing the temporary one at Bridgman Place, and that August they opened Trent Valley Junction station adjoining the company's said junction at Lichfield.

Exercising running powers over the Midland Railway contained in the original TVM&GJ Act, the SS began to operate a service between Walsall and Derby consisting of three trains in each direction daily, with a fourth working short to Lichfield. In conjunction with this new service, the LNWR operated a connecting service between Birmingham and Bescot Junction, thereby providing their passengers with an alternate route to Burton-on-Trent and, with a further change, to Derby.

The success of the SS north of Walsall masked the difficulties it was having in completing its line between Dudley and Pleck. Although short, only six miles in length, the line passed through a heavily industrialised area littered with past and present mine workings and criss-crossed by canals. There was one further problem: a deadline. Under the powers granted to the BW&D line,

Above left:
The junction between the former OWW and SS lines at Dudley is shown in this 2 May 1964 shot of a two-car Park Royal DMU set working the 17.18 local to Walsall along the latter. This service was withdrawn five weeks later.
Michael Mensing

Above:
Walsall (SS) station of 1849 in Station Street, photographed in 1976, a year or so before it was demolished. Opened on 9 April 1849, the station was built to designs in the Elizabethan style by the London architect, Edward Adams. Already the third station to serve Walsall, it was prone to flooding and was replaced by a new station, fronting the adjoining Park Street, which opened on 1 January 1884. In the autumn of 1978, both buildings were swept away when the town centre site was redeveloped for a shopping centre. This incorporates a new station whose gloom out-dims even that of New Street.
Michael Mensing

Below:
Bescot was a junction for the GJ and SS companies' lines. It is seen here on 17 March 1962 as the 15.10 service to Rugeley departs. In the top centre of the picture is the site of the new marshaling yard at Bescot, then under construction.
Michael Mensing

subsequently vested in the GWR and then building between Birmingham and Wolverhampton, if the SS failed to open its line from Dudley by 1 November 1849, they would have powers to reach Dudley via Swan Village. Not only would this admit a competing company to the SS's 'heartland' but it would also give a toe-hold in the district to the GWR's broad gauge. Complying with this ruling was a close run thing, a measure of the SS's confidence in being able to open the line by the date required being given by the fact that they constructed it to mixed gauge dimensions (just in case).

Opening and early train services

In the event, they just made it. On 1 November 1849, the company's engineer, John Robinson McClean, allowed a special train, with the Directors on board, to ply its way, very cautiously, along the line to Dudley, passing the line's three incomplete stations. A token gesture maybe, but it satisfied the letter of the SS and BW&D Acts. The actual opening of the line came four months later; goods services between Dudley and Walsall commencing on 1 March 1850, with a series of sidings at Great Bridge, linking the line with the Birmingham Canal, coming into use on the same day. Passenger services, from a temporary station at Dudley, started two months later, on 1 May 1850, with the opening of stations at Dudley Port, Great Bridge and Wednesbury. There was a basic weekday service of 11 trains from Dudley and 10 from Walsall daily, two and three of these, respectively, being LNWR services; the Sunday service consisting of three SS trains in each direction. With this opening, Dudley was also linked to Birmingham by rail for the first time; coaches traveling from Dudley being joined onto trains from Walsall, at Bescot Junction, and proceeding to Curzon Street via the GJ line. This practice continued until competition from the more direct Stour Valley (opened 1 July 1852) and BW&D (opened 14 November 1854) routes forced its withdrawal. Later in 1850, around November, to integrate its services with the SS's, the LNWR closed their Bescot Bridge station and started to call only at Bescot Junction.

Behind the scenes, the company's Directors were attempting to secure the long-term future of the its lines. Both the LNWR and Midland Railway were approached to see if they would lease the line, but satisfactory terms could not be agreed. Outside bids were then sought, and British railway history was made on 21 January 1850 when the terms offered by the company's engineer, Mr McClean, were accepted and operation of the line was leased to him for 21 years. This arrangement was confirmed by the SS Act of 1 August 1850, becoming the first instance in this country of a railway being leased to a private individual.

Under McClean's control, the SS developed and prospered throughout the 1850s. A link with the Stour Valley line, between Sedgley Junction and Dudley Port, which was authorised by the SS Act of 24 July 1851, came into use on 2 January 1854, also giving the LNWR running powers into Dudley station. In April 1856 an extra station, possibly temporary and styled Ryder's Hays, was opened between Pelsall and Brownhills, but this was soon dispensed with, closing in May 1858. Two years later, on 1 February 1858, the company opened a line from Ryecroft Junction in Walsall to Cannock, with stations at Birchills (opened 1 April 1858; downgraded to a halt from 1 March 1909;

Above left:
Brindley Heath station on the former Cannock Mineral Railway, which opened on 7 November 1859. The station opened on 3 August 1939, to serve an RAF base nearby, but passenger services on the line did not quite make their centenary, being withdrawn on 7 April 1959.
P. J. Shoesmith

Left:
The SS Railway opened a link between their Dudley-Walsall line and the LNWR's Stour Valley line on 2 January 1854. Immediately upon leaving the latter, this line curved sharply westwards, crossing the Birmingham Canal by means of a heavy girder bridge, which is seen here in a view from 1960. *Michael Mensing*

closed from 1 January 1916) Bloxwich, Wyrley & Church Bridge (Wryley & Cheslyn Hay from 1 December 1912) and Cannock; together with a mineral branch to Norton, which left the company's Walsall-Wichnor line just north of Ryder's Hays station. Both lines were sanctioned by the SS Act of 2 June 1854. Two further short mineral branches, to Walsall Wood and Wyrley, were authorised by an Act of 23 June 1855 and opened at about this time.

North of Cannock, the SS line was continued to a junction with the TV line at Rugeley by a separate scheme, the Cannock Mineral Railway. This began as the impressive sounding Derbyshire, Staffordshire & Worcestershire Junction Railway, adopting the shorter title with the passing of a new Act on 14 August 1855. The line opened on 7 November 1859, with a solitary station at Hednesford, and was leased to the LNWR from that date, being formally vested in the latter from 12 July 1869.

Thus, by the early 1860s, the SS was hemmed in by the LNWR, with whom it had, of necessity, developed a close working relationship; so much so that the latter was prompted to make another offer to lease the line. J. R. McClean was disposed towards this offer and it was sanctioned by the company's Board on 1 February 1861; effectively ending all but the SS's nominal independence. It was therefore under LNWR control that the last four SS line opened. Two of these served the heart of the Black Country, one being a single line, which looped its way between James Bridge, on the GJ line, and Wednesbury, on the SS; with a station at Darlaston. This was christened the 'Darlaston Loop' and opened on 14 September 1863, having been authorised by an Act dated 23 June 1855, and granted additional construction time by an Act of 13 August 1859. Sanctioned and time extended by the same acts was a line between Tipton Junction, with the Stour Valley line, and Wednesbury on the SS. This also opened on 14 September 1863, with intermediate stations at Princes End and Ocker Hill (opened 1 July 1864)

Six years after leasing the SS, the company was vested in the LNWR by that company's New Works & Additional Powers &c Act of 15 July 1867. No new additions were made to the former SS system by the LNWR, other than the doubling of the Darlaston Loop line, which came into use on 22 December 1872, and the opening of the 'Tipton Curve' on 1 October 1883, a second link between the Stour Valley line and the former SS's Tipton to Wednesbury line, this one facing Tipton station. Indeed, both of the SS's Black Country passenger lines suffered badly in the face of competition from other forms of public transport, in particularly tramways, from around 1883 onwards. In response, the LNWR cut once intensive services, accelerating their decline and prompting closure; the Darlaston Loop passenger services being withdrawn from 1 November 1887. Exactly three years later, on 1 November 1890, the passenger service was also withdrawn between Tipton and Wednesbury, with both Princes End and Ocker Hill stations closing; tramway competition being cited as the reason in both instances. But, despite poor patronage, local people felt incensed by these closures and lobbied for both lines to be reopened. They had partial success, the Tipton-Wednesbury line reopening on 1 July 1895, but the Darlaston Loop remained firmly closed, the station at Darlaston having been demolished. Later, Rushall station, between Walsall and Pelsall,

Below:
The Princes End branch enjoyed an intermittent passenger service. These began when it opened on 14 September 1863, but were withdrawn between 1890 and 1895 and again, permanently, from 1 January 1916. From then the line was used by goods trains and diversions, one of the former, hauled by ex-LMS 8F No 48082, being photographed in July 1965.
W. J. A. Hoskins

Above:
Lichfield (Trent Valley) station on 29 August 1961 as No D325 (later Class 40 No 40125) heads north with an extra down train. The Lichfield (City) to Burton-on-Trent line crosses behind and two of the newly erected overhead wire gantries can be seen.
Brian Haresnape

was closed completely from 1 March 1909, tramway competition again being blamed, and the Tipton-Wednesbury service was withdrawn again as a wartime economy from 1 January 1916, never reopening.

The Trent Valley Railway

By virtue of having been built as two independent schemes, the combined GJ and L&B route from Liverpool/Manchester-London via Birmingham was neither straight nor direct. The difficulties that were to result from working this route were not lost to some, even before any part of it opened, and in 1836 at least two groups were eyeing-up alternatives. One such was the GJ company itself, whose engineer, Joseph Locke, lighted upon a shorter and more direct route following the Trent Valley; he surveyed this during the year. The same route was also favoured by the Manchester & Birmingham Railway, an ill-fated scheme to build an independent line between Manchester and London, allegedly conceived by a group of Manchester traders in a fit of pique following the short shrift given to a delegation of their number visiting the GJ company in 1834. Both envisaged links with the GJ line at Stafford and the

Right:
An example of Trent Valley Railway architecture: Lichfield station, which opened with the line on 1 December 1847. This was superseded by a new station, opened by the LNWR on 3 July 1871, and eventually became a private residence. It is seen here in the early 1960s, just before work began on the electrification of the line.
R. S. Carpenter Collection

L&B at Rugby, saving roughly 50 miles on the proposed route and by-passing Birmingham altogether. The GJ did not proceed with their line and the latter's proposal, which was encapsulated in the Manchester & Birmingham Extension Railway Bill of 1839, was defeated in the House of Commons.

Other attempts to build a similar line followed, including one to link up with the B&DJ line at Tamworth and to by-pass the GJ completely by forging a route to Manchester via the Churnet Valley and the M&B's Macclesfield branch. In 1845, suitably encouraged by such renewed interest, the Manchester & Birmingham extension line's proposers put forward a new line, under the title of the Trent Valley Railway. This received the backing of the L&B, who concluded a provisional agreement to absorb it, together with the M&B and 'Churnet Valley' companies, at a later date. Upon learning of this arrangement the GJ company took umbrage and their relations with the L&B worsened until matters were resolved by the success of the Trent Valley Bill and the failure of the 'Churnet Valley' one; the latter scheme being redrafted and re-emerging a year later as part of the North Staffordshire Railway.

The Trent Valley Railway, which was authorised by an Act of 21 July 1845, ran from a junction with the L&B line at Rugby to one with the GJ at Stafford. Construction began on 13 November 1845, when the Prime Minister, Sir Robert Peel, MP for Tamworth, ceremonially cut the first sod. Before it was completed, the L&B, GJ and M&B had united as the LNWR and together purchased the line on 14 April 1846. It opened in sections during 1847: a spur at Tamworth to the Midland Railway opening on 12 June; limited traffic between Rugby and Stafford commencing on 15 September; the line opening fully on 1 December, with stations at: Stretton (renamed Brinklow from 1 February 1870), Shilton, Bulkington, Nuneaton (Nuneaton Trent Valley from 2 June 1924), Atherstone, Polesworth, Tamworth, Lichfield, Armitage, Rugeley and Colwich.

Improvements on the line have included the opening of a new station at Lichfield on 3 July 1871, situated a quarter of a mile south of the original one, and the quadrupling of the line between Nuneaton and Atherstone, and Armitage and Rugeley; work sanctioned by the LNWR (New Works &c) Act of 31 July 1902.

Local services along the line were very poor to begin with, just three trains in each direction each day, taking an average of 1hr 55min for the journey. Even with improvements, by the 1920s this service had only increased to six trains in each direction per day, taking an average of 1hr 20min each. Despite this, the majority of the local stations remained open, with only Bulkington closing completely on 18 May 1931. Express services fared better. Between Rugby and Stafford, most expresses only called at Nuneaton and Tamworth, and in 1855, allowing for these stops, they were covering the 49.75 miles in 1hr 40min. Advances in locomotive design, and the quadrupuling mentioned above, improved these times, so that by 1921 the equivalent journey took just 1hr 15min, the best non-stop time between Rugby and Stafford being around 58min.

The LNWR's Coventry-Nuneaton line

At the height of the Railway Mania, various projects set their sights on Coventry. The only railway company to actually serve the city was the L&B, which was determined to retain its exclusive access there. Wind of a planned line to Nuneaton provoked the company to propose a 'spoiler'; a rival plan for a railway along a near identical course, designed to delay the progress of the other bill through Parliament. Spoilers were rarely designed to be built, but in this instance the bill was successful, receiving the Royal Assent on 3 August 1846. By then the L&B was no more, and the LNWR inherited its constituent's powers, gaining authority to raise the necessary capital to build the line in an Act passed on 2 July 1847.

Against the background of railway skulduggery going on elsewhere in the West Midlands at that time, the Coventry-Nuneaton line was completed with a minimum of fuss or interruption, opening on 2 September 1850, with intermediate stations at Counden Road (renamed Coundon Road from 1 November 1894), Foleshill, Longford & Exhall, Hawkesbury Lane (to passengers only), Bedworth and Chilvers Coton. A basic service of seven trains in each direction was operated on weekdays, two of which missed out all of the intermediate stops; a Sunday service of two slow trains in each direction was also provided, the journey times being: slow, 45min; non-stop, 20min. All of this came to an abrupt halt on 26 January 1857, when 23 arches of the viaduct carrying a section of the line between Coventry and Counden Road stations collapsed. Too major a collapse for a quick repair, the LNWR re-thought the engineering of the line at Spon End and opted for a smaller replacement viaduct and an embankment. An Act authorising this work was obtained on 23 July 1858 and the completed work came into use on 1 October 1860, nearly four years after the collapse!

Subsequent events on the line were few. Hawkesbury Lane station was opened to goods traffic from 21 May 1889, and a new stop, Daimler Halt, was opened between Coundon Road and Foleshill on 12 March 1917. At a time when the LNWR was pruning-out a lot of similar stops, this suggests that the halt was designed, as its name suggests, to serve the adjacent BSA/Lanchester/Daimler works, then engaged in important war-related production. Just after World War 1, passenger services mainly worked through from Leamington Spa, with one or two trains daily continuing on to Leicester. The LMS recast this timetable, making a number of the trains serving local stations between Coventry and Nuneaton ones which were running through from Atherstone, Leicester or Northampton; one, on Fridays only, even came from Blackpool! These services survived past Nationalisation, the only major change coming at that time being the complete closure of Longford & Exhall station on 23 May 1949.

The Rugby & Leamington Railway

Following the opening of their railway between Coventry and Warwick on 9 December 1844, the L&B planned a short extension of it to continue the line along the comparatively short distance to Leamington. Powers authorising this were contained in an Act of 27 July 1846. Meanwhile, a number of schemes had been promoted to link this extended L&B branch to Rugby; one, the Rugby & Leamington Railway, succeeding in obtaining an Act authorising its construction between Leamington Priors, at a junction with the proposed L&B extension, via a single line to Rugby, at a junction with the L&B main line. This Act also included a clause which permited the L&B to purchase and vest the Rugby & Leamington Railway company in itself, which is exactly what the succeeding LNWR did, on 17 November 1846.

Above right:
Foleshill station on the Coventry-Nuneaton line. One of the latter shed's BR Standard Class 4s, No 75035, has just arrived with a workmen's service for Nuneaton one weekday in July 1963. The line was opened by the LNWR on 2 September 1850, but threatened with closure when this shot was taken.
A. W. Flowers

Right:
Birdingbury station, on the LNWR's Rugby & Leamington line, showing the arrival of the last train to call there, the 19.54 Rugby-Leamington service, on 13 June 1959. A lone local, carrying a doll dressed like Lord Nelson and waving a flag, appears to be all there was, apart from the photographer, to mark the occasion. The locomotive, 2-6-2T No 41227, is adorned with the legend 'Oh Sir Brian', a reference to Sir Brian Robertson, Chairman of the BTC, who caught the stick for rail closures before the days of the beloved Doctor.
Michael Mensing

75035

41227

Left:
The LNWR doubled most of the line between Leamington and Rugby in the early 1880s. The section between Rugby and Dunchurch was the first part to be completed, coming into use on 27 March 1882. Passenger services were withdrawn on 15 June 1959 but the line saw sporadic use thereafter as a diversionary route. On 9 August 1960, un-named 'Britannia' No 70047 works a trains past Bilton Sidings box.
Michael Mensing

Right:
Monument Lane station, looking towards New Street, in the early 1930s. The train is being hauled by a Watford Tank Class 0-6-2-T locomotive and is probably bound for the Harborne line.
Lens of Sutton

Below:
The characteristic scenery of the Stour Valley line is captured well in this wintry view of the 12.25pm Hereford-New Street DMU nearing the end of its journey on 19 January 1985. The building to the extreme left is a canal pumping engine house which has been extensively restored since this photograph was taken.
Chris Morrison

Having safely fought off another rival, the LNWR was less than motivated actually to build the line. Abandonment was actively considered, but the Board succumbed to pressure applied by a deputation of Warwick people and set to building it in 1850. Work was completed early the following year and the line opened on 1 March 1851, with intermediate stations at Birdingbury and Marton (renamed Marton for Southam on 1 July 1853, reverting to Marton in October 1860, changing back to Marton for Southam in January 1877 and reverting to Marton once more from 1 August 1895). The initial passenger service was equally unenthusiastic, only five trains each way, on weekdays only, taking 40min for the journey.

An additional station, Dunchurch, was added between Birdingbury and Rugby, opening first to goods, on 1 February 1871, then to passengers, on 2 October that year. Two sections of the line were doubled in the early 1880s; the first being that between Rugby and Dunchurch, which came into use on 27 March 1882, the second being between Marton and Leamington, which opened to traffic on 28 January 1884. This left only the section between Marton and Dunchurch as single line. By the time of the Grouping, the LNWR service along the line was little improved from that it had opened with, consisting of nine trains in each direction on weekdays only, taking 35min for the journey. The LMS slightly improved this service, increasing the number of trains to 13 in each direction per weekday, one of which was a workmen's service and six of which were worked by steam railmotors.

After Nationalisation the viability of the line seemed doubtful. Goods facilities ceased at Birdingbury station from 3 August 1953, and the passenger service between Leamington and Rugby was withdrawn on 15 June 1959.

The Birmingham, Wolverhampton & Stour Valley Railway

A railway linking Birmingham and Shrewsbury was first proposed in 1830, and stabs at building the line were made more or less every two years subsequently. After a failed Bill early in 1845, one further attempt was made, as part of which the cost of constructing the line was split three ways. One was a section between Shrewsbury and Wellington, to be built jointly by the promoters and the newly formed 'Shrewsbury & Birmingham & Shropshire Union Railways & Canal Company'. Second was the portion between Wellington and Wolverhampton, which was to stay the responsibility of the line's proponents; and third was the remainder of the line, between Wolverhampton and Birmingham, which was renamed 'The Stour Valley Railway'; and was to be built by a new company, funded equally by public subscription, the Shrewsbury line's promoters, the L&B, and the Birmingham Canal companies; its title coming from a planned branch along the valley of the River Stour, from Smethwick to Stourbridge and Stourport. On 1 January 1846, the company behind the Shrewsbury line adopted the title of the 'Shrewsbury & Birmingham Railway Company' (S&B), and the Stour Valley line became

Lifebuoy
Soap
VIM

known as the 'Birmingham, Wolverhampton & Stour Valley Railway Company' (Stour Valley).

These cost-cutting motives suited those of the emerging LNWR. As the GJ and L&B amalgamation approached, the two companies were planning a new station to be erected on a vast site of derelict housing adjoining Navigation Street. Although offering a more advantageous location, this site also lengthened the journey to Wolverhampton, where the S&B were to build a more centrally located station. Therefore, if the S&B were to be assisted with building their line to Birmingham, the newly created LNWR could split the cost of constructing a line they had to build in any case, and control both who used this and who gained entry into their new station.

The Stour Valley Railway was authorized by an Act of 3 August 1846. Construction was divided into three sections: Birmingham-Winson Green, which included an 845yd tunnel approach to Navigation Street; Winson Green-Oldbury, and from there to Bushbury. Then, in 1847, the LNWR strengthened its control of the Stour Valley line, in three ways. Firstly, by taking over the Birmingham Canal Co; secondly, by leasing the line, under the terms of an Act passed on 1 July 1847, which also gave the S&B use of it unless they became 'leased to, or purchased by, or amalgamated with, the Great Western'; and thirdly, in a further Act of 9 July 1847, by making the Wolverhampton General station, and the line from there to Bushbury, joint property with S&B. Having therefore secured control of the Stour Valley line, they could proceed with construction more slowly, and 1848 1849 and 1850 each passed without its completion. The line was eventually declared fit to open on 21 November 1851, and this was announced for 1 December, when the S&B fully expected to be able to run their trains through to Birmingham. This was not to be so.

The LNWR had learned of a draft agreement to amalgamate with the GWR at some time in the future, in 1856 or 1857, which the S&B had signed on 8 May 1851; and so they invoked the terms of their 1847 agreement, and denied the company the use of the Stour Valley line; setting the scene for a prolonged disagreement. The Stour Valley line eventually opened to goods on 1 February 1852, and for passengers, to a temporary platform just inside the Navigation Street site, on 1 July 1852. There were stations at: Smethwick; Spon Lane; Oldbury & Bromford Lane; Dudley Port; Tipton; Deepfields, and Ettingshall Road & Bilston, additional ones being opened at Bushbury (2 August 1852); Albion (1 May 1853); Monument Lane (1 July 1854), and Monmore Green (1 December 1863).

Meanwhile, the S&B, weakened by their fight with the LNWR, brought forward the date for their proposed amalgamation with the GWR, this becoming effective from 1 September 1854. The problems with the LNWR were finally resolved on 29 May 1854, almost four months after the latter had finally allowed them to run their trains over the Stour Valley line into Birmingham New Street, which they did between 4 February and 13 November 1854, being granted an extension of running powers following a bridge collapse at Handsworth, on the GWR's BW&D line, on 26 August 1854.

New Street Station

During the summer of 1845, divergent interests began to converge in Birmingham. The not-so-cold war that had existed between the GJ and L&B companies began to thaw and formal talks were held from early August. Crafty schemes had gone awry and the idea of working as a proper through route was emerging. That decided, attention turned to the point at which the two lines met: the Curzon Street stations. A decade earlier, blinkered protectionism had ruled out 'butt-ending' the lines, to correct this now would have been very costly. Curzon Street was also a far from ideal location; passenger complaints were on the up. It was over half a mile from the town centre and the stations occupied very cramped and fully developed sites. Into this poured the burgeoning services of three railway companies and, by 1845, it was obvious that a larger, more central, station was needed.

At the same time, the Birmingham Street Commissioners and Council were looking at ways of improving the town centre; especially at clearing the many cluttered courts and slum areas which lay just off the main streets. One such was commonly referred to as 'The Froggery' because its damp conditions were said to favour the breeding of frogs. It included Peck Lane and King Street, plus other alleys, and a number of important buildings, such as the Old Dungeon, the Old Meeting House and a Jewish synagogue and cemetery.

The L&B took the lead in finding a site for the new station. They approached the town Council, and guess what they were offered? The Froggery! Both parties were pleased: the L&B would get their central railway station and the town council would get a slum cleared at someone else's expense. A Bill was prepared and presented to the 1846 Parliamentary Session; this sought permission for the compulsory purchase of the land required and the construction of a passenger station, with the stopping up of Peck Lane and the construction of a public footpath in lieu of King Street, which was to be obliterated. The Bill also included an extension line between Curzon Street and the new station. It received the Royal Assent on 7 August 1846, three weeks after the Act formally merging the GJ, L&B and Manchester & Birmingham railways as the LNWR.

Land and property purchasing began immediately and the site was gradually cleared, including the demolition of three churches: The Chapel, The Welch Chapel and Lady Huntingdon's Church, the exhumed bodied being reburied elsewhere, including those from the Jewish cemetery, which found their 'final' resting place in Granville Street. In addition to being cleared, the site had also to be lowered, by about 25ft; this work taking until 1850. The job of setting out the Joint Central station, as it became known, fell to William Baker, the LNWR's Chief Engineer. As at Curzon Street, although the trains it would serve ran on a north-south axis, the site favoured a layout arrayed along an east-west axis.

Two lines were approaching the site, the L&B authorised Curzon Street extension, and the nominally independent Stour Valley Railway, the latter opening to goods in February 1852 and to passengers on 1 July 1852, working from a temporary platform at the west-end of the Joint Central station site, by the Navigation Street road bridge. Access to this platform was via steps leading from Navigation Street, which may account for its name being applied to the station at this time. On the same

Below:
A portion of a plan of Birmingham dated 1836, showing the area where New Street station was built. Note the names Peck Lane, King Street and The Froggery; Queen Street would later become part of the station as Queen's Drive. The location of the Old Meeting House is also shown, between King Street and Peck Lane.
Authors Collection

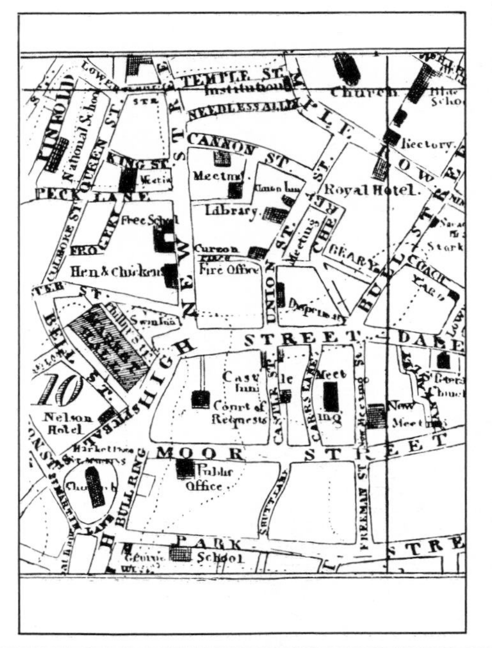

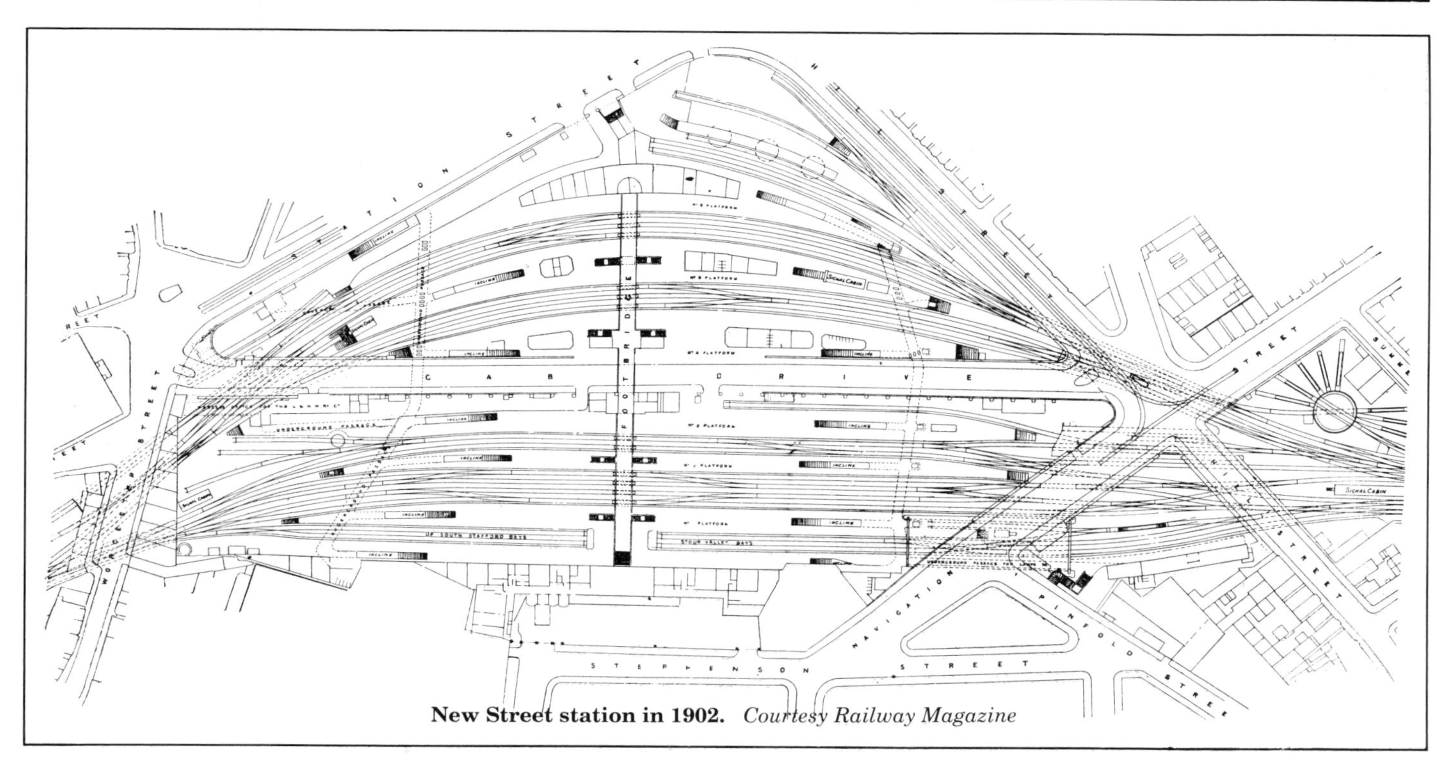

New Street station in 1902. *Courtesy Railway Magazine*

day a single line linking Navigation Street and Curzon Street stations came into use to allow the transfer of through stock.

1852 was also the year when the LNWR decided to include a hotel in the Joint Central station scheme. Reporting on the progress of the work on 5 June 1852, *The Builder* noted: 'the works at the central station in New-street, Birmingham, are now in active progress. It is intended to erect a stone building, of the Doric order, broken up into a projecting centre, five stories high, with a wing on either side. The wings and second floor of the centre will be a hotel. The whole frontage length of the building will be 314 feet, and the height 88 feet from Stephenson-place, and 109 feet above the level of the rails. These arrangements are independent of the plans for the business department of the station, which provide for a refreshment saloon 70 feet long, and more than 33 feet wide; various waiting rooms, officers' apartments, &c. on the ground floor; and on the second floor, approached through the colonnade in Stephenson-place, the booking offices of the six different companies whose passenger traffic will concentrate at the station.'

The main work of finishing the station was occupied in erecting the overall iron and glass roof, which had the largest span, at 212ft, of any in the world at the time. For expertise in the design and construction of this the LNWR turned to the Smethwick firm of Fox, Henderson & Co, who, with their engineer E. A. Cowper, erected the Crystal Palace between July 1850 and April 1851. Cowper's design for the Joint Central station was breathtaking and was described, together with another progress report, in *The Builder* on 29 January 1853: 'The Grand Central Station at Birmingham – This immense erection, which has been in the course of construction for many months past, is fast approaching completion. The offices, hotel, &c are being proceeded with by Messrs Branson & Gwyther, and the first section of a rib arch for the vast roof has been raised. . . The rib arches (are being) erected under the supervision of Mr Phillips, superintendent of works for Messrs. Fox, Henderson & Co, (and) are each composed of three sections, the weight of each rib is 25 tons. There are 45 of these in the roof, at distances of 24 feet apart, and at a height of 75 feet from the rails: nevertheless they look light and fragile. The difficulties have been enhanced by the circumstance that no interference with the traffic on the Stour Valley line could take place. Consequently, a gigantic traversing scaffolding has been constructed, reaching from one side of the station to the other, and of the most ponderous character, by which the work is being carried on without blocking up the rails at any point. The roof will be

Left:
Is this a view of New Street station under construction? It is very difficult to authenticate such a claim, but if it is correct then the photograph must date from c1853. That's some ladder in the foreground. The locomotive over to the right is a 2-4-0 of the 'Crewe Goods' class.
Don Powell Collection

Right:
This modest LNWR advertisement for the fayre at the 'Bestotel' in Birmingham dates from 1913. Their claim to be the only railway hotel comes from the fact that the Great Western Hotel had closed seven years earlier, which is fair enough, but Birmingham had been a city for 24 years by then! Did Billy Butlin ever stay here?
Pete Glews Collection

BIRMINGHAM.

—NORTH WESTERN RAILWAY COMPANY'S—

QUEEN'S HOTEL

The

ONLY Railway Hotel in the Town.

RED COAT PORTERS MEET ALL TRAINS.

Well-known for Comfort and Good Food.

Telegrams: "BESTOTEL" Telephone: 5531 Central.

filled with fluted glass, of which a vast quantity will be used, and which is to be supplied by Messrs Chance.'

The designation 'New Street' was first applied to the station in LNWR timetables of November 1852 and so it was as such that it formally opened on 1 June 1854. No one had seen anything quite like it, as evinced by the tone of this description published in *The Illustrated London News* of 3 June 1854: 'The entrance is at the bottom of Stephenson-place, where is a plain gateway leading to the main front of the station and hotel. . . . Entering the Station by an arcade, we arrive at the booking-offices for the respective railways; and passing through these, emerge on a magnificent corridor or gallery, guarded by light railing, and open to the Station (but enclosed by the immense glass and iron roof), from whence broad stone staircases, with bronze rails, afford access to the departure platform. We then stand on a level with a long series of offices, appropriated to the officials of the Companies; and a superb refreshment room, about eighty feet long by forty broad, divided into three portions by rows of massive pillars.' Beneath the roof were four through platforms and two pairs of bays, which were allocated for the arrivals and departures of the various companies.

The Queen's Hotel

The Queen's Hotel opened with the rest of New Street station on 1 June 1854. It comprised the whole of the left wing, the centre block except the ground floor, and the third storey of the right wing of the station frontage; the remainder being in railway company use. It included first and second-class refreshment rooms for the station, coffee and smoking rooms, plus 60 bedrooms. In the late 1850s more of the office space was taken over to provide an extra 26 bedrooms. From its opening the manager was Walter Scott, who leased the hotel from the LNWR in 1858. Its name was changed to the North Western (Queen's) Hotel in June 1872 to prevent the 'North Western' mantle being assumed by another hotel then in the course of erection opposite (now the Midland Hotel). A successful gambit, the name was soon changed again to the Queen's & North Western Hotel. Scott retired in 1871 and from 31 December 1881 the LNWR terminated its leasing arrangement, resuming the hotel's management.

By 1911 the Queen's was as large as it could be within its original buildings, and so that October the LNWR authorised an improvement scheme involving the demolition and rebuilding of the west wing, to incorporate 94 new bedrooms, a dining room, winter garden, banqueting and tea rooms, lounge, smoking, writing and billiards rooms. A typewriting room and ladies hairdressing saloon were also provided, the main hotel entrance being moved to the centre of the new wing. Between 1914 and 1917 an addition was made to this new part of the hotel, coming into use on 9 August 1917. The *Railway Gazette* described this extension as: 'furnished and equipped in the most up-to-date fashion. On the ground floor are three paneled rooms of fine proportions – a dining room, a lounge and a smoke room. On the first floor is another capa-

Right:
Front of the Grand Central Railway Station, at Birmingham, from the *Illustrated London News* for 10 June 1854, which featured a major article on the opening of New Street station. The opening to the station was through the colonnade at street level, the rest of the building housing the station offices and the Queen's Hotel. In the latter, on 3 June 1854, a banquet was held in honour of Edward Watkin, the LNWR Chairman, who was moving to the Manchester, Sheffield & Lincoln Railway.
Illustrated London News/Author's Collection

cious room, oak paneled, which will be available for public dinners and meetings. The extension more than doubles the bedroom accommodation hitherto provided.' Shortly after its formation, the LMS further enlarged the hotel by adding an extra two storeys on top of the original centre block. This work was completed in March 1925 and was part of a major renovation of the building, which embraced redecoration and saw individual gas fires fitted to each room.

Enlarging the station

Almost from when it opened, improvements began at New Street station: a number of small turntables, installed to facilitate the movement of carriages between the lines, were replaced by crossovers; the bay platforms were narrowed to increase the surface area of Platform No 1 and in 1874 a wider and stronger footbridge was installed. But this was just tinkering, and by the mid-1870s it was clear that an even larger station was required.

Although the enlarged portion of New Street is usually referred to as the 'Midland side', it was built and paid for by the LNWR. Through their New Lines, &c. Act of 24 July 1876 they obtained powers to buy land and property on the south side of Great Queen Street, which formed the then southern boundary of their land. These included land lying between Summer and Navigation Streets and part of Swallow Street, also gaining the authority to stop up Vale and Bread streets. Their Act of 6 August 1880 added land on the south-east side of Navigation Street and the southwest side of Hill Street to this list, plus more land in Swallow and Summer streets; another Act of 18 July 1881 adding land between Great Queen, Dudley, Old Meeting and Worcester streets. The same Act also authorised the taking of Great Queen Street within the station property and the opening out of some of the station's approach tunnels. One last Act, of 12 July 1882, authorised the purchase of more lands in the area of the newly formed Station Street and Dudley Street.

Construction began in 1881, with the demolition of the properties in the streets described; building work beginning in 1883. Four through platforms were provided, with sidings and loading docks, covered by two semi-circular roofs, with 58ft spans and lengths of 620 and 600ft. Two subways were also added, running beneath both the old and the new parts of the station. One was used for Porters to transfer luggage and parcels, but was also used by passengers until around 1920; the other was for the mails and continued into the main Post Office sorting offices in nearby Hill Street. The total scheme cost £500,000, the main contractors for the buildings being T. Nelson & Co of Carlisle and for the roof being Horton & Sons. A new street, named, appropriately enough, Station Street, was built in lieu of the roads obliterated by the expansion of the station; with Hill Street, this formed the new southern perimeter of the New Street site, which now covered 14½ acres, eight of which were under cover.

The former Great Queen Street was renamed Queen's Drive, and platforms on the old side of the station were renumbered 1 to 3, those on the new side being Nos 4 to 6; the first of these coming into use on 8 February 1885. The Midland Railway opened its extension of the Birmingham West Surburban line into New Street station on 1 June 1885; the whole of the new portion of the enlarged station coming into use on 1 October that year, when Midland expresses were able to run through for the first time. For the next four years, both halves of New Street were used by the LNWR and Midland companies: some of the former's local services using the new Platform No 5, some of the latter's trains still using the South Staffordshire bays on Platform No 1. This practice ended from 1 October 1889, when the new half of the station became the exclusive province of the Midland Railway.

On 1 April 1897, New Street became a joint station, being operated under a joint management scheme by the LNWR and Midland Railway. It had long been an open station, the public right of way which existed over the main footbridge preventing an easy means of closing it from being implemented. Tickets were therefore collected at the nearest local stations: Dudley Port, Monument Lane, Vauxhall,

Above:
The splendour that was New Street. A view of the North Western side of the station in the 1890s, taken from the steps of No 1 signal box, looking towards Wolverhampton. The trio in the centre are taking levels amidst a fine array of ageing LNWR rolling stock.
British Rail

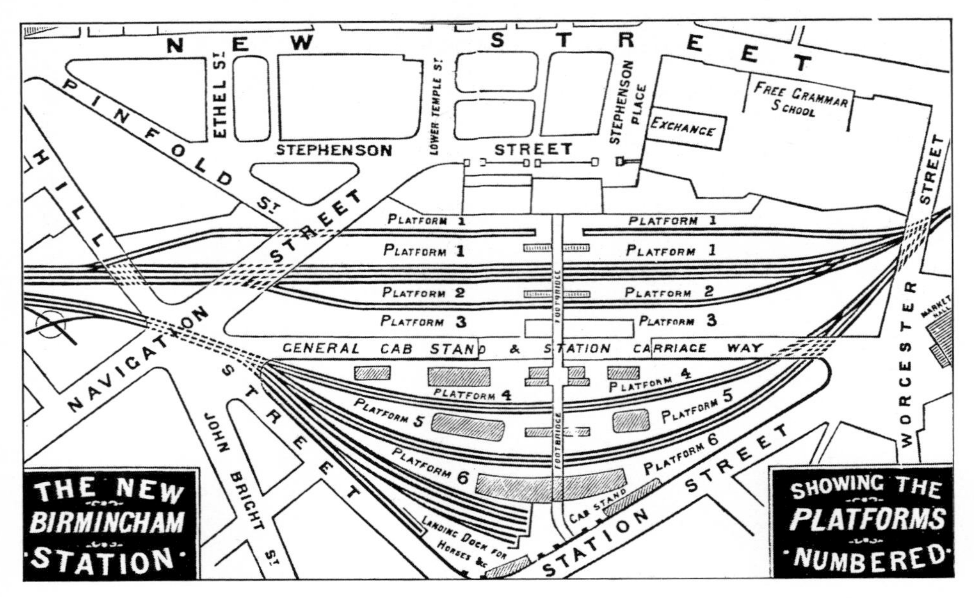

Left:
The 'New Birmingham Station' was 21 years old when this sketch plan was published with James Upton's *Birmingham ABC Railway Guide* in 1904; but when you've a perfectly good block already, why waste it! This does serve as a useful reference to the enlarged station, showing the confusion that resulted from having more than one platform No 1!
Author's Collection

Below left:
A view across the North Western side of New Street station from the Queen's Hotel in September 1885. The footbridge at right maintained a public right of way through the station and was the main reason why it could not be 'closed'. The daylight in the centre is coming from Queen's Drive and the piles of building materials centre left indicate that whilst the Midland side of the station came into use on 8 February that year, the work involved was not yet completed.
NRM

Stetchford, Adderley Park, Saltley, Camp Hill and Kings Norton all being used for this at one time or another.

A number of improvements were made to New Street station over the years. In 1912, two additional through lines were added and in 1924 colour light signals were installed on two platforms, more being added in 1946. The station lighting was improved under a scheme completed in January 1925; a total of 188 Sugg's five-light 'Littleton' gas lamps being installed, hung in rows following the centre-line of each platform. These boasted the unusual feature of being remotely controlled and lit from a central point on each platform. A 40ft wide, double-sided, Benn & Cronin train indicator, then the largest in the country, was installed as the entrance to Platform No 4 from Queen's Drive in August 1928; this incorporated collapsible gates, the services being displayed on interchangeable enamelled-iron plates.

From the time of its expansion, New Street station, excluding the Queen's Hotel, gave employment of around 600 people. It was also an extremely busy place, with an average of 190 arrivals and 180 departures daily. Appendix 2 gives a portrait of the latter over a one hour period during 1938. New Street was controlled by six signalboxes: No 1 had 63 levers, two signalmen controlling movements to and from platforms Nos 1, 1a, 3, 4, 5 and 6, plus all up and down Western lines at the London end of the station. No 2 box had 75 levers with which one signalman controlled movements to and from platforms Nos 7 to 10, plus the Midland Division lines at the London end of the station. No 3 box shared duties with No 1 box, one signalman controlling dwarf signals at platform level; it was abolished in 1946 as part of the LNWR side roof removal. Box No 4 had 73 levers through which one signalman controlled platforms Nos 7 to 11 and the back sidings at the Gloucester end. The biggest box was No 5, having three signalmen and 153 levers which controlled movements to and from all platforms and sidings at the Wolverhampton end of the station. Box No 9 was the smallest, having only 18 levers with which one signalman operated crossover points and movements at the end of platforms Nos 1 and 1a.

Routine maintenance on such a large building was an on going task; the roofs presenting a costly fight against corrosion. They were inspected at least twice a year and cleaned and painted in yearly sections in rotation, starting at one end and working along to the other. programming the work over a number of years so that by the time it was completed it was time to start again. After cleaning, minor repairs would be effected and the metal work painted with red lead, which would be followed by an undercoat and a top coat of deep cream paint, this shade being the one found to show through the begriming pall of smoke which pervaded the station the longest.

During the war, New Street station suffered considerable air-raid damage, especially between 1940 and 1942; the roof of the former LNWR side receiving a direct hit on the night of 28 July 1942. Troops in transit were accommodated on the station, not at the Queen's Hotel, but in makeshift barracks set-up in the lamp room at the extreme end of Platform No 1, in between the Navigation and Hill Street bridges.

By the end of the war, New Street station was beginning to show its age. Letters of complaint began to appear, such as this one of 15 October 1945 in the *Railway Gazette* : 'Of our larger stations it would seem that none would have a better claim for early attention than Birmingham (New Street) . . . .

Right:
An unusual view of New Street, taken from No 5 Signal box on 17 August 1954. The building to the left was the lamp-room and is one of the few portions of the original station to have survived the station's rebuilding. During the war, troops in transit were allowed to bed-down for the night in there. Thank goodness gricers don't congregate like this on the new station. Over to the right, someone has dropped his pencil!
Donald Kelk

Why should all the expresses for Liverpool, Manchester and the North start from No. 3 Platform? this is more like a parcels dock . . . . Only half of the coaches of a train can be accommodated, which necessitates a double pull up before (departure) . . . . These trains . . . have deteriorated . . . they now consist of non-corridor stock . . . In one train recently (there was) an amazing collection, including a M.R. narrow 4-coach rake, a Caledonian third brake, and an LYR. composite. New Street, however, can take first place for its loudspeaker system: one has no doubt, when staying in the hotel, that the 11.5pm is going to call at Motherwell, etc.'

This produced another letter to the same journal, written on 5 November 1945: 'The chaotic conditions prevailing there on a Saturday during the summer have to be seen to be believed, and the stupidity of giving one number only to platform 2, an island platform with two faces, adds to the confusion and leads to such conundrums from the loudspeaker system as: 'The train standing at the London end of Platform 2, facing Platform 1,' etc. (There is also) the inordinate delay caused by the need of collecting tickets at such stations as Stetchford, Vauxhall, Monument Lane, Dudley Port, etc. It is surely time that this anachronistic relic of Victorian travel finally was discarded.

Two of these complaints were dealt with sooner *and* later. From 7 October 1946 a new platform numbering scheme was introduced, giving each platform face, including those in the bays, a number. Thus the 'LNWR' side became platforms Nos 3 to 6 and the 'Midland' side Nos 7 to 10. Nine years later, in March 1955, a new public address. system was installed, featuring 149 loudspeakers and five powerful amplifiers delivering 300W. Meanwhile major work was also carried out. In November 1945 the LMS began the task of removing the damaged roof from the 'LNWR' side; this was undertaken by the aptly named Altitude Contracting Co Ltd, of Birmingham, who employed a similar travelling scaffolding gantry, mounted on rails on the platforms, to the one used 90 years earlier to erect it. The trusses were cut down with oxy-acetylene equipment; the work being completed by February 1947. Temporary awnings, of corrugated asbestos and perspex, were put up over the platforms and these were to be replaced by more permanent versions in work scheduled to begin in April 1948. More ambitious was the replacement of the Hill and Navigation Street road bridges with stronger and wider steel structures carrying slab concrete beds. This began in February 1948 and was completed in 1951, by which time a second phase of roof repair work had begun, affecting platforms Nos 7 to 10 and Queen's Drive.

Right:
The information that the Altitude Contracting Co of Birmingham are responsible for the removal of the roof over the North Western side of New Street station is not withheld from the public in this view of the operation from the Queen's Hotel on 26 October 1946. Note the movable staging in the foreground, and the erection of the replacement canopies, bottom right.
Modern Transport

Above:
New Street's platform canopies were intended to be only temporary, but as this view from the top floor rear of the Queen's Hotel shows, they were still there in 1960. Note the draughty rooflights in the centre cover Queen's Drive and the buildings which used to flank all corners of the Hill/Navigation/John Bright street corner.
British Rail

It was therefore a much altered New Street station that celebrated its centenary in 1954. An exhibition was held there between 1-3 June, which included items of historic rolling stock (drawn from that in service?). There were four coaches: a 50ft Midland non-corridor third of 1910; a 57ft LNWR corridor third of 1905; Queen Victoria's 60ft LNWR saloon of 1895 and a 17ft royal saloon of 1842; plus three locomotives: a Midland Kirtley (No 20002) of 1866; the LNWR 2-4-0 Precedent class *Hardwicke* and LMS 4-6-2 No 46235 *City of Birmingham*. These celebrations were just in time as in October 1957, exploratory talks began between British Railways and Birmingham Corporation to relate the modernisation of New Street station to the Council's planned Inner Ring Road scheme.

Birmingham, Erdington & Sutton Coldfield Railway

By the early 1840s the residents of Sutton Coldfield, six or so miles northeast of Birmingham, were beginning to feel isolated from Birmingham, and all of the other surrounding towns which were starting to flourish through their proximity to the railways. Local traders were especially disadvantaged as goods and raw materials were made more expensive through the need to transport them via the town's unreliable roads. They needn't have worried for long. Sutton Coldfield is well situated, being directly en route between Birmingham and Tamworth and but a small deviation in a line drawn between the former and Lichfield. Sooner or later, the thinking went, someone would want to build a railway between Birmingham and one or both of these places, and then the town would benefit. It was right too, but things took just a little longer than most had anticipated.

The first railway schemes to encompass Sutton Coldfield were hatched at the height of the 'Railway Mania' in 1845. One may even carry the distinction of being the shortest lived railway company: the Birmingham & Lichfield Railway Co being formed on 16 September 1845 and amalgamating with the more ambitiously titled Lichfield & Manchester Railway, just two days later, to form the Birmingham, Lichfield & Manchester Railway Co (BL&MR)! The line was surveyed by J. R. McClean. It was to run from a junction with the GJ line at Aston to one with the Trent Valley line at Lichfield, with a branch to Sutton Coldfield. An Act authorising its construction was obtained on 27 July 1846, but the scheme was taken over by the LNWR that September and not proceded with in favour of their own line to Lichfield, which revived the name of the short-lived Birmingham & Lichfield Railway Co. Another Act was duly obtained, on 9 July 1847, but construction did not begin, nor was it to, despite extension of time Acts which ultimately gave the LNWR seven years grace to build the line. In fairness the company was otherwise distracted locally, with the building of New Street station and in its punative 'war' with the S&B company over use of the Stour Valley line, and so it abandoned the Lichfield line in 1853.

Other schemes followed on the heels of this abandonment but came to nothing and attention now moves forward to June 1857 when further attempts to promote a railway to Sutton Coldfield began. Distrustful, with good cause, of the LNWR, discussions were also held with the Midland Railway. Debate and dissention followed, with two camps being formed, each promoting a different line. The Birmingham, Erdington & Sutton Coldfield Railway favoured a line, from a junction with the Midland Railway near Erdington Hall, which kept to the east of the main turnpike through Sutton Coldfield, whilst the Birmingham, Erdington & Sutton Coldfield Railway (Western Line) favoured the tried and tested route from the LNWR at Aston, which kept to the west of the same turnpike. Squabbling between the two companies occupied most of 1858 until, tired of the stupidity of it all, some of those involved began moves towards reconcilliation.

The LNWR was also roused. They made overtures to the backers of the rival 'eastern line', were rejected, and duly adopted the 'western line' proposal as their own, taking the company over. Unfortunately, *both* companies had submitted bills to Parliament in November 1858 and, with neither showing any sign of withdrawing, matters had to be resolved by a House of Commons Select Committee, which met between 4 and 7 July 1859 and came out in favour of the LNWR's bill. Hastily its title was changed to the LNWR, Sutton Coldfield Branch Bill and it received the Royal Assent on 8 August. Although torturous to plan, constructing the line was relatively easy. It opened on 2 June 1863, with stations at Gravelly Hill, Erdington, Wyld Green (Wylde Green from August 1864) and Sutton Coldfield. There was a basic daily service of seven trains in each direction (with three on Sundays), with local people now able to take just 25mins to complete a journey that had taken 20 years to make possible.

This may have seemed a reasonable conclusion to matters, but even as the line to Sutton Coldfield opened, others were planning to extend it on to Lichfield; and history was about to repeat itself. The Birmingham & Sutton Coldfield Extension Railway proposed a line from a junction with the LNWR there to the same company's former SS line at Lichfield, obtaining an Act authorising this on 21 July 1863. But the 'Railway Mania' was long over; investors were more wary of speculative railway ventures and, sadly for this line's promotors, investors were not forthcoming; its powers lapsed. Almost 10 years later, the Birmingham & Lichfield Junction Railway was promoted to build the same line, obtaining an Act on 6 August 1872, but despite extension of time Acts in 1875 and 1878, they also failed to build it. These successive failures were felt hardest by the LNWR, to whose advantage the line was. Unable to have others build it before taking it over, they were forced to do the job themselves.

The LNWR (Sutton Coldfield and Lichfield) Act of 29 June 1880 authorised the company to build a line, 8 miles 3 furlongs 8 chains and 40ft long, by a junction with their Sutton Coldfield Branch Railway, terminating by a junction with their South Staffordshire railway in Lichfield; included in these proposals were new stations at Sutton Coldfield and Lichfield. Construction proceded without undue difficulty and the line was opened to goods traffic on 1 September 1884. Two months later, on 3 November, the almost completed station at Lichfield, designated 'City', came into use, in place of the original South Staffordshire station there. Finally, on 15 December 1884, passenger services began to operate through to Lichfield and the new station at Sutton Coldfield came into use. There were intermediate stations at Four Oaks, Blake Street and Shenstone. The timetable was recast to provide a much more intensive service than on the original branch, although few of the trains worked all the way through to Lichfield. A basic service of 35 trains from and 36 trains to Birmingham was operated on weekdays, with a vastly reduced service of only five trains in each direction on Sundays, only working to and from Sutton Coldfield. Of the daily services, most only ran as far as the latter, with just five making the through journey between New Street and Lichfield, some of which were semi-fasts, not calling at any stations before Sutton Coldfield. An additional service of six trains provided a shuttle service between there and Lichfield.

Below:
Shenstone was one of only three intermediate stations built on the LNWR's Sutton Coldfield-Lichfield line. Opened on 15 December 1884, its elaborately decorated frontage is seen in this view taken in the early 1960s. *R. S. Carpenter Collection*

LNWR miscellaneous improvements 1855-1872

Locomotive sheds

Upon its formation, the LNWR's main locomotive shed in Birmingham was at Curzon Street; which was used in conjunction with the accommodation at the ex-GJ temporary terminus at Vauxhall. The latter was also temporary and very limited in size, having only two tracks and room for just six locomotives. It was enlarged once, in 1839, when the GJ's move to its new terminus at Curzon Street freed land at Vauxhall, and again in 1855; the LNWR Board authorising the latter on 8 December 1854. The 'new' shed was in fact a redundant wooden structure, transported from Camden, which was extended progressively over the next three years, until it was declared fit for use by the Locomotive Department late in 1858. This appears to be all the work that was carried out on the shed, which was soon too small for its allocation, most of which stood outside. Construction of a new shed at Aston began in 1882 and when this opened Vauxhall shed was closed and demolished soon afterwards.

The LNWR also built a locomotive shed at Monument Lane in 1858, which had its origins as the Edgbaston Depot of the Stour Valley line. Reference is made to this shed being in use in a report dated December 1850, but little else is known about it, other than that it may also have been used by the S&B company to stable one locomotive overnight during their brief nine month use of the line and New Street station in 1854. Monument Lane shed proper was built in 1857/8, coming into use in November 1858. Initially it was a 200ft long three road shed with accommodation for only 12 locomotives; the Carriage Department having occupation of one of the roads. It was built to allow the original roundhouse at Curzon Street to be demolished to make way for enlargements to the goods facilities there; the latter's allocation of locomotives and crew arriving at Monument Lane in 1859. Thus overcrowded, space was relieved slightly in 1870 with the removal of the Carriage Department to

Left:
Monument Lane shed in 1959. Progressively down-graded since the mid-1930s, by this time it had also become a DMU stabling point. The poor state of the buildings, especially that to the right, is all too apparent. Monument Lane's steam allocation was officially ended from 12 June 1961, steam workings from there lasting until 16 February 1962. *R. S. Carpenter Collection*

Above:
Class 24 No D5005 passes the junction of the Harborne Railway with the Stour Valley line, near Winson Green, in September 1963. The branch closed two months later on 4 November.
Ian Slater

a new shed nearby, but full relief did not come until the erection of a new building in 1884. Known as the 'New Shed', this was 150ft long and covered six roads, but only accommodated 12 locomotives. A 42ft diameter turntable, coal stage and water tank were also added at this time.

Monument Lane shed could therefore accommodate just 30 locomotives under cover, 18 in the old shed and 12 in the new, and by the late 1880s its allocation was already up to 37. It was a sub-shed to Aston and coded 10M, itself being responsible for a small shed at Tipton, supplying motive power for a variety of services, including main line turns, Stour Valley line locals and the Harborne branch. No major improvements were made there for 50 years, until the early 1930s, when a new 60ft diameter turntable was installed and the old shed demolished to make way for mechanical coaling and ash disposal plant; this work being completed by 1934. A water softener was added in 1938 and new shed offices in 1939. During and after the war Monument Lane lost its express duties to Bushbury, and in the LMS shed reorganisation of 1935 it became a sub-shed to Bescot and renumbered 3E; becoming 21E under BR(LMR) shed changes on May 1960 and 2H under Tyseley in September 1963. DMUs were allocated to Monument Lane by 1957, its allocation for 27 July that year including Nos 79173-75/8-80; its steam allocation being officially ended from 12 June 1961, but, as ever, a few locomotives hung on until steam workings ceased from it on 16 February 1962.

Other improvements

The shared use of New Street station brought the LNWR and Midland companies into close daily contact at Birmingham, an arrangement which bore fruit in a number of ways. One such was the reciprocal granting of running powers, an example being the LNWR's use of the Midland's line between Burton and Wichnor Junction which began on 1 December 1861. Eleven years later, on 1 January 1872, LNWR goods trains began to work through between Wichnor Junction and Derby, passenger trains following suit on 1 March that year. LNWR cooperation even extended to the GWR, and at Leamington a joint junction line to the west of the latter's station there was brought into use on 26 January 1864.

The Harborne Railway

The village of Harborne was mentioned in Domesday. Situated on the then fringe of Staffordshire, four miles southwest of Birmingham, it became much favoured by the town's 'new gentry', its businessmen and senior city workers, as *the* place to live. By the mid 19th century Harborne had developed into a high class suburb of Birmingham which lacked little other than a quick and efficient means of conveying its residents to and from their places of work. Moves to rectify this situation began in 1865, resulting in the formation of the Harborne Railway Company. To counter any difficulties the company may have encountered steering a bill through Parliament, it established its offices in London. But this was an uncontroversial proposal, the Harborne Railway Act receiving Royal Assent on 28 June 1866, authorising construction of a 2 mile 42 chains long line from a junction with the LNWR's Stour Valley line, just beyond its Edgbaston station (renamed Monument Lane in March 1874), to Harborne.

Initial enthusiasm for the scheme quickly waned and the company had to present a second bill to Parliament,

Above right:
Harborne station, terminus of the Harborne Railway, in 1906. The line opened on 10 August 1874, and featured an extremely intensive service, tailored to suit the needs of the businessmen who resided in this affluent suburb. Part of the timetable was designed so that they could travel home for lunch.
Don Powell Collection

Right:
After closure to passengers the Harborne line became a favourite with enthusiasts specials. This one, organised by the SLS on 30 May 1959, is seen passing beneath Selwyn Road and emerging, with dramatic effect, upon the site of the former Rotton Park Road station.
A. W. White

three years later, to extend its powers. The Harborne Railway Act which received Royal Assent on 1 August 1870 extended the time allowed for land purchasing until 1 August 1872 and the time allowed for construction to 1 January 1873. The Act also leased the line to the LNWR, for which they would receive 50% of the gross receipts from it. Completion of the line outreached even these powers and it finally opened to passengers on 10 August 1874; goods traffic commencing on 1 October that year. The line was single throughout and built on a steady gradient, which dropped at 1 in 66 from the point at which the line had crossed the Birmingham Canal Navigation, through Icknield Port Road, Rotten Park Road and Hagley Road, three of its four stations; dropping to 1 in 74 for the final approach to Harborne. The line's only branch, a connection to Mitchell's & Butler's brewery at Cape Hill, which opened in July 1879, was added in 1909. This left the line near to Rotton Park Road station.

The service was operated from New Street, with an intermediate call at Monument Lane, and was particularly

Right:
The Harborne Railway had four stations, of which this, Hagley Road, was the last before its terminus. It is seen here in 1910. Passenger services were withdrawn on 26 November 1934 but Hagley Road remained open for goods and coal traffic.
Don Powell Collection

intense, consisting of 20 trains to Harborne and 19 to New Street, Mondays to Fridays, with 17 and 18 trains respectively on Saturdays; there being no Sunday service. Motive power was provided by LNWR 4ft 3in 0-6-2Ts, based on Monument Lane shed. Journey times varied between 17 and 23mins, depending on the time of day, and fares were low; even at closure a return cost only 3d (1.5p) and a weekly third class season ticket just 2s (10p)! Equally distinctive was the service frequency. The first train left Harborne at 05.35, and between then and 09.13 there were no fewer than nine trains to New Street, but only two, at 06.35 and 07.22, in the other direction. Over three hours then elapsed without any trains at all, until a lunchtime service of 'expresses' began; trains which missed out some or all of

the intermediate stations and were designed to enable businessmen to get home for lunch. The service then became hourly until around five, when a more intensive service, including one 'express', commenced. Later trains were less frequent, but ran until 22.04 (from Harborne) and 22.40 (from New Street).

Few improvements were made to the line. New station buildings were opened at Rotton Park Road on 2 September 1902 and a passing loop was put in there in 1903. Nonetheless it was very remunerative and the Harborne Railway Company remained independent until it was grouped into the LMS in 1923. Bus competition reduced the number of passengers using the line, and although it survived the LMS's pruning of local services in 1931, other factors were working against its survival. Much as with Stourbridge line services today, slotting 20 or so trains in between expresses and other services plying their way along the Stour Valley line was problematic and the Harborne trains regularly suffered long delays. Icknield Port Road station was closed completely on 18 May 1931, in an attempt to speed up services on the branch, but this was in vein, and its last regular passenger services ran on 24 November 1934. Rotten Park Road station was closed completely, leaving only Hagley Road and Harborne open for goods traffic. Coal merchants had developed businesses operating out of the yards at each station, and goods trains serving these, and the brewery at Cape Hill, sustained the line until the early 1960s. These were worked by Ex-Midland Railway Class 2F 0-6-0s until June 1961, when their duties were taken over by small diesel shunters. In its later years the branch became a great favourite for enthusiasts specials, one such, organised by the SLS for 3 June 1950, producing many of the photographs of the line seen today.

Below left:
Taking the direct line to Berkswell at Kenilworth Junction, on the former L&B Coventry-Warwick line, is the 09.30 service from Northampton to New Street on 23 July 1961. This line opened on 2 June 1884, but was latterly, as here, only used for diversions; this one being occasioned by electrification work.
Michael Mensing

The Kenilworth & Berkswell Railway

By the 1880s, the LNWR's West Midlands network was substantially complete and the company set about melding its rather rag-bag assemblage of lines into an efficient rail system. At certain points, they determined, cut-offs would greatly improve train working. One such was at Coventry, where services bound for Leamington had to pass through the city's station to gain the line. A great saving, in both time and delays, could be achieved if the city could be by-passed by these services. An opportunity existed to link the Leamington line, just north of Kenilworth, with the L&B line at Berkswell, at a point where the latter veers sharply

Below:
James Bridge Junction, from where the 'Walsall Junction Railway' linked the GJ line with the SS Railway one mile away. This link was opened on 1 March 1881 and had one intermediate station, at Pleck. It is seen here in the depth of winter during March 1947.
Author's Collection

eastwards. Accordingly, the LNWR proposed the Kenilworth & Berkswell Railway, a line between Kenilworth Junction and Berkswell, in its 1881 Act. This received the Royal Assent on 18 July 1881, and also allowed for the doubling of that portion of the line between a point 500yd southwest of the Milburn Grange viaduct (in Kenilworth) to a point 500yd north of the booking office at Milverton (for Warwick) station.

The Kenilworth & Berkswell Railway took three years to construct, opening to goods on 2 March 1884; the same day as the doubled line between Kenilworth Junction and Milverton (for Warwick) station came into use. Passenger trains first used the line between Berkswell and Kenilworth on 2 June 1884; there were no intermediate stations. Primarily of use to goods services, the line saw scant use by passenger trains, an average of three New Street-Leamington locals using it in each direction on weekdays.

LNWR miscellaneous improvements 1877-1884

Locomotive sheds

The LNWR opened a large shed at Walsall in the late 1870s. This was situated in the centre of the four-way junction to the north of Walsall station, at Ryecroft, the name by which it became commonly known. It was a 12 road shed that could accommodate 48 locomotives and was authorised in October 1877. Coded 9 by the LNWR, it became 3C under the LMS in 1935; 21F under BR(LMR) in May 1960 and 2G, as a sub-shed to Tyseley, in September 1963. Mechanical coaling and ash disposal apparatus was installed in 1937; new offices opening in 1938. Roof repairs were delayed after the war, and Ryecroft was converted to diesel use, with the addition of new offices and oil tanks over 1956/7; DMUs being introduced on the Birmingham to Lichfield service on 5 March 1956. The depot's last steam locomotives were reallocated to Bescot and Aston in June 1958.

As noted above, the LNWR decided to build a new locomotive shed at Aston in 1882, in the newly created fork in between the company's GJ and Aston to Stetchford link lines. This came into use c1884 and consisted of a 12 road shed and 42ft turntable capable of housing 60 locomotives. Aston shed was coded 10 by the LNWR becoming 3D, and a sub-shed to Bescot, under the LMS in 1935. At about that time it was equipped with the standard LMS mechanical coaling and ash disposal apparatus and a larger, 60ft, turntable; the roof being renewed in 1944. It was recoded 21D by BR(LMR) in May 1960, becoming 2J, under Tyseley, in September 1963, being kept in use through receiving the locomotive allocations from other local sheds, such as Monument Lane and Ryecroft, as they closed

Cut-offs and related improvements

By the mid-1870s, the LNWR was sufficiently established in and around Birmingham to turn its attention to making minor improvements to its lines, particularly at junctions. Three such were identified: between the L&B and GJ lines at Aston; between the Midland Railway owned W&W line at Wolverhampton, over which the LNWR had running powers, and its own GJ line at Wednesfield; and between its own GJ and SS lines at James Bridge. Authority to build link lines or cut-offs at all three of these points were granted under the titles of The Aston & Stetchford Junction; The Wolverhampton Junction and the Walsall Junction railways, respectively, in the LNWR's New Lines Act of 28 June 1877

The first to be completed was the first named, the 2 miles 6 furlongs line opening to goods between Stetchford and Aston on 7 September 1880 and to passengers on 1 March 1882; it had no intermediate stations. From this date the LNWR began a practice of dividing and uniting its expresses at Stetchford, a fast portion traveling non-stop via the GJ line, a slow portion going along the Stour Valley line, calling at all the stations. A month earlier, on 1 February, the company had opened a new station at Stetchford (renamed Stetchford for Yardley that May), west of the original L&B one, which was closed. The new station was better suited for uniting

Below left:
The LNWR's Aston-Stetchford line opened to passenger services on 1 March 1882. Enabling certain express services to by-pass New Street by gaining the GJ line at Aston. Here, two-cylindered Stanier-designed 2-6-4T No 42544 hauls its load of six coaches over the Birmingham & Warwick Junction Canal near to the line's Aston end. *Michael Mensing*

Below:
Below, the viaduct extending the GJ line from its temporary terminus at Vauxhall on to Curzon Street; above, the viaduct carrying the GJ lines into New Street. This curious, double-decked structure came into use on 7 May 1893 as part of a scheme to quadruple part of the approach to New Street station. It is seen here on 23 February 1982 as the 10.50 Four Oaks to Redditch Cross City line service approaches Proof House Junction.
British Rail

and dividing expresses; its relocation also allowing the replacement of an inconvenient level crossing: 'Yardley Gates' by a road overbridge.

Both of the remaining lines authorised in 1877 opened on the same day: 1 March 1881. The 1 mile long Walsall Junction Railway linked the GJ line, at a new 'James Bridge Junction', with the SS line, at a new 'Pleck Junction'. There was one intermediate station at Pleck, which opened on 1 October 1881, and remained open until 1 January 1917, when its was closed to passengers as a wartime economy measure, reopening on 1 May 1924. Although almost the same length, at 1 mile 2 furlongs, the Wolverhampton Junction Railway did not have any intermediate stations. Indeed its construction had eliminated one; the junction on the GJ line being on the site of Portobello station, which had closed on 1 January 1873. On the same day, the LNWR began to run trains over the Midland Railway's line between Heath Town Junction and Wolverhampton, also reopening the GJ line between the new Portobello Junction and Bushbury to passenger services.

In August 1881, the LNWR brought two additional running lines at Walsall station and Ryecroft Junction into use, and on 1 October 1883 they opened a goods line between Tipton station and the Princes End line (Tipton Station Junction to Tipton Curve Junction).

The Soho Loop line

By the late 1870s, the LNWR was finding New Street station increasingly difficult to operate. The new lines and services the company had introduced were beginning to clog-up the station; something which was not helped by the number of goods services which had to pass through there for want of any other way for them to go. Two solutions were proposed. One was the Aston to Stetchford line, noted above, which relieved services working from the east of Birmingham, but was of no use to those approaching from the west, along the Stour Valley line, as no link existed between it and the GJ line on that side of New Street station. Therefore, one such line was proposed in the LNWR (New Railways) Act of 1883.

Titled the Soho, Handsworth & Perry Barr Junction Railway, it was to be a 2 miles 4 furlongs line, linking the Stour Valley line at Soho with the GJ line at Perry Barr, both ends to have junctions facing in each direction. Authority to build the line was received on 16 July 1883 and it opened, in stages: Perry Barr to Handsworth Pool, 2¼ miles, to goods on 30 October 1887; Handsworth Pool to Soho Junction, 1 mile 45 chains, to goods on 1 March 1888 and the Winson Green Branch, to goods and passengers, on 1 April 1889. The line was built in conjuction with track quadrupling and other improvements in the vicinity, which also opened on 1 April 1889. There was an intermediate station at Soho Road, which was joined, on 1 January 1896, by one at Handsworth Wood; the line becoming known as the 'Soho Loop'. Its passenger services were provided in part by certain peak hour New Street to Wolverhampton GJ line trains, which were routed via the loop to relieve conjestion in the former at busy times. Other services were provided by a special New Street circular service, which had an avergae of 12 services per day and also called at Monument Lane, Winson Green, Perry Barr, Witton, Aston and Vauxhall & Duddeston stations; taking 53mins for the whole journey. This survived until 5 May 1941 when the LMS withdrew it as a wartime economy, both Soho Road and Handsworth Wood stations closing entirely.

Top:
Perry Barr North Junction, between the Soho Loop line and the Grand Junction line, is seen to good advantage in this view of a pair of three-car Metro-Cammell DMUs taking the SLS 50th Anniversary Railtour Special on to the latter en route to Bescot.
Michael Mensing

Above:
By the time that this empty stock six-car DMU set (two x Metro-Cammell; two x Birmingham RCW and two x Gloucester RCW) passed along the Soho Loop line on 1 August 1959, Handsworth Wood station, which had once stood here, had been demolished.
Michael Mensing

LNWR miscellaneous improvements 1889-1914

Bescot shed

Together with the development of extensive sidings at Bescot on its GJ line, the LNWR built a 200ft long, eight road, shed capable of accommodating 32 locomotives; this was also equipped with the usual 42ft turntable, coaling stage and water tank, etc. Its duties were mainly connected with goods services, and it soon came to have an allocation twice the size of its covered capacity. Numbered 6 by the LNWR, Bescot became 3A under the LMS, receiving mechanised coaling and ash disposing equipment in 1936. It was recoded 21B by BR(LMR) in April 1960 and 2F in September 1963; steam duties being retained beyond this date.

Relief and connecting lines

Despite all of its improvements in recent years the LNWR still had insufficient capacity at the east (London) end of New Street station. The Soho Loop line reduced the number of goods and passenger services required to work through the station, but the line capacity they created was soon taken up improvements to other services. Their solution to this was twofold. Firstly, the former GJ line would be quadrupled between Aston No. 1 Signal Box and Erskine Street, with alterations to the approaches to Curzon Street goods station to provide separate lines connecting it with the former L&B and GJ lines. Secondly, the New Street approach lines would also be quadrupled, from where the former L&B and B&G and B&DJ railways converged, in between Landor and Garrison streets, and the station; thereby providing the LNWR and Midland companies with independent up and down lines.

Work began on the first scheme in mid-1888. This required the widening of Vauxhall viaduct to twice its original width, by the construction of a contiguous parallel structure, which was completed by May 1889. Once laid with rails, the GJ passenger lines were transferred to the new viaduct; the old one having its rails removed to allow a second new viaduct to be built on top of it; producing a unique double-decked structure which still dominates the approach to the station to this day. When the lines across the latter were brought into use on 7 May 1893, the GJ passenger lines were separated from those serving Curzon Street, which could now be operated without interfering with passenger train movements. In the midst of this work, the quadrupled lines between Aston No. 1 Signal Box and Erskine Street were brought into use, the up and down fast ones on 15 February 1891; the up and down slow ones two days later.

A scheme was also devised to improve the Midland Railway's access to the eastern side of New Street station, which, although mainly to that company's benefit, was devised and undertaken by the LNWR. The basic idea was to provide the Midland's former B&G and B&DJ routes with their own independent up and down lines into the station, converging at the mouth of a new south tunnel which would conduct them through to the Midland side of New Street. This involved the widening of the station approaches paralleling Landor Street, slewing the B&DJ and, a new set of, B&G lines to the south side of Exchange sidings. An opportunity was also taken to improve the junctions of the various lines converging at that point. All of this work took three years, involving, as it did, one of the most intensively used sections of line in the area. The new lines came into use on 17 May 1896, with the new south tunnel first seeing use around August that year.

More track widening was undertaken on the west (Wolverhampton) side of New Street station at this time. The LNWR Act of 27 July 1893 authorised the widening of the Stour Valley line in between Sheepcote Lane and Harborne Junction, past Monument Lane shed and through the station there; this coming into use around 1895. Thirteen years later, the LNWR and GWR brought a new east facing junction into use at Leamington, linking the GWR to the former's Rugby line. On the same day the companies introduced a new through service between Cardiff and Yarmouth (Vauxhall) which used the new link.

LNWR station improvements 1876-1908

With all of the attention paid to its lines and motive power, the LNWR did not forget the needs of its passengers and it embarked upon a continuous programme of station rebuilding and upgrading from the mid-1870s. New stations were opened on the GJ line at Witton (renamed Witton [for Aston Lower Grounds] in February 1878) on 1 May 1876, and at Winson Green, on the Stour Valley line, on 1 November that year. In 1881, a new station, called Wood Green (Old Bescot) was opened on the GJ line, on site of the former Bescot Bridge station; this had been closed during 1850, but its replacement fared better, surviving until complete closure on 5 May 1941. Two years later, a new Milverton (for Warwick) station was opened, a short distance south of the original L&B one, which was closed; its nameboard probably having been worn out through all the name changes it had gone through! That same year, the company completed work on enlarging their station at Walsall, the new one opening on 1 November.

Hampton station, on the L&B line, was replaced by a new building on 1 September 1884, being situated ¼-mile southeast of the original one, which closed. Two years later, in July 1886, this was given its more familiar name of Hampton-in-Arden. On the Stour Valley line, Albion station was enlarged, the first portion of the new buildings coming into use during August 1889. One year later, on 1 August 1890, new buildings came into use at Smethwick as part of a scheme which had also replaced two level crossings by an overbridge. At the turn of the century, two replacement stations were opened on the GJ line, south of the originals, which were closed: Great Barr opening on 25 March 1899, and Newton Road on 1 January 1902, the latter closing entirely on 7 May 1945. Finally, a new Deepfields station (renamed Coseley & Deepfields on 25 August 1952) was opened on the Stour Valley line, south of the original one, on 10 March 1903.

The Coventry Loop Line

The industry of few places can have undergone greater upheaval than that of Coventry. From the mid-1850s the city entered a period of cyclical slumps, which began with a depression in its staple watch trade. Unsure of a recovery, local industrialists eagerly sought alternative manufactures, lighting upon that of sewing machines. A decade later, that trade slumped too, and was replaced by bicycle manufacture, honing the skills that would serve the motor car manufacturing industry well when it took hold in the city during the mid-1890s. Many of the city's larger companies had built their works adjacent to the Coventry-Nuneaton line, but 'latecomers' began to develop the area to the east of the city, which was poorly served by direct rail links. Recognising this, the LNWR proposed a double track, goods only, line to run for 3½ miles from a junction with their L&B line near Pinley, to a junction with their Coventry to Nuneaton line near Lythalls Lane, Rowley's Green. This was authorised by an Act of 26 July 1907, eventually opening on 10 August 1914 with depots at Gosford Green and Bell Green.

The Development of Passenger Services

Being at the heart of the LNWR's constituents, Birmingham enjoyed a high quality of both local and express passenger services from the company. These were made all the better by the keen competition they enjoyed on many of their routes from the GWR; a rivalry which spawned a kind of one-upmanship, out of which the citizens of Birmingham gained an excellent rail service, most particularly on the route to London.

1 – Local passenger services

Many of the local services which the LNWR operated along its secondary and branch lines in the Birmingham area have already been described. The company also provided local services along its main lines, and put a considerable amount of effort into trying to generate passenger traffic for these, most notably through the provision and resiting of stations.

Local trains along the GJ line ran either to Walsall or, reversing there, continued on to Wolverhampton; an average of eight and five services, respectively, making these journeys in each direction daily. At both ends of the line, from Wolverhampton through Willenhall, Darlaston to Walsall, and from Perry Barr into Birmingham, local GJ passenger services came under serious competition from tramway and omnibus services, to which the LNWR did not have any satisfactory response, other than to cut fares, as the former won hands down with regard to convenience. Despite this, from shortly after the opening of the Stour Valley line, which handled most of the local passenger traffic to Wolverhampton and express workings through Birmingham, north to Stafford; the company began to make changes to the stations along the GJ line.

The first of these was on 1 October 1854, with the opening of Lawley Street station, situated immediately after Curzon Street. One month later they also opened a station to serve Aston, and a third station, Bloomsbury & Nechels, between Lawley Street and Aston, was opened on 1 August 1856. Both this and Lawley Street proved unviable, the former also being inconveniently located at the busy junction of the GJ lines to Curzon Street and New Street stations, and so they closed together, on 1 March 1869. Further out from Birmingham, Hamstead & Great Barr station, between Perry Barr and Newton Road, was opened on 1 October 1862. This was more of a success, being renamed Great Barr on 1 May 1875. It was replaced by a new station of this name, built slightly to the south, which opened on 25 March 1899. The aforementioned Newton Road underwent this experience twice, the original one being replaced by a new station, built a short distance to the north, on 1 March 1863. This was named West Bromwich, but renamed Newton Road for West Bromwich two months later, and changed back to Newton Road in December 1870. A third station was opened there, south of the second one, on 1 January 1902; the latter closing; this new station itself being closed entirely on 7 May 1945. To replace Lawley Street station, on the day it closed a new station was opened at Vauxhall, about a ¼mile north of the site former GJ terminus there, and from 1 November 1889 the LNWR renamed this Vauxhall & Duddeston.

Along the L&B line, local services operated to Coventry and Leamington. Of the former there were 13 trains in each direction, most of which called at all stations, except one, which missed out Adderley Park, and three, which were semi-fasts, calling at Stetchford to set-down only. Two additional Coventry workings were provided by through running of weekday morning trains from Dudley and Walsall; each having a corresponding return evening working. There were also 13 trains in each direction to Leamington, only five of which were through workings of Birmingham-Coventry locals.

A number of stations were also added along the L&B line between Birmingham and Coventry. One of the first of these was Allesley Gate, between Coventry and Hampton, which developed out of a request by local people to

Above:
'Snow where? – Never heard of it mate'. The date and occasion are unknown, but it is a genuine photograph. Ex-GWR diesel railcar No W22W has somehow worked its way onto platform No 5 at New Street station and has stopped in front of Signal Box No 2 for advice from a passing bod, who is touching it to see if it is real!
Ian Allan Library

the LNWR's Traffic Sub-Committee for trains to stop there. This was so ordered on 19 May 1847; buildings being provided there in 1848, the station being renamed Allesley Lane in September 1863 and the more familiar Tile Hill in April 1864. Between I January and 30 April 1855, the lines to Coventry and Leamington were also the subject of one of the LNWR's experimental fare reduction schemes. Under this, the first-class fare to Coventry was reduced to 6d (2.5p), but it was raised to 9d (4p) that March, and the experiment was scrapped the following month.

Almost 30 years passed before another new station, at Hampton, a ¼ mile southeast of original L&B one, was opened, on 1 September 1884; the latter closing on the same date. In July 1886, the LNWR renamed this as Hampton-in-Arden. Two new stations were added on the line as World War 2 began; Lea Hall, between Stetchford and Marston Green, opening on 1 May 1939, and Canley Halt, between Coventry and Tile Hill, built to serve Air Ministry Shadow Factories at the nearby Standard Motor Company Works, opening on 30 September 1940.

The history of the Stour Valley line was described above, but, at Dudley Port the line had a junction with a short 1½ mile branch to the town of Dudley, which had an important connection with the LNWR, as it was the home of Sir Gilbert Claughton, the company Chairman from 1911 until his death in 1921. There were no fewer than 55 passenger trains over the short branch each day in Sir Gilbert's time, most of which were worked by 2-4-0 and 2-4-2 tank locomotives with two or more bogie coaches fitted to work as motor trains. A number of improvements were also made to the Stour Valley line. Albion station, the next after Dudley Port towards Birmingham, was enlarged during 1888/89, the first stage of the completed work coming into use in August 1889. One year later, a rebuilding scheme at Smethwick (now Smethwick Rolfe Street) was completed, with an overbridge replacing two level crossings in July 1890, and new station buildings coming into use on 1 August. Ironically, Albion was the one of the few Stour Valley line stations to be closed to passengers before 1962, closing on 2 February 1960. The others were: Soho (23 May 1949); Winson Green (16 September 1957) , and Monument Lane (17 November 1958)

Just past Albion station, at Galton Junction, the line connected with the GWR's Stourbridge Extension line. When this opened, on 1 April 1867, the LNWR began a through passenger service over it and the ex-WM line to Kidderminster, Worcester and Hereford; a service which ran for almost 50 years, being withdrawn on 1 January 1917 as a wartime economy, and never reinstated.

A final variation in local services became possible on 1 April 1889 with the opening of the Soho loop line. In addition to the circular service already described, four distinct services were now possible between: Great Barr, Winson Green and Birmingham; Perry Barr, Winson Green and Birmingham; Great Barr, Soho and the Stour Valley line and Perry Barr, Soho and the Stour Valley line. Only journeys of the first two kinds were performed by ordinary passenger trains as New Street bound trains, along either the GJ or Stour Valley lines, could now enter the station from either its Wolverhampton or London end; but from Birmingham it was used by four afternoon GJ line Wolverhampton trains, to eliminate the need for locomotive run-rounds in New Street

Above:
In 1936, Armstrong-Siddeley Motors experimented with the building of railcars. They were powered by a V-12 engine and ran on pneumatic tyres, being tried out on a number of lines in the Birmingham/Coventry area. Here, Railcar No 1 is seen being given the once over in Coventry Goods Yard in June 1936, before entering trial service with the LMS.
Rolls Royce Heritage Trust

station at peak times. Also, through a combination of the loop line's circular service, and stops made by Walsall and Wolverhampton trains routed that way, its intermediate stations at Soho Road and Handsworth Wood were afforded an excellent daily service of 13 trains from the Monument Lane direction and 15 from the Perry Barr end.

Major changes in the operation of these local services by BR(LMR) came about through the use of DMUs. These were first introduced on the Birmingham-Lichfield service on 5 March 1956, being the first time the units were seen in regular passenger service anywhere in the Birmingham area. Two years later, on 17 November 1958, DMUs were introduced on the majority of the former LNWR routes in the area; Birmingham-Coventry-Rugby, Wolverhampton-Stafford, Walsall-Rugeley; Dudley-Walsall, Leamington Spa-Nuneaton and Rugby-Nuneaton-Stafford.

2 – Express passenger services

In 1841, a train journey from Euston to Birmingham by the L&B was only for the hardy. Third-class, by the slowest trains, it took 8½ hours, first-class, by the fastest mail train, a mere 4¾ hours. By 1855, with a united railway, and new lines and station at Birmingham, 95mins had been taken off the third-class journey time, whilst first-class passengers could now travel the distance in 3hr 40mins flat.

The acceleration of the LNWR's London-Birmingham expresses is charted in the company's timetables. Major improvements were made in 1845 through the elimination of intermediate stops. That January, a journey from London to Birmingham took 4hr 2 mins, but by May it had been reduced to 3hr 7mins. From 10 September 1848, by eliminating refreshment stops, and not calling at the majority of the intermediate stations, this was reduced to a straight 3hr, but reductions below this appear to have taken much longer to achieve. By May 1859, it was down to 2hr 55mins, but 22 years later the best timing was still 2hr 45mins. Beyond Birmingham matters were even worse. The 12¾ miles of the Stour Valley line, with its dozen stations and saw-tooth gradients, offered little opportunity for speed; being generally disliked by most drivers, who, in more polite moments, described it as a 'Fred Karno's backyard'. A remedy for this came on 1 March 1882 with the opening of the

Below:
Berkswell began on 9 October 1844 as a stopping place on the L&B called Docker's Lane. On 29 November that year the L&B Board ordered that booking huts and platforms be erected there and from 1 January 1853 the station became known as Berkswell, and from 1 February 1928, it was styled, as here in this 13 September 1959 view, Berkswell & Balsall Common. The train is the 16.35 New Street local to Coventry.
Michael Mensing

Aston-Stetchford link line, enabling expresses to be divided at Stetchford, the front portion going fast to Wolverhampton via the GJ line and Portobello Junction, the rear portion continuing on through New Street, and working to Wolverhampton as a Stour Valley line stopping service.

Away from its more traditional territory, the LNWR offered connections with other regions by the use of through carriages. New services using these were inaugurated from time to time, such as on 2 November 1879, when a through coach was introduced between Birmingham New Street and Norwich, via Rugby and Peterborough. But most of the company's efforts and resources went into edging nearer to the 'magical' two hours point-to-point timing on the London-Birmingham route. Ultimately, this took until the turn of the century, and was achieved through a combination of locomotive developments and the eventual realisation that such a time could only be achieved on a non-stop run. The LNWR came close to a two hour run when it inaugurated its first non-stop Euston to Birmingham expresses on 2 June 1902; the 11.25 departure from New Street taking 2hr 5mins to Euston; but the first true two hour service came two months later, on 1 August 1902, with a new 17.00 New Street-Euston (up) and 18.55 Euston-New Street (down) service; the locomotive used on the first day being No 1960 *Francis Stephenson*. More expresses working to these timings were introduced on 1 March 1905, when a service of three daily non-stop trains was introduced. Nonetheless, these crack services were seen by many as jewel in an otherwise dingy crown; their timings not being reflected in the majority of the expresses linking Birmingham with London. Indeed, the Birmingham Chamber of Commerce lobbied the LNWR for further improvements, especially to its breakfast trains, and on 1 July 1908 the company retimed its 07.20 breakfast train to leave Euston at 08.00 and accelerated it to reach New Street by 10.30; an improvement of 45mins over previous timings.

As the opening of the new GWR route approached in 1910, the LNWR made a number of service improvements, including the introduction of a slip coach for Leamington on the 18.55 service from Euston, which was slipped at Rugby. They also ran a number of acceleration runs between Euston and New Street, one on 28 November 1909 achieving an impressive 1hr 51mins, hauled by 4-4-0 'Precursor' No 1387 *Lang Meg*. With an eye to the prestigious business traveller, on 1 February 1910 the LNWR inaugurated its 'City to City' expresses between Wolverhampton and London (Broad Street); then the company's only named express. It was formed by four specially constructed large bogie coaches, those at each end being corridor compartment cars. In between were a first, second and third-class dining and refreshment car, on which breakfast and dinner could be taken. From 1 May 1910, one of these compartments was converted into an office, equipped with typewriter and typist, for urgent correspondence; and from March 1911 the LNWR entered into a contract with the Underwood Typewriter Co for carrying this out. This slightly bizarre service was first worked by locomotive No 1918 *Renown*, a unique Whale converted Webb compound that was virtually a 'Baby Precursor', used due to North London line restrictions out of Broad Street. Two daily City to City expresses ran until 1914 when, that 1 April, the

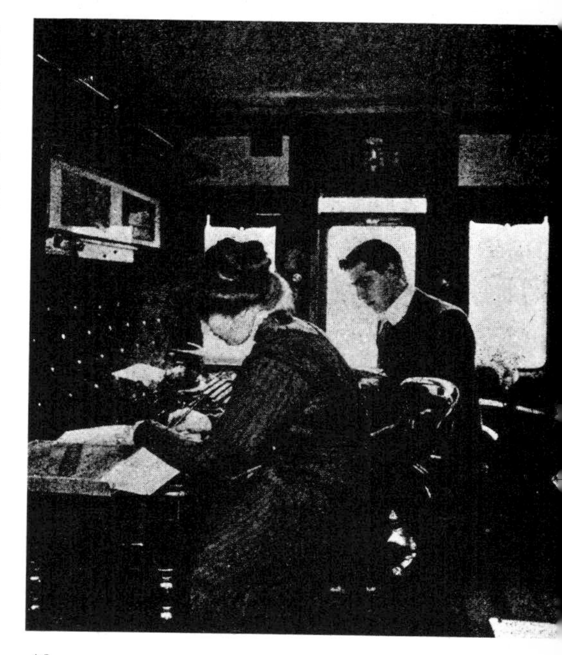

Above:
The typewriting bureau in one of the LNWR's 'City to City' expresses, where businessmen could take breakfast and catch up on their correspondence.
Railway Gazette

Below:
An outstanding LNWR poster for their new service of three non-stop trains between Euston and Birmingham introduced on 1 March 1905. These worked to a two hour timing, but served only to show up the rest of the timetable on this route. More and greater improvements were to come.
British Rail

L. & N.W.R.

TRAVEL BETWEEN

BIRMINGHAM

AND

LONDON

— BY THE EXPRESSES OF THE —

L.&N.W.R.

40 TRAINS DAILY 40

(Including Ten Non-Stop Two Hour Expresses) between New Street Station and London (Euston and Broad Street Stations).

SHORTEST & MOST DIRECT ROUTE
to
LIVERPOOL, MANCHESTER,
SCOTLAND & NORTH WALES

ILLUSTRATED GUIDE BOOKS TO CHARMING HOLIDAY RESORTS OF

—North Wales, English Lakes,— Blackpool, Morecambe, Ireland, Scotland, &c., &c.

may be obtained free at Stations and Town Office

For particulars of Cheap Excursions, Through Carriages, Works, School and Pleasure Parties, apply to Mr. R. T. MORCOM, District Superintendent, New Street Station, Birmingham.

For particulars of Goods Trains Traffic apply to Mr. J. G. HUMPHREYS, District Goods Manager, Curzon St. Station, Birmingham.

FRANK REE,
Euston Station. General Manager.

The Business & Pleasure Line.

Left:
What a difference five years can make. The LNWR's London-Birmingham service finally came into its own in 1910, and by 1913, when this advertisement appeared, the company was offering no fewer than 10 non-stop two hour expresses out of a total of 40 trains between the two cities daily.
Pete Glews Collection

07.50 (up) service was withdrawn, and on 13 July, the 17.25 Broad Street service was replaced by new 17.50 train which included a corridor connected slip coach for Coventry and carried the typewriting compartment. The final City to City working, the 08.20, was officially suspended due to World War 1, but was never reinstated.

Other parts of the timetable were not ignored at this time though. On 2 October 1910 the LNWR introduced the first Sunday two-hour service: (Up) Wolverhampton High Level 10.55, Dudley Port 11.05, New Street 11.30, Willesden and arriving at Euston 13.35; (Down) – the two-hour service – 17.20 from Euston in Birmingham by 19.20; then to Dudley Port and on to Wolverhampton High Level by 19.55. Services elsewhere were also augmented. On 10 July 1908 a joint LNWR/GWR passenger service was introduced between Cardiff and Yarmouth via a new line at Leamington; this ran until 30 September 1908, and again between 16 July and 30 September 1909, but not thereafter. From 1 October 1908, the LNWR also introduced through trains to Leicester and Nottingham via Leamington; LNWR and Midland companies providing one set of coaches each to work the service. Finally, 1 October 1910 saw the introduction of a joint Manchester-Bournemouth West service, also with the Midland. This avoided Wolverhampton by running along the GJ line from Bushbury, then via the Midland to Bath and finally along the Somerset & Dorset Joint line; carrying the distinction of being the only regular passenger service to use the Bushbury-Portobello

Above:
LMS unnamed 'Patriot' class locomotive No 5544 draws its stock forward from Monument Lane Carriage Shed en route to New Street station during the mid-1930s.
Don Powell

Below:
On 29 June 1957, ex-LMS 4-6-0 'Jubilee' class locomotive No 45596 *Bahamas* pulls forward with the 23.45 Birmingham-Edinburgh express.
Michael Mensing

section of the Grand Junction. Developed out of a through coach service, this train ran until 1914 but was reinstated after the war, being named the 'Pines Express' in 1927.

Second-class accommodation was withdrawn from all LNWR services from 1 January 1912, and so the new two-hour service, the 20.00 New Street to Euston, introduced on 1 July 1913 to compete with a new GWR service introduced on the same date and running at the same time, carried only first and third-class carriages. A further innovation was introduced on the 08.40 and 18.55 Euston services from 16 February 1914. Each carried slip coaches for Coventry, which remained corridor connected until a few minutes before slipping. Wartime economies led to the withdrawal of a number of the LNWR expresses serving Birmingham, coal shortages also seeing the non-stop Birmingham-London expresses decelerated to 2hr 10mins between 1 January 1916 and 3 October 1921; from when they were the province of LNWR 'George V' or superheated 'Precursor' classes, until in LMS days, when these were displaced in turn by Midland compounds, 'Jubilees' and finally 'Royal Scots'.

Re-accelerating the expresses after the war was a slow process, not aided by the many problems inherited by the LMS upon the Grouping. Two hour timings were reinstated in the 1920s and by the early 30s it became possible to insert additional stops whilst retaining these. For instance, on 1 April 1932, the LMS accelerated the 16.50 Euston express. With an additional stop at Coventry, this covered the 88.75 miles to Willesden in 87 mins, an average of 61.2 mph, and was the fastest timed express for such a distance on the LMS; but overall, the journey time to Birmingham was still 2 hours. The 1930s was also an era of summer excursions. On 10 February 1933, the LMS and The General Steam Navigation Co announced a new type of summer excursion for the people of Birmingham and the surrounding towns: a one day combined rail and river trip from New Street to Margate, which ran daily between Whitsun and September that year. A special train left New Street at 07.00 and ran direct to Tilbury, where

passengers embarked on the new oil-burning paddle steamer *Royal Eagle* for Margate; spending just 1½ hrs there before returning; being due back in Birmingham by 22.00 – all for a fare of 15s 6d! (77.5p). Sleeper services were not a feature of LNWR/LMS services from Birmingham until the 1930s, but on 6 June 1936 the latter introduced one between New Street and Glasgow; the 22.05 departure, which called at Dudley Port, Wolverhampton and Stafford, carrying composite first and third-class sleeping coaches, which were also carried on the 21.30 train from Glasgow.

Express timings were reduced during World War 2 as they had been during the First, and the newly nationalised railways were just as laggardly in returning timings to their pre-war levels as the railway companies had been almost 30 years earlier. Appalled by these matters, representatives from Birmingham City Council and the Chamber of Commerce met with BTC officials in London on 2 May 1950 to discuss the poor performance of the London-Birmingham express services. They received assurances that timings of 2hr 10mins would be restored by the summer timetable of 1951 and that a new named express, plus an early morning breakfast car train would be introduced with the winter timetable that September. Accordingly, on 25 September 1950, 'Royal Scot' No 46140 *The Kings Royal Rifle Corps*, inaugurated 'The Midlander' restaurant car express, the first one pulling into New Street at 11.00 that morning. This also boasted new stock: 11 BR Mark 1 coaches in the new 'blood and custard' livery. There was a complementary breakfast car service which left Euston at 08.55, arriving at New Street at 10.29, calling at Watford and Coventry only. But all parties had to wait a further two years for the reintroduction of the two-hour expresses, which finally returned with the summer timetable in 1953.

In the 1950s, Birmingham's LMR services were dominated by two things: dieselisation, and then electrification, and the allied resignalling work. DMUs, first introduced on the Lichfield service, began to be spotted on other lines, as on 11 March 1956 when they worked the Leamington-Coventry-Nuneaton service, and on weekday evenings when they were seen on the Walsall-Birmingham-Burton run. That summer, DMUs substituted for some express workings, forming the Saturdays only 07.15 service to Llandudno and its 14.25 return; also being used on the 08.48 service to Peterborough and its 13.45 return on 2 July. Diesel No 10203, an 1Co-Co1 Type 4 locomotive introduced in 1951, was used regularly on the London expresses in March 1957, being seen on the 08.50 ex-Euston, 13.55 ex-Wolverhampton, 17.50 ex-Euston, and working the Birmingham to London night parcels service.

Above:
With most of the London trains withdrawn for electrification and resignalling work, Class 40 No D315 (later No 40115) waits to depart New Street with the 09.40 Wolverhampton-Euston service on 19 February 1961.
Michael Mensing

Preparation for electrification and resignalling work began in 1958, the winter timetables showing decelerations on the London expresses to allow for engineering slacks. An extra 7-8mins was added on timings to Wolverhampton, and an extra 16-20mins down to London. The major impact of the work was not felt until the introduction of the winter timetables in 1959. This was delayed from 14 September until 2 November through a printers strike, but it saw almost the complete withdrawal of the entire LMR service between Birmingham and London. A compensatory service was introduced on the WR from Snow Hill, but the withdrawals hit Wolverhampton High Level, New Street and Coventry stations very hard. Only five semi-fast services remained to Euston: 06.40, 09.30 and 16.00 ex-Wolverhampton; 17.00 and 19.40 ex-New Street; plus four from Euston: 08.45, 16.25, 18.55 and 21.20. There were compensations too, in the form of unusual diversions, such as on Sundays 22 and 29 August 1961 when, due to closure of the Stafford-Wolverhampton line for electrification work, Birmingham and the North services were sent over the Princes End branch.

Away from the London route, improvements in services were maintained; the summer timetable which came into force on 18 June 1962 showing better links between the West Midlands and Lancashire towns and Scotland. There were new Birmingham connections with the up and down 'Caledonian' and a new six hour service to and from Glasgow. The winter timetable that year brought less glad tidings though, as the 'Pines Express' was re-routed to run south of Crewe via Market Drayton and Snow Hill, Oxford, Reading and Basingstoke. To 'compensate' for this, the DMU service between Snow Hill and South Wales was revised to start from New Street.

The Development of Goods Services and Facilities

The L&B's Birmingham Goods station was built on the opposite side of Curzon Street from the company's passenger accommodation, on a site also bordered by Grosvenor Street, access to which was over a level crossing in the public highway. This served the LNWR after the former's amalgamation with the GJ company, and upon the transfer of passenger services to New Street in June 1854, an opportunity was afforded to redesign the now redundant passenger side of Curzon Street to meet the ever expanding needs of the LNWR's goods department. Although certain of the passenger facilities there could be readily adapted to this changed role, others were either unsuitable or simply in the way. This applied particularly to the roundhouse locomotive shed at Curzon Street, which blocked the neck of the site. Accordingly it was vacated and demolished to make room for the fan of lines which eventually diverged to all parts of the expanded station.

Above:
Curzon Street station c1858. Locomotive No 189 was built by Jones & Potts in September 1848. Work is about to start on the conversion of the station into goods accommodation. The inscription on the far right bay reads 'Platforms for Gloucester, Bristol & Derby'.
Locomotive Publishing Co/IAL

In the space of five years this was transformed into a modern goods station through the addition of covered accommodation, cattle pens, loading docks, etc; the former hotel and main station frontage buildings being converted into offices. These alterations took care of the station's fabric, but generating and sustaining the goods traffic it needed to survive was down to its staff and, in particular, the Birmingham Goods Manager. The first holder of this office at Curzon Street following its transformation was John Mason, who was succeeded by William John Nichols in May 1870. He was born in London in 1831 and from his appointment at Birmingham he spearheaded the growth of goods business in the town. The LNWR had been happy to regard Birmingham as a mere adjunct to its neighbouring, and their largest, Goods District, South Staffordshire, which was centred upon Wolverhampton. Serving a large mineral rich area, the latter's pre-eminence was perhaps predictable, but Nichols saw no reason why this should overshadow Birmingham; was it not the nation's manufacturing centre?

Through sheer hard work and determination, Nichols built up the goods traffic using Curzon Street. The company rewarded him in 1873 by creating a separate Goods District for the town, with Nichols as its first District Goods Manager. In 1874 he caused quite a stir by being the first person on any railway in the country to employ female clerks. He also took a paternal interest in the welfare of his staff, installing a coffee house in the basement at Curzon Street and taking an active role in organising social activities. His manner was firm but kind, it being said of him: 'I'd rather be discharged any day than have such a talking to as he can give. He does it so kindly that you feel thoroughly ashamed of yourself'.

A measure of Nichols' value to the company, and the regard in which he was held, comes from the fact that when he turned 60, and, under LNWR rules, was supposed to retire; the Board passed a special resolution, on 25 May 1892, which allowed him to stay on. He eventually retired in 1897 at the age of 66. Under his direction five major goods installations had been built in the city and the staff at Curzon Street had grown from 427 in 1878 to 1,079 in 1893; the latter comprising 315 clerks, of which 45 were women; 380 porters and 384 carters, plus another 150 in the employ of Pickfords. The station had also been expanded. A coal wharf came into use on 16 December 1878 and additional stables and offices were provided in the early 1890s. It was now open from 03.00 on a Monday until 12 Midnight on a Saturday, and within 15 years of Nichols' departure employed 2,000. There were over 600 horses, housed in two-storey stable blocks; 54 cranes and 26 turntables, the latter being worked by hydraulic capstans arrayed in front of the main shed, the power for these, and for ones at New

CURZON STREET GOODS STATION.
(From a Photograph by our Own Artist.)

Right:
Curzon Street Goods Station, Summer 1893, near the end of William Nichols' tenure as District Goods Manager. The former station offices and Queen's Hotel there had been turned into the office of the Birmingham Goods District. In 1874, this was where the first lady clerks to work on any railway in the country had been employed.
Author's Collection

Street and Monument Lane, coming from two on site 150hp engines, working alternately. Bonded stores were provided in the passages and cellars beneath the loading decks; the station also being an early user of motor vehicles, having 10 petrol lorries and one steam lorry by 1912.

All kinds of traffic could be handled at Curzon Street. It dealt with all of the produce for the Birmingham markets; fruit and vegetables being handled in the old L&B goods station, which was known as 'Top Yard'. Rolling stock manufactured by the Metropolitan Railway Carriage, Wagon & Finance Co was despatched from Curzon Street, which also handled many valuable metals; it not being uncommon for there to be over £¼ million worth of copper, brass or silver in store there on an ordinary working day. By far the biggest consignee for these was ICI Metals at Witton, and a goods shed, plus 225 wagon capacity sidings, were built there especially for this traffic. By the 1930s, Curzon Street Goods had a capacity of 1,095 wagons, of which 163 could be accommodated in its coal wharf, 165 in the grain depot, 137 in the vegetable depot, 412 in the goods shed and yard, 60 in the fish depot and 158 by the cattle dock in Banbury Street. An idea of the traffic passing through the station can be gained from the list of departures on 10 October 1935, reproduced as Appendix 3.

Above:
Stetchford, 5 June 1961. Ex-LMS Class 5 locomotive No 42956 shunts over the hump onto the down yard.
Michael Mensing

Above right:
In addition to the larger goods installations, many of Birmingham's NW stations also had small goods yards. One example was here at Stetchford, where, at 12.07 on 31 May 1961, Stanier Class 5 2-6-0 No 42974 stands with a brake van, whilst the businesses trading from the yard behind are a hive of activity.
Michael Mensing

Curzon Street's traffic soon far exceeded its capacity and so nine additional facilities were built within the Birmingham area to accommodate this. Six of these installations were built within William Nichols' time, the first being Windsor Street depot and wharf. This was authorised by an Act of 22 July 1878, and located at the end of a short branch which left the GJ line by its junction with the Aston-Stetchford link; opening on 1 March 1880. A large new goods warehouse was added at Windsor Street, coming into use in September 1901; making the depot's total capacity, in its coal and goods yards, up to 334 wagons. Birmingham also lacked any room for marshaling sidings and so these were developed at Bescot on the GJ line; up sidings there first coming into use on 1 December 1881 and new sorting sidings being opened on 17 October 1892. Eventually,

Below:
Most of the alterations to Curzon Street throughout its years as a goods station were made quite sensitively, preserving many of its original features. This view of the former station entrance shows the L&B coat of arms surmounting a modest declaration of its later usage.

Road station. A new goods shed was built there in 1890, and new stables added in 1911; the yard holding 486 wagons. Soho Pool specialised in coal and coke, timber, scrap metal, ale finings, grain and flour, oil and petrol, plaster, buscuits, cement, limestone, empty barrels, hay and straw and bricks; in 1936 handling 225,009 tons of goods of which 142,687 were coal and coke and 82,322 goods and minerals. A new goods depot was opened at Aston, situated by Windsor Street Wharf, on 14 October 1901; with its associated yard there was a wagon capacity of 280 to which the neighbouring Walter Street Goods Depot Sidings added a further 243. The depot specialised in timber, iron and steel, machinery, bricks, coal, cotton, stoves, wood pulp, wet and dry bonded goods, grain and paper, in pulp or reel form. In 1936 it handled 866,324 tons of merchandise, of which 585,206 were coal and 281,118 were goods and minerals.

This was the last of the major LNWR goods installations to be built, although two additional facilities were added on the company's former lines by its successors. On 11 August 1924 the LMS opened Smethwick High Park mineral sidings, a coal, mineral and cattle depot by Soho station; having a 110 wagon capacity yard, and on 8 October 1951, BR(LMR) opened a depot at Perry Barr Wharf.

Goods and passenger services were separated on the LNWR from 1 November 1889, when the company ended the practice of running mixed goods and passenger trains, over its entire system. In later years BR and the BTC also ended a century or more of canal/rail interchanging by stopping its boatage services; those between between Wolverhampton, Kidderminster and Stourport being withdrawn from 1 November 1950, and all boatage services ending on canals in Birmingham region from 1 April 1954.

Bescot came to have a staggering capacity of 2,876 wagons, comprising, on the Down side: Reception Sidings, 175; Ground Frame Sidings, 314; Reception Sidings, 208; Old Yard Sidings, 437, and New Yard Sidings, 584; Total: 1,718. On the Up side, there was: Brook Sidings, 316 wagons; New Brook Sidings, 316 and Top Yard, 253; Total: 1,158. Bescot was worked in conjunction with sidings at Stetchford, which could hold 544 wagons, 362 in Down Marshaling Sidings and 182 in the Up Yard. Wagons for the north went to Bescot to be made up; those for the south going to Stetchford.

Closer to Birmingham, plans for new goods warehouse at Monument Lane were produced in 1885, the first portion coming into use on 3 August 1886. New stables were added in 1896 and a new goods shed in 1898, with alterations being made to the goods warehouse, and a new loading dock and offices added, in 1912. The yard had coal sidings and a canal wharf, loading docks, two warehouses plus a goods shed, and could hold 404 wagons. It principal traffic was iron and steel, copper, minerals, coal and coke, boated tea, timber and bedsteads! In 1936 it handled 212,114 tons of goods, of which 124,888 was coal and coke and 87,226 goods and minerals. Nearby, on 16 November 1885, a new goods shed was opened by the passenger station at Soho; having a capacity of 415 wagons. There was also a 53 wagon capacity coal yard, and a 268 wagon 'New Storage Sidings' were added on the opposite side of the Stour Valley line to the goods shed; the site of the latter now forming the Soho DMU and EMU stabling point. Soho's goods shed was enlarged in 1938, increasing its wagon capacity by 41.

The confusingly named Soho Pool was opened on 1 April 1889, and was situated at the end of a short branch which left the Soho Loop line by Soho

Right:
Dwarfed by the Queen's Hotel, ex-LMS 2-6-2T No 40129 stands in Platform No 1A at New Street station with a rake of parcels vans on 11 July 1959.
Michael Mensing

3: The Midland Lines to 1962

In the early 1830s, away from Birmingham, four railways were promoted which were to become founding or constituent members of the Midland Railway. Three of the schemes were based around Derby: the North Midland (NM), Midland Counties (MC) and Birmingham & Derby Junction (B&DJ) railways, the fourth was promoted from Gloucester: the Birmingham & Gloucester Railway (B&G). Collectively, and in particular the last two schemes, these came to underscore Birmingham's importance as a rail centre, providing links with the east Midlands, northeast, west and southwest.

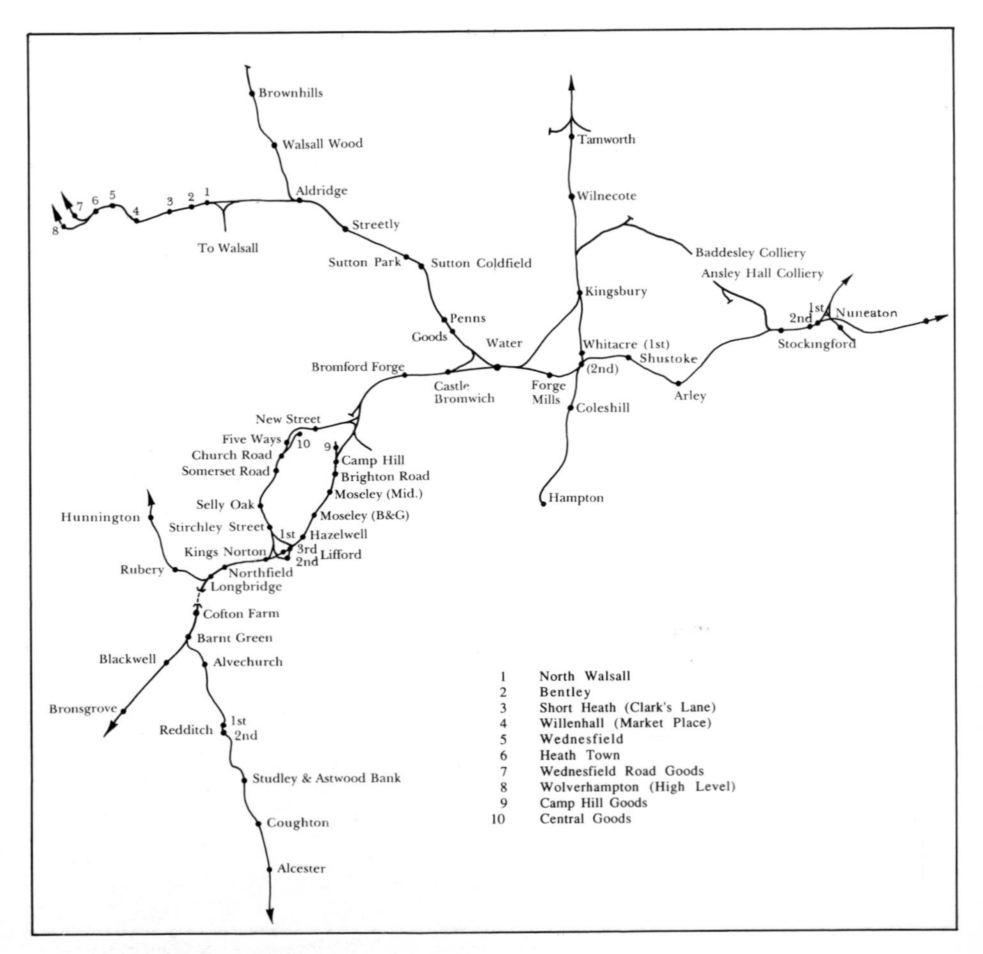

The Birmingham & Derby Junction Railway

The NM Railway's promoters proposed to build a line between Leeds and Derby. Their scheme was well advanced by 1834. That summer, the notion of a complementary line, extending the NM south to a junction with the planned L&B at Birmingham, was promoted. A provisional committee was formed, made up of businessmen, predominantly from Birmingham. They engaged George Stephenson to survey the route, who fitted this into his busy schedule during the early months of 1835. Reporting back in April that year, Stephenson commented that no difficulty existed in constructing the line and recommended a junction with the L&B at Stetchford, enabling the use of the latter's line to, and use of their planned station at, Curzon Street. As the proposed B&G line intended to use this station too, an easy transfer of passengers and goods would be effected between Leeds, Derby and the southwest.

A second branch was also recommended, from the B&DJ's main line at Nether Whitacre, to another junction with the L&B near Hampton; this would facilitate the transfer of traffic to and from London. Stephenson's proposals were welcomed by the Birmingham to Derby line committee, but did not please the promoters of the MC line. They had designs on the L&B too, planning a line to join it at Rugby; so they saw the Birmingham-Derby line as a very definite threat. A dispute arose between the 'rival' scheme's promoters but an accommodation was reached. Under this the Birmingham-Derby line committee agreed to drop its plans for a line to the L&B at Hampton in return for the MC committee deleting a proposed branch to Pinxton. This had been intended to connect up with the Mansfield Railway, but was opposed by the Birmingham-Derby committee's allies, the NM, who saw it as likely to draw traffic from its planned system.

Matters settled, in November 1835 the Birmingham-Derby committee were therefore more than a little surprised, upon reading the newly published MC Railway Bill, to find the Pinxton branch still included. An oversight or fast sleight? Too late to amend their own Birmingham & Derby Junction Railway Bill, minus its much needed Hampton line, the committee hastily made the

Left:
Hampton station on the B&DJ Railway c1839. This was built adjacent to the L&B main line (to the left), giving the company a link to Birmingham without having to build a direct line there initially. In the centre distance is the company's original locomotive shop.
Ironbridge Gorge Museum Trust

missing line the subject of a separate Bill: The Stonebridge Railway, which they hoped to consolidate with their main Bill as both passed through Parliament. Both a clever and successful move, the combined bills were passed by the Commons on 30 April 1836 and the Lords on 22 April; receiving the Royal Assent on 19 May that year. This authorised a line from a junction with the L&B at Stetchford via Castle Bromwich, Whitacre and Tamworth to Derby; with a branch from Whitacre to Hampton. By mistake, only one year had been allowed for the compulsory purchase of the land required and an 'emergency' Bill was rushed through Parliament to extend this to two years; receiving the Royal Assent on 30 June 1836.

The newly incorporated B&DJ Railway Co held its first meeting in Birmingham on 22 September 1836. Recommendation was given to proceeding with the Hampton line first; consideration also being given to the promotion of a new line from their main line at Tamworth to the L&B at Rugby. This would link up with the proposed Manchester South & Union Railway; an ambitious scheme which planned to by-pass the GJ by building a new route via the Potteries to Tamworth, enabling the line to Hampton to be abandoned in favour of this alternative, which was seven miles shorter to Rugby. All right on paper, all hell broke loose when its embodiment in a Bill was submitted to Parliament. Most opposition came from a not unexpected source, the GJ Railway, who so finely picked it through that they succeeded in having it rejected on a technicality under Parliamentary Standing Orders. The following year, another B&DJ Act, of 27 July 1838, varied the junction with the L&B at Hampton to avoid land on the estate of Lord Aylesford; eventually producing a cramped site with less room than required for the erection of locomotive shops, etc. The same Act also extended the time allowed for construction to 19 May 1843.

Meanwhile, work had been proceeding on the B&DJ. All 18 contracts had been let, George Stephenson having been replaced by his son Robert through the former's commitments to the NM Railway. The 38¾-mile line was unusual in that it did not require a single tunnel and only a few deep cuttings, and despite two very wet winters in 1837/8 and 1838/9, on 13 February 1839 Robert Stephenson and his assistant Robert Birkenshaw reported to the Directors that the line would be ready by that July. All of the ructions of previous years had made the B&DJ's Directors keen to see their line open as soon as possible, so that they could have first bite at the traffic available. By late May, the line was virtually complete and on 29 May a special train took a Director's party over the whole route. Robert Stephenson personally inspected the line on 15 July 1839 by driving the Locomotive *Derby* from Birmingham to its namesake and back. He found everything but the minor station buildings to be complete; these were apparently deliberately left as temporary structures so that the company could determine the demand for travel from each *before* being committed to the expense of building permanent ones.

The opening of the B&DJ

The B&DJ was formally opened on 5 August 1839; a special train leaving Curzon Street station at 10.20 and arriving at Derby by 13.10, where a lavish banquet was held; returning to Birmingham by 16.00. One week later, on 12 August 1839, the line opened to the public. There were intermediate stations at Tamworth, Kingsbury, Coleshill (renamed Maxstoke from 9 July 1923) and Hampton. Three trains in each direction ran on weekdays, with two on Sundays. The fastest journey was two hours. At Hampton B&DJ passengers were transferred to the L&B for travel on to London; journeys in the other direction, to Birmingham, being worked there by the former's own locomotives and stock. Through carriages were also conveyed to London by the L&B; but for whatever use the B&DJ made of that company's lines, it had to pay a toll of 1s 6d (7.5p) per passenger.

Five weeks after opening the B&DJ hit trouble. On 21 September 1836 the L&B banned the company from working their locomotives to Curzon Street, insisting that their trains be worked by L&B locomotives alone; the 1s 6d toll to continue, of course. By 1840 the basic B&DJ service had been increased to six trains in each direction on weekdays, with four on Sundays. Birmingham departures left at 07.05, 10.30, 13.00, 15.45, 17.03 and 18.45; Derby ones at 08.00, 10.40, 12.00, 14.15, 16.40 and 20.25.

The L&B toll began to take its toll on the B&DJ's revenue, which was not helped by it having been the first of the 'Midland' network to open. A bit like an early guest at a party, the B&DJ began to feel a little on its own. To the north, eight months would elapse before the NM Railway opened between Sheffield and Derby on 11 May 1840 and another month before it opened throughout from Leeds on 1 July that year. To the south, 15 months were to pass before the first section of the B&G Railway opened, and another nine months before it too ran trains into Curzon Street.

But there were more immediate concerns. On 30 June 1840 the MC Railway opened between Leicester and Rugby. Even though this was only to a temporary station someway from the L&B at the latter, it effectively broke the B&DJ's 'monopoly' of London traffic. And so the latter tried to protect both companies 'mutual interests' through negotiation with the MC Railway, but this came to nought. Therefore, having tried to play fair, they began to play dirty; lowering their first-class fares to London from 35s (£1.75) to 29s (£1.45) and their second-class ones from 24s (£1.20) to 19s 6d (£0.97). The bulk of the journey being over the L&B, the only way this could be achieved was by slashing fares on their part of the journey, for through passengers only, from 8s (40p) to 1s 6d (7.5p) for first-class and from 6s (30p) to 1s 6d (7.5p) for second-class. A familiar sum? The B&DJ were in effect only raising the L&B toll from its through passengers, and were

therefore deliberately running at a loss.

The MC Railway had a ready rejoinder to all of this; they went to court, but lost. Nonetheless the cost of this litigation, plus their drastically pared income, was wearing down the B&DJ. Goods returns were equally poor. Hampton was in the middle of nowhere, and the cost of cartage to and from Birmingham was so high, and took so long, that there was little advantage to be gained from using the railway at all. An obvious solution to all of these problems was building an independent line to Birmingham, and just such a line was the subject of a Parliamentary Bill in 1840. This sought authority to abandon its Whitacre to Stetchford line (authorised in 1836) and to build a line from Whitacre, via Castle Bromwich, to a Birmingham terminus on the east side of Lawley Street, 40ft below the fork created by the convergence of the GJ and L&B lines; this bill received the Royal Assent on 4 June 1840.

No time was lost in building this line. It was staked out from 8 July 1840; tenders were invited from 28 October and the main contract was let on 23 December that year. Over 1,200 navvies worked on the line, which opened to the public on 10 February 1842, with intermediate stations at Whitacre, Forge Mills (for Coleshill) (shortened to Forge Mills in April 1904; renamed Coleshill from 9 July 1923), Water Orton, Castle Bromwich and Bromford Forge (opened on 16 May 1842 and closed, after it proved unremunerative, in May 1843). A new terminus was provided at Birmingham. Lawley Street station had a long elegant frontage which housed the B&DJ's head office as well as the usual passenger facilities. An engine and carriage shed opened later in June 1842.

From the opening of this line the L&B began to be progressively relieved of the L&B's crippling toll. But, by this move, their passengers were also denied easy transfer to the L&B, soon having to travel the whole length of the journey

Above:
Whitacre was the meeting point for the B&DJ's original main line and the company's Birmingham extension, plus a later Midland Railway line to Nuneaton. The first station there was replaced by the one shown on 1 November 1864, and is seen here after closure and removal of the buildings in the 1960s.
Don Powell Collection

Below:
Lawley Street station when converted to goods use, seen in a block from Measom's *Guide to the Midland Railway* published in 1875. The original station building is the block in the centre, the one with the chimneys. Services were diverted to Lawley Street from 10 February 1842, and from there to Curzon Street from 1 May 1851.
University of Birmingham

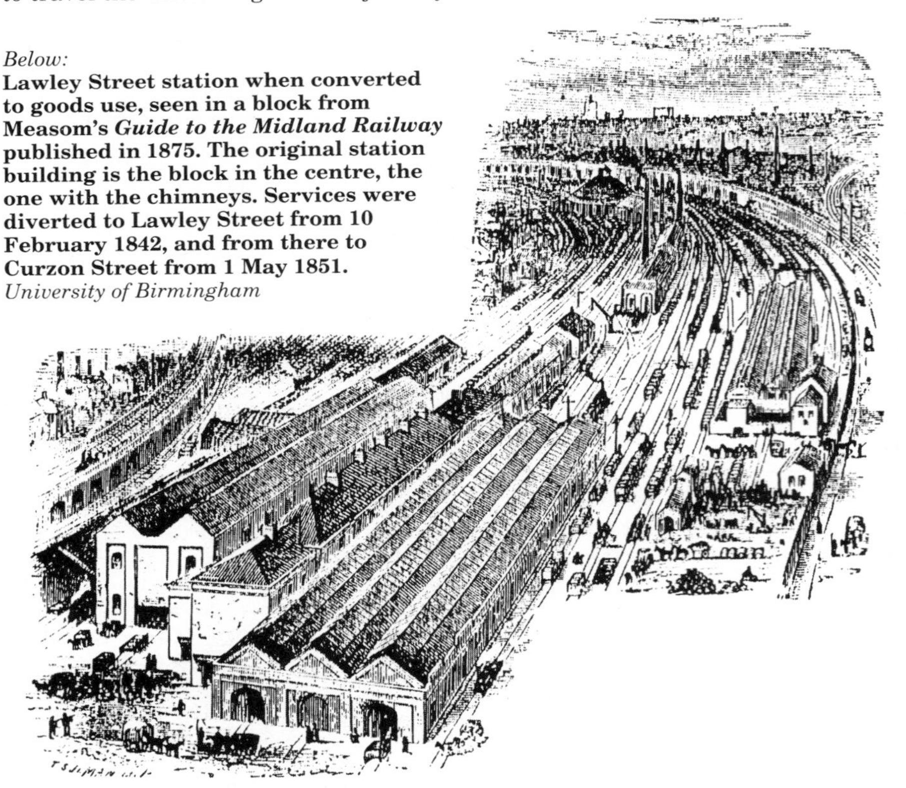

Above:
The original B&DJ station buildings at Coleshill c1933, the last station before Hampton, on the company's former main line. This was singled following the opening of the line into Birmingham (Lawley Street) on 10 February 1842; retaining a passenger service of one train per day each way until 1 January 1917. The station was retained for goods and renamed Maxstoke on 9 July 1923, closing finally on 1 May 1939.
Don Powell Collection

to London via the latter, and being required to walk from the subterranean Lawley Street to nearby Curzon Street via a footpath 'conveniently provided' by the B&DJ for their use, to boot. The Hampton line quickly declined. It was used by goods services until 11 April 1842, when an incline, linking Lawley Street with the GJ and L&B lines, came into use. Mail trains also ran via Hampton until 1 July 1842 from when the line from Whitacre was downgraded; being singled between August 1842 and March 1843.

The B&DJ became part of the Midland Railway from 10 May 1844. Most of the company's lines enjoyed a profitable existence in the greater company and its heirs, save for the aforementioned Whitacre-Hampton line. After singling, two daily trains continued to convey through coaches to and from Euston along it until some time in 1845. Three daily local passenger trains maintained a service to Coleshill and Hampton, but from 1859 one of these was cut out, and from May 1877 onwards, only one train remained. The passenger service was withdrawn as a wartime economy from 1 January 1917,, leaving only a daily goods working, which, from 24 April 1930, until it was withdrawn on 30 April 1939, served Maxstoke only, from the Whitacre end. Most of the line was lifted between July and October 1952, leaving just ¾-mile at each end for use as sidings.

The Birmingham & Gloucester Railway

About 1820, merchants in Bristol, some 90 miles southwest of Birmingham, began to formulate proposals which would eventually result in two railways being built to the latter. Developed as a port from the Norman Conquest, by the early 19th century Bristol's fortunes were on the decline. The abolition of slavery in Britain in 1772 dealt a severe blow to the sugar trade, one of the city's staple imports. Increases in the tonnage of vessels using its quays were also putting a great strain on the capacity of the tidal rivers Avon and Frome to cope with them. In 1803, to combat the latter, a Dock Company was formed to divert the Avon through a 'New Cut' and to convert the Frome and Avon waterways into a floating harbour which would retain its water irrespective of the tide. Completed in 1809, the harbour was an engineering triumph but a commercial disaster as the high charges levied to use the new facilities served only to drive trade elsewhere. Desperate for new business, Bristol merchants eyes' lighted upon London and Birmingham as potential sources of extra traffic and upon railways as the way of bringing this to their city.

Two schemes were hatched in 1824, one for a line to the capital: the London & Bristol Railroad, a scheme later realised by the GWR; the other for a line to Birmingham, styled the Bristol, Northern & Western Railroad (BN&W), which was outlined to a public meeting held in Bristol on 13 December 1824. The arguement was persuasive: Bristol was an established outlet for the products of Birmingham and South Staffordshire, but the established routes to the city, via road, canal and the River Severn at Worcester, were slow and quite unsuited for delicate and perishable items. True, a new canal, the Gloucester & Berkeley Ship Canal, was under construction (it would open early in 1827, linking Sharpness with Gloucester), but this could not compare with the practicality and efficiency of railways, which could do in hours what rivers and canals might manage in days. Enough of those present were swayed by this reasoning for the project to go forward and a full survey of the route, via Gloucester, Tewkesbury and Worcester was made by Josiah Jessop in 1825. Unfortunately, following this the confidence of the project's backers flagged, especially when the enormity of the engineering work involved was fully appreciated. The BN&W scheme foundered in 1826.

This set back apart, its promoter's reasoning was sound enough but, as with so many other of the early railway schemes, its timing was out. A brief revival in 1829 also came unstuck, but a year later, the success of the Liverpool & Manchester Railway gave it a much needed fillip. Now the impetus came from Birmingham. Local tradesmen engaged a certain Isambard Kingdom Brunel to survey a line between there and Gloucester, from where the Gloucester & Berkeley Ship Canal would complete the link to Bristol until a separate railway, then being promoted between there and Gloucester, was built. This, Brunel was briefed, should avoid major population centres to minimise the sums to be paid for the land and property required. Duly completed, Brunel's survey provoked an outcry from the businessmen in Stourbridge, Kidderminister, Droitwich, Worcester and Tewkesbury, all of whom felt, with some justification, that the line should pass through or near to their town.

To enforce their view a rival line was promoted 'joining these dots', provoking a counter proposal from the Birmingham camp, who engaged Capt W S Moorsom to survey another route for them, this one taking the shortest route between the two places, again skirting major towns, but this time driving straight up the Lickey Hills, to be worked by stationary winding engines, to join the proposed L&B line in Birmingham. More howls of protest were heard from the circumvented towns of Droitwich, Kidderminster, Stourbridge and Dudley, all of which would eventually be served by the OWW, but the line's promoters, who had twin committees in Birmingham and Gloucester, persisted; formally adopting Capt Moorsom's route at a meeting on 25 September 1835. With the aim of presenting a Bill before Parliament during its 1836 Session, work began to placate objections to their proposals. Most resistance was met over two sections of the proposed line. A rival scheme, the Cheltenham & Great Western Union Railway, was seeking permission to build along an almost identical route between Gloucester and Cheltenham, and the people of Worcester felt that the 'B&G' line should come closer than its planned three miles from the city.

The majority of the time and effort expended by both committees, in the period leading up to the submission of the B&G Railway Bill by 30 November 1835, was directed towards soothing these sources of opposition; in which pursuit they were sufficiently adept to ensure that, once it had begun its passage through Parliamentary procedure, their Bill became an Act with as little fuss as possible. This it did, receiving the Royal Assent on 22 April 1836. The end of one chapter . . . for sure, but the beginning of a second one that was to prove every bit as trying. The newly incorporated company faced formidable problems and opposition from interests in the towns and cities at its southern end, most notably Cheltenham, Tewkesbury and Worcester. These are well chronicled elsewhere, and their relevance to the present account is more in what they did not achieve, namely any progress in the building of the main B&G line to Birmingham, than anything else.

After obtaining their Act there was keenness, zeal even, amongst most of those involved in the company to see construction underway as soon as possible. This was not to be. Over a year passed with very little to show for it. Difficulties were encountered on three main fronts: firstly, certain landowners, affected by the compulsory purchase of their land to build the line, had tried to obtain the highest price possible; sums which the company could not afford. Secondly, no contractors could be found who were willing to undertake the various contracts required at the prices estimated by the compnay's engineer, Capt Moorsom. Finally, the exact course of the line, and in particular the fate of a branch to Worcester, was dependent upon the progress of another Bill, for the Grand Connection Railway, through Parliament. Agreements had been made in conjuction with the promoters of this line, and when it was thrown out, in May 1837, the B&G were left with binding commitments to build a branch which they did not want.

At around this time, some of the B&G's investors began to look for a scapegoat; rounding upon Capt Moorsom. They approached Joseph Locke, engineer of the soon-to-be-opened GJ Railway, effectively to check Moorsom's figures. Sadly, for them, Locke, reporting back in September 1837, said that it was a well selected line, only expressing some reservations over the gradients on the Lickey incline. Exonerated, the following month, Capt Moorsom reported to the Board that work would start the next month; contracts being advertised on 31 October. By the New Year there were freshly completed earthworks to seen at various points along the southern portion of the line, which it was hoped would be opened by mid-1839.

Progress and opening

1838 saw good progress, by September, work was well advanced between Camp Hill and Moseley, near Birmingham, and the permanent way was being laid on the southern section of the line by November. It had been planned that the first section to be opened would be that between Cheltenham and Droitwich, but that same month this was postponed until the line was ready through to Bromsgrove, a town 13 miles from Birmingham, which had good coaching facilities. By late May 1840, a single line was completed between Cheltenham and Bromsgrove and on 30 May a Director's special travelled the line. Its opening to the public was delayed until 24 June 1840 when a 09.10 departure from Cheltenham became the first public passenger service along the line, arriving at Bromsgrove by 10.50; a coach service completing the journey to Birmingham.

From that date, the remainder of the line opened in sections: Bromsgrove-Cofton Farm, a temporary station at the rear of what is now part of 'The Austin' works at Longbridge, on 17 September 1840, with intermediate stations at Blackwell (opened 5 June 1841), at the summit of the Lickey incline, and Barnt Green; Cofton Farm (which closed) to

Below:
Characteristic B&G architecture: Droitwich Road station, between Dunhampstead and Stoke Works below Bromsgrove; seen in the 1930s, when it remained open for goods.
Don Powell Collection

Camp Hill, with intermediate stations at Longbridge (closed in April 1849), Lifford (closed in November 1844) and Moseley (renamed Kings Heath from 1 November 1867) on 17 December 1840; and Camp Hill-Gloucester Junction, with the L&B, on 17 August 1841. B&G trains were finally able to run into Curzon Street station, stopping just short of Gloucester Junction, at a platform where passengers' tickets were checked and collected. This also gave the company a rail link with the B&DJ Railway for the first time.

Camp Hill became a goods station, that traffic first running in October 1841; and, on 15 November 1841, it was partially reopened to passengers; the 15.30 departure and 13.40 and 19.10 arrivals, being goods trains which also conveyed passengers. The basic service was weekdays only and consisted of eight trains in each direction. Curzon Street was hardly buzzing with B&G trains either. The first arrival, the 08.15 ex-Gloucester, did not reach there until 11.18 and the first departure was not until 12.44; the second arrival worked to Camp Hill, the third reaching Curzon Street by 14.21, 49min before the second B&G departure of the day; and so on. Fares for the complete journey were: first-class, 13s 6d (65.5p), second-class, 9s (45p), and third-class, 5s 6d (27.5p). On 14 November 1842 a service of through first-class coaches was introduced between London and Gloucester, jointly with the L&B; the 09.45 ex-Euston conveying carriages which arrived in Gloucester at 1715; the 13.00 ex-Gloucester conveying carriages

Above:
'The Philadelphia Engine ascending the Plane, rising One in 37 with a train of loaded Wagons. The total weight moved, 74 tons – The maximum Speed, 9¾ miles per hour'. Caption to a famous print showing the Lickey Incline in June 1840. This section of the B&G did not open to passengers until 17 September 1840, and the company did not start conveying goods until October 1841, so this is either a trial, or material being transported to construction work further up the line. In the distance, the other line is being worked on.
E. I. Dolby/Modern Transport/IAL

Left:
Once clear of the Lickey incline and Cofton Tunnel, the B&G line's approach to Birmingham was relatively free of engineering difficulties save for Moseley Tunnel, seen here c1960 with Class 4F 0-6-0 No 44411 emerging with a down Gloucester freight.
R. S. Carpenter Collection

which arrived in Euston at 21.00. Passenger services continued to use Camp Hill until November 1844.

The B&G's outstanding feature was the 2 mile 1 in 37.7 gradient Lickey incline. Edward Bury, the noted authority on locomotives of the time, had been engaged by the company in 1838 as their agent and advisor. He ordered four locomotives from the Liverpool firm of George Forrester & Co., and two were purchased second-hand, one from the Leicester & Swannington Railway, another from the London & Southampton line. Bury also set to work designing the winding engines for the Lickey incline, but Capt Moorsom was determined that this should be worked by locomotives. He was aware of the hill-climbing prowess claimed for the locomotives built by the American firm of Norris Bros. of Philadelphia, and in November 1838 he persuaded the B&G Board to order one locomotive of that company's most powerful design, the Class A Extra, and they contracted to buy no fewer than nine other, lesser powered, Norris engines. Bury was delighted with this news. The principal Norris design was in fact one of his, which the latter had pirated!

One of the lighter Norris locomotives arrived in March 1839, but the Class A Extra was not delivered until May 1840, helping to delay the opening of the line up the Lickey incline. Late delivery of locomotives wasn't the B&G Locomotive Department's only problem; far from it. By all accounts the Department, and its works at Bromsgrove, operated on a heady mix of incompetence in its officers and cheeseparing from the company, which, more than once, produced the kind of disaster it was bound to. Ironically though, the line's most famous incident cannot be directly attributed to this. In November 1840, the B&G took delivery of an experimental locomotive for trial purposes: *The Surprise*. This had been built in Birmingham in 1837, to the designs of an American, one Dr Church, and was unusual by any standards. Its configuration was 0-2-2 and it had a vertical boiler and two cylinders, the footplate being formed by a sunken platform between these; the crew therefore riding in front of the boiler, without any protection from the elements!

The locomotive had been 'doing the rounds' a bit, having been tried by both the L&B and GJ companies, and it had spent quite a long time in a siding at the latter's Vauxhall station in Birmingham. Too long in fact, as rainwater, admitted by the uncapped chimney, had corroded away a portion of the boiler plating. On the evening of Tuesday 11 November 1840, after a day of trials, *The Surprise* was waiting at Bromsgrove to act as a banking engine on the Lickey. Its relief valve was set at 45lb per square inch, but hadn't been checked, so when pressure began to rise the boiler burst, dumping its contents ,

BIRMINGHAM AND GLOUCESTER RAILWAY.—ALTERATION OF TRAINS.—On and after Tuesday, the 1st of August, this Company's Trains will run as follows, until further notice :—

FROM BIRMINGHAM.	FROM GLOUCESTER.
H. M.	H. M.
12 44 Night (Mail.)	5 15 Morning, goods with passengers.
3 10 Morning (Mail.)	8 15 Morning.
5 15 Do. Goods with passengers.	10 30 Do.
8 40 Do.	1 0 Afternoon.
12 15 Noon.	3 0 Do.
2 45 Afternoon.	4 15 Do. Goods with passengers.
4 15 Do. Goods with passengers.	7 15 Evening (Mail.)
6 45 Evening.	9 0 Do. do.

First and second-class Carriages with all the Trains.
Third-Class with the Goods Trains only.

The Company cannot guarantee the Goods Trains so keeping correct time as to secure passengers being forwarded by the Trains of other Companies.

For the accommodation of Passengers between London and Worcester, Cheltenham and Gloucester, *First-Class* Carriages of this Company will be attached to the London and Birmingham Company's Mail Train, leaving the Euston Station at a ¼ to 10 in the morning; and the 4 o'clock afternoon Train from Birmingham. Both these Trains call only at First-Class Stations.

From London, quarter to 10 in the morning.
Arriving at { Worcester.... half-past 4. / Cheltenham .... 5. / Gloucester quarter-past 5.
From Gloucester, at 1 in the afternoon.
" Cheltenham, 20 minutes past 1.
" Worcester, 25 minutes to 2.
Arriving in London at 9 in the evening.

By order,
GEORGE KING, Secretary.

Above:
An 'Alteration of Trains' notice for the B&G dated 1 August 1843. In the early years of operation, most railway companies changed their service frequently, often from month to month, and notices like this one were a means of passing this information on to the travelling public. It also gives a good impression of what travelling by the B&G must have been like.
Author's Collection

Left:
The memorials to Thomas Scaife and Joseph Rutherford in Bromsgrove Churchyard, before they were renovated by BR. Both men were killed in a boiler explosion on the B&G on 11 November 1840. The locomotives shown are both Norris designs, all the stonemason had to sketch, but the one which killed the men was an experimental design.
Author's Collection

and those of the firebox, through the firebox door into the sunken footplate. Both men on the locomotive, a banking engine driver, Thomas Scaife, aged 28, and the Locomotive Foreman at Bromsgrove, Joseph Rutherford, aged 52, were killed. The locomotive went on to be rebuilt, and survived in Midland Railway ownership until around 1874.

Both of its victims were buried side-by-side in Bromsgrove churchyard, their graves being marked by matching stones erected in 1840 and 1841, paid for by Scaife's colleagues and Rutherford's widow, respectively. These are inscribed with lines and verses commemorating the accident, plus carvings depicting two Norris locomotives, which often gives rise to comments that it was one such which exploded, killing the men. But they were so featured because that was all that was available for the monumental mason to sketch when he visited Bromsgrove Locomotive Works. Over the years the stones became dilapidated and on 7 July 1959 the Rev F. G. Shepherd, the Vicar of Bromsgrove, launched an appeal for money to restore the lettering on them. This was paid for by British Railways, London Midland Region, and the restored stones were unveiled at a ceremony attended by the Rev Shepherd, local civic dignitaries and representatives of British Railways, in mid-September 1959.

Joseph Rutherford's death set in train (sic) a chain of events which culminated in the appointment of James Edward McConnell as Locomotive Superintendent at Bromsgrove on 2 July 1841. He was a young, then only 26, and able man, who put the B&G's ramshackle collection of locomotives into good order, going on to design the first purpose-built Lickey banker. It is a pity that the same could no be said about the rest of the B&G's operations; its story reading more like 'how not to run a railway'. Most of their difficulties were not concealed behind the Boardroom door either. The company's problems were given a full airing by an anonymous 'Whistle-blower' (sic), one of the first such, who hid behind the nom de plume 'Veritas vincit' and conducted his business through the columns of such journals as the *Railway Times* .

At Gloucester, the B&G joined the Bristol & Gloucester Railway, a broad gauge line, and so there was a break of gauge there, which meant that passengers, their luggage, and particularly goods traffic; *all* had to be transferred between what were in effect different railway systems. Breakages, losses and general confusion abounded, with appropriate accusations about just whose fault it was. Matters came to a head in 1844. The Bristol & Gloucester Railway had hoped for a deal of goods traffic from the GWR at Bristol, but in the event found that most of this came from Birmingham, via the B&G, in the other direction. Having thus a common interest (Birmingham goods traffic), and a common problem (the gauge break), the two companies began talks which resulted in a decision to merge.

Therefore, from 14 January 1845, they began to work together as the Birmingham & Bristol Railway, resolving to offer the united companies to the GWR. A meeting was arranged with the latter for 30 January; two members of the late-B&G Board travelling down to London via the L&B the day before. At Rugby, who should get into their compartment but John Ellis, Vice-Chairman of the newly formed Midland Railway. Pleasantries turned to chat about railway matters, various and specific, including the purpose for the trip; at which point Mr Ellis said that if the GWR turned them down they should come and see him. They did, and so *they* did; an initial leasing to the Midland company coming into effect on 7 May 1845. All of this was happening against the background of the Gauge Commission's deliberations, which held up the formal consolidation of the B&G within the Midland Railway until the passing of an Act on that famous date: 3 August 1846.

The Formation of the Midland Railway

Although planned as more or less a through system, by the early 1840s, the three railways that converged upon Derby, the North Midland, Midland Counties and B&DJ, were performing as something less than this; the returns in particular leaving much to be desired by their shareholders. Capital was exhausted and resources overstretched, but salvation was at hand in the form of the North Midland's enigmatic and ebullient Chairman: George Hudson.

Hudson was the son of a Yorkshire farmer, who had been catapulted into the business world in 1827 upon his inheritance of £30,000, with which he elected to start a joint-stock bank. From this point, Hudson's story would have been remarkable only if he had *not* become involved in railway promotion, such was the hold this had on the nation's commercial interests following the opening of the Liverpool & Manchester line in 1830. Through a large holding of North Midland Railway shares, Hudson became involved with the running of the company, participating in an Committee of Enquiry into this, and being elected its Chairman in November 1842, at a stormy meeting at which the committee's findings were being reported. He assumed responsibility for dire problems, which were highlighted the following spring when the North Midland was forced to sell 60 carriages as 'surplus to requirements'.

Hudson saw the solution to all of this as a true merger of the three 'Derby' companies, to form a single, unified system, under one management. He began immediate negotiations with the other parties. The Midland Counties Railway were agreeable and sanctioned the move at its quarterly meeting on 21 September 1843; but the B&DJ proved harder to convince. They had other allies, and physical connections with both the L&B and B&G companies, and their assent to Hudson's proposal was only just secured in time for a 'Grand Midland Amalgamation' Bill to be submitted to Parliament by 30 November 1843; in time for the Parliamentary Session of 1844. This bill received the Royal Assent on 10 May 1844, from which date all three companies began to function as one system, under the title of the Midland Railway.

Midland Railway Locomotive Sheds 1855-1894

The B&DJ Railway built locomotive maintenance and repair shops at Lawley Street, to replace earlier facilities at Hampton; the former coming into use in June 1842. These also offered limited locomotive accommodation and served the Midland Railway from its formation

Below:
0-6-4T No 2001 stands adjacent to the mechanical coaler at Slatley shed on 9 May 1936. Saltley shed opened in 1855, closing in March 1967.
H. C. Casserley

Above:
Class 5 No 44691, introduced in 1950, and Class 9F No 92138 were amongst those stabled at Saltley shed in 1964, when this view of the latter being prepared for express duties was taken.
Michael Mensing

in 1844 onwards; but by the end of the decade they were inadequate for the company's expanding needs, and in a poor state of repair. In 1851 a site was therefore sought in Birmingham on which to construct a new, purpose built, locomotive shed; convenient land being identified and purchased in Saltley, adjacent to the former B&DJ main line. Then, for some reason, this much needed improvement was delayed; plans not being prepared for three years and building work not beginning until 1855. The completed round-house shed came into use about 1856 and had 24 roads, arrayed around a 39ft diameter turntable; plus a repair shop, smithy and stores. Improvements, including the addition of a larger turntable in the yard, and refurbishment, followed quite quickly, but, within 10 years, this new shed was also too small, and in a location with little or no room for expansion.

A second new site was sought, land being bought near by, on the opposite side of the company's main line, in between it and the Birmingham & Warwick Canal. A new shed opened here in 1868, and was followed by a second, No 2 Shed, in 1876; the former being designated No 1 Shed, and having a new fitting shop extension built on to it. With this, the old Saltley shed was abandoned, although it was not removed until around 1900, following the addition of a new No 3 Shed on the 'new' site there. Saltley's locomotive allocation grew and grew, eventually reaching almost 200, most of which worked goods trains, although a stable of tanks was housed to work the Midland's circular suburban services, and expresses to run turns to Bristol, Derby and certain services through to Peterborough. Saltley was coded 3 by the Midland Railway but became 21A under the LMS reorganization of 1935; the following year also receiving the usual mechanical coaling and ash disposal plant with which the company was equipping most of its larger depots at the time. After the war all three sheds were re-roofed and subsequently rebuilt. Saltley closed to steam with the commencement of full electric working in the Birmingham area on 6 March 1967, its comparatively modern sheds being demolished, although the yard remains in use as a diesel depot.

Away from the centre of Birmingham the Midland Railway also had locomotive depots at Bromsgrove, Redditch, Walsall and Bournville. Bromsgrove depot served the banking engines stabled there to assist trains up the Lickey Incline, the three-road shed being built by the B&G Co. The basic building they erected c1840 served until the end of banking duties on the Lickey following the withdrawal of steam. A number of alterations were made to the shed, but these were in the nature of additions of plant and outbuildings to the main building. Originally coded 4A, as a sub-shed to Worcester, Bromsgrove became 21C, under Saltley in 1934, remaining so until inter-regional boundary changes brought it under Worcester (WR) shed and a recoding to 85F in February 1958. This was altered to 85D in January 1961. The shed finally closed on 27 September 1964.

Redditch shed had a single road and was situated about half a mile north of the station there. It was built about 1873, its allocation of no more than half-a-dozen locomotives being supplied by Saltley to work services to Ashchurch, the East Midlands and Birmingham. Designated 3C, it was later made a sub-shed to Bournville, becoming similarly associated with Bromsgrove following the February 1958 boundary changes noted. It had minimal facilities: a coal stage, office and store; its allocation having dwindled to just three locomotives by the early 1960s, one for passenger work, one for parcels and one to serve as a yard pilot; and its future looked dim following the withdrawal of passenger services beyond Redditch to Ashchurch in October 1962. The shed, however, lasted for a further 18 months before closure on 1 June 1964.

The Midland Railway built a three-road shed at Pleck in Walsall in 1880, adjoining the Wednesbury Road, with a capacity of 12 locomotives to work local passenger and goods turns. Coded 3B under Saltley, Walsall was closed on 2 September 1925; the newly formed LMS regarding the larger neighbouring shed at Ryecroft (ex-LNWR) to be far superior. Despite this, the shed remained in use as a depot for coaching stock.

With the success of its suburban services, many of which centred upon Kings Norton, the Midland Railway decided to provide additional accommodation for the locomotives working these nearby, on land at Lifford, to the southwest of Birmingham, by the junction of the West Suburban and Camp Hill lines. Opened in 1895, Bournville shed could accommodate 25 locomotives 'displaced' from Saltley, but its allocation rarely, if ever, exceeded this number by many. By the 1930s it had begun to loose some of its work and its importance was on the wane, which is possibly why it was missed out of the LMS shed improvement scheme of c1935; the only change in that period being one of coding, from 3A, under the former Midland Railway scheme, to 21B, in 1935. Further prestige was lost with the withdrawal of the New Street circular passenger service, via the West Suburban and Camp Hill lines, in 1941, and in 1956 the turntable was put out of action by a stray engine, from which time locomotives were 'housed' in the yard outside. Closure had seemed inevitable for a number of years, and finally came on 14 February 1960. All of the shed buildings have been demolished, but part of one of the perimeter walls survives to echo to the sound of Cross-City line services as they pass by.

The Redditch and Evesham & Redditch railways

Before its expansion as a 'new town', Redditch was a quiet village at the heart of a rich agricultural district. Although only 13 miles due south of

Birmingham, it was an unlikely place for any industry, let alone one with a world-wide reputation. Nonetheless, a local craft of making fish hooks had spawned (sic) a major industry; that of needle manufacture. With the opening of the B&G Railway, some seven miles to the west of the town, the thoughts of local industrialists and townspeople turned to connecting Redditch to it, thereby providing the town with a speedy and reliable link to the all important markets of Birmingham and the Black Country.

Early schemes foundered, but the promotion of the Redditch Railway Company in the mid-1850s resulted in the submission of a bill to Parliament in November 1857 and in the securing of an Act on 23 July 1858 which authorised the construction of a line between a junction with the Midland Railway at Barnt Green and a terminus in Redditch at or near to Brock Hill Lane. Construction began at once, and the line opened to passengers on 19 September 1859 and to goods on 1 October that year. At first there were no intermediate stations, but one was already under construction at Alvechurch, this opening in November 1859. With a guaranteed goods traffic, and passenger support, the line fared well. In 1862, the Midland Railway, who worked the line, made an approach to the company's Directors to absorb it; terms being duly agreed, this was effected by the Midland Railway (New Lines & Additional Powers) Act of 21 July 1863.

One week earlier, on 13 July, a scheme to build a railway which continued the Redditch Railway on to Evesham, the Evesham & Redditch Railway, was successful in obtaining a Parliamentary Act. This opened in two stages: between Alcester and Evesham, to goods on 16 June 1866 and to passengers on 17 June, and between Redditch and Alcester, with stations at Studley & Astwood Bank, Coughton and Alcester, on 4 May 1868. A new station was also provided at Redditch, ¼-mile south of the original Redditch Railway one, which was closed on the same day. Services were again operated by the Midland Railway, who vested the Evesham & Redditch company into their own with effect from 1 July 1882, by an Act dated that 12 July.

Above:
Barnt Green was one of the original B&G stations, opening on 17 September 1840. A branch to Redditch opened from there on 19 September 1859, and in this view from c1900 a Midland goods train is taking the latter.
Don Powell Collection

The line between Barnt Green and Redditch was worked by a passenger service from New Street which only stopped at stations from Kings Norton, an average of 10 trains in each direction making the journey on weekdays, there being no Sunday service. Four of these weekday services ran on beyond Redditch to serve the Evesham and Redditch line, working through to Ashchurch; a further two trains running short workings between New Street and Evesham. Passenger services between New Street and Redditch were turned over to DMU operation on 25

Below:
Alcester station on the Evesham & Redditch Railway, which opened on 4 May 1868, seen c1905 with a Midland goods train. The line south to Evesham opened on 17 June 1866.
Don Powell Collection

Right:
The original Redditch station opened with the line from Barnt Green on 19 September 1859 but was replaced by the building shown here on 4 May 1868, when the Evesham & Redditch Railway opened. This station is a ¼-mile south of the old one and is seen on 18 June 1960 with the 14.30 service from New Street. Passenger services beyond this point ceased from 1 October 1962 when the BR Engineer responsible refused to sanction use of the line.
Michael Mensing

April 1960, the units being housed at Monument Lane; trains working beyond Redditch continuing to be steam hauled. The latter section of the line had begun to present engineering difficulties, and on 1 October 1962 passenger services between Redditch and Ashchurch were withdrawn because the BR Engineer responsible refused to accept responsibility for the safety of trains on its Broom Junction to Evesham section, leaving only a solitary daily goods service to operate as far as Alcester.

The Whitacre & Nuneaton line

Before the mid-1860s, Midland Railway passengers bound for Leicester from Birmingham faced a roundabout journey involving a change at Burton. Consider one such journey in 1860, via the 09.50 from New Street. This took until 11.21 to reach Burton where an 11.25 service left for Leicester, arriving at 12.40; almost 2hr 50min to travel 62 miles; some clear room for improvement! The company's solution was to propose a direct line striking eastwards from Whitacre to Nuneaton, where it would form two junctions with the LNWR, one with the Trent Valley line station, the other with the South Leicestershire Railway, then under construction, and still independent, but destined to become part of the LNWR in 1867.

Authority to build the Whitacre & Nuneaton line was contained in the Midland Railway Act of 7 June 1861, and it opened on 1 November 1864, with intermediate stations at Shustoke, Arley (renamed Arley & Fillongley from March 1867), Stockingford and Nuneaton (Midland), plus a new station at Whitacre at the junction with the new line; the original B&DJ station there closing. Goods services began a month later, on 1 December 1864. The junction with the LNWR's Trent Valley line station came into use on 21 March 1867, but only for goods services (it would not see regular use by passenger trains until 1 January 1909). A new Nuneaton (Midland) station (renamed Nuneaton, Abbey Street from 2 June 1924) was opened on 1 September 1873; it was situated 150yd west of the 1864 one, which was closed. Twelve years later, a branch was opened to Stockingford Colliery. This left the line just west of Stockingford station and was authorised by the Midland Railway Act of 28 July 1873, coming into use on 3 April 1876, with a branch off, to Ansley Hall colliery, opening that September.

A basic service of around six trains in each direction ran on weekdays, with two on Sundays; the new line reducing the journey time between Birmingham and Leicester to 1hr 20min or so. Few changes were made to the service or the facilities along the line until November 1960, when goods services were withdrawn from Stockingford station from the 4th, and Arley & Fillongley station was closed completely from the 7th. Passenger services were withdrawn from Shustoke station the following year, from 24 July.

The Wolverhampton & Walsall Railway

A railway, to run between a junction with the GWR at Wolverhampton, and the South Staffordshire Railway at Ryecroft Junction, was authorised by five Acts; the first of which was given the Royal Assent on 29 June 1865. Styled the Wolverhampton & Walsall Railway (W&WR), its junction in the former

Right:
Construction of the Whitacre & Nuneaton line meant great upheavals at the former location. A new station, seen here, was built, opening to passengers on 1 November 1864. On Sunday 3 May 1964 English Electric Type 4 No D381 (later No 40181) approaches the junction to take the Nuneaton line (to the right) with the diverted up 'Ulster Express', occasioned by electrification work on the Trent Valley line.
Michael Mensing

place was transferred to one with the LNWR's Stour Valley line by a second Act of 23 July 1866. This necessitated the construction of an extra three-quarters of a mile of line, but the W&W gained running powers over a portion of the Stour Valley line when their railway was completed. Another deviation, at Walsall, was authorised by a third Act of 12 August 1867, which also extended the time allowed to build the line until 12 August 1870. The same Act granted the Midland Railway running powers over the SS lines of the LNWR, and over the latter's lines between Bescot and Wolverhampton; rights which were first exercised on 1 September 1870. Authorisation to build a road at Walsall, to avoid the need for two level crossings over the SS line, was contained in a fourth Act of 13 July 1868, and the construction period was extended until 1 December 1872, by a fifth Act, of 20 June 1870; the line finally opening, just in time, on 1 November 1872.

From its opening the W&WR was worked jointly by the LNWR and Midland Railway, having intermediate stations at: Heath Town; Wednesfield; Willenhall (Market Place); Short Heath; Bentley; and North Walsall. It was worked for three years, under an agreement which required both companies to use the line to send all of their traffic between Wolverhampton and Walsall, plus any traffic for which it formed the shortest route. Unfortunately, differences of interpretation arose between the LNWR and the Midland over this agreement, resulting in legal action. It emerged that the LNWR had been sending much of the goods traffic that should have gone via the W&W, via alternate routes. In settlement, they offered to purchase the line; partly to relieve themselves of the meticulous book-keeping that its joint operation required, and partly as an investment, suspecting that the Midland Railway would be interested in acquiring it once the Wolverhampton, Walsall & Midland Junction line (WW&MJ), in which they were also interested, opened. On 1 July 1875, the W&WR was vested in the LNWR, who sold it on to the Midland Railway on 1 July 1876; ending their services over the line on 31 July 1876.

Passenger services along the line were combined with those on the WW&MJ when the latter opened three years later, providing a Birmingham-Wolverhampton via Walsall service. Curious operating practices developed too. Midland services to Birmingham, using the WW&MJ line from Walsall, arrived via the GJ line to avoid reversing; whilst LNWR Walsall local services ran via the Midland owned W&W line. Therefore, in each direction daily, the Midland's stations on the W&W received an average of nine LNWR trains, but only one from their own company. Despite such a frequent and well spaced service, passenger returns from the W&W line stations were never spectacular. As a result, over its years of operation some stations were closed through being unremunerative. The first to go was Bentley, which closed on 1 October 1898, followed by Heath Town on 1 April 1910 and North Walsall on 13 July 1925. By that time the weekdays service was reduced to five

MIDLAND RAILWAY.

IMPROVED TRAIN SERVICE
FROM AND TO
SUTTON COLDFIELD,
WALSALL & WOLVERHAMPTON

BROWNHILLS AND ALDRIDGE.

WOLVERHAMPTON ART & INDUSTRIAL EXHIBITION.

NEW TRAINS will leave Birmingham for Walsall and Wolverhampton at 11.5 a.m., and Wolverhampton for Walsall and Birmingham at 1.0 and 10.5 p.m. Other additions will also be made to the train service between Birmingham, Walsall, and Wolverhampton during the period of the Exhibition.

CHEAP TICKETS, including admission, will be issued on the shilling admission days from all stations within a radius of 50 miles. See special bills.

JOHN MATHIESON, General Manager.

Derby, May 1st to June 30th, 1902.

Bemrose & Sons, Limited, Printers, Derby, London and Watford.

Above:
Both the W&W and WW&MJ lines were worked as a through route by the Midland and LNWR companies. This poster is advertising an improved train service in connection with the Wolverhampton Art & Industrial Exhibition of 1902. Note also the timetable for the Walsall Wood branch.
British Rail

trains in each direction, plus one working by a railmotor. Willenhall (Market Place) station was renamed Willenhall, Stafford Street, on 2 June 1924 as the LMS sought to remove certain confusions that existed between the names of former LNWR and Midland stations. From 1930 onwards, the LMS cut back on its loss making local services in the Birmingham area, closing the W&W line, and its remaining stations, at Short Heath, Willenhall and Wednesfield, to passengers from 5 January 1931.

Birmingham West Suburban Railway

In July 1864 the Worcester & Birmingham Canal Co were busily promoting the West Birmingham Railway & Canal Co. a line to run alongside their canal between New Street station and the Midland Railway at Kings Norton. But by 3 January 1865 the project had failed, owing to the depressed state of the money market. Nonetheless, the idea was sound enough, and five years later it was revived under the title of The Birmingham West Suburban Railway (BWS). This was promoted by an independent group of local businessmen who were mindful of the fact that villages in Birmingham's developing south western suburban outer ring, including Selly Oak, Bournville and Stirchley Street (the latter being a favourite country outing place for weary town workers), were poorly served by railways. In 1870 they proposed a solution: the BWS, a single line, which would commence at Albion Wharf in Bridge Street, Birmingham and follow the western bank of the Birmingham & Worcester Canal as far as Breedon Cross, Lifford; where it would form a junction with the Midland Railway's B&G line. A bill to authorise construction of the BWS was presented to Parliament in November 1870, receiving the Royal Assent on 31 July 1871.

Construction work was delayed by difficulties with both the purchase of the land required and building a railway in such close proximity to a canal. These required a number of small deviations in the course of the line, which strayed beyond those authorised by the company's Act, and so a new bill was presented to Parliament in November 1872, gaining the Royal Assent on 7 July 1873. This authorised deviations between Bridge Street and Suffolk Street, also extending the time allowed for construction until 7 July 1876. The company's original Act had included a clause formalising an agreement signed with the Midland Railway for the latter to work the BWS from its opening. In 1874, as that date came ever closer, the Midland entered into negotiations with the BWS's Directors, signing an agreement to vest the line into the former from 1 July 1875; this arrangement being sanctioned by the Midland Railway (New Lines & Additional Powers) Act of 29 June that year.

As built, the BWS was cut back at its Birmingham end to a new terminal station at Granville Street. This was a single wooden platform, with a very basic shed-like booking office, offering minimal protection to passengers under a projecting awning. The line opened on 3 April 1876 with intermediate stations at Church Road, Somerset Road, Selly Oak (renamed Selly Oak & Bournbrook from 1 October 1898, reverting to Selly Oak from 1 April 1904) and Stirchley Street (renamed Stirchley Street & Bournville from 1 March 1880; reversed to Bournville & Stirchley Street in July 1888 and simplified to Bournville from 1 April 1904). Trains ran through to Kings Norton, and two months later, on 1 June 1876, an additional station was opened at Lifford, by the BWS's junction with the Birmingham & Gloucester line.

The BWS was well patronised, soon highlighting the inadequacy of the single line and its mainly wooden stations. Also, at Bournville, in 1878, the Cadbury Brothers announced plans to build a new works for their burgeoning cocoa

Left:
A very rare picture: Stirchley Street station (later Bournville) on the BWS in 1879, only three years after the line opened and whilst it still terminated at Granville Street. All of the original stations on the line, including the latter, were of this basic design.
Author's Collection

Above:
A view from Islington Row over the parapet of the BWS line on 27 May 1957 revealing Five Ways station 13 years after closure on 2 October 1944. Note that the platform edges have been removed. Over to the left is the original course of the BWS to its terminus at Granville Street, extended and converted to run into Central Goods following the extension of the BWS into New Street from 1 July 1885.
Lens of Sutton

business; the BWS being well situated to provide transport for the firm's 230 employees, all of whom were based at their premises in Bridge Street, adjacent to the line's terminus in Birmingham. The first phase of the new Cadbury's factory opened in September 1879 and the likely acquisition of their goods and workforce traffic acted as a great impetus to the Midland Railway to improve the accommodation along the BWS.

Little time was wasted. The Midland Railway conceived the idea of doubling the line and extending it on into New Street station; in that way it could both take greater traffic and act as a more direct link for main line services, avoiding the rather roundabout B&G route via Camp Hill. Preparation for this began in their Additional Powers Act of 3 July 1879 which authorised 'The BWS Improvement'; work to upgrade the line along a 2 mile 5 chains section between Five Ways and Selly Oak. Two years later, their Additional Powers Act of 18 July 1881 authorised the widening and deviation (doubling) of 2 miles 4 furlongs and 5 chains of the line, between Church Road and Stirchley Street & Bournville stations, as well as the 'BWS New Street Extension', a 1 mile 6 chains 11yd line, commencing at or near the engine turntable at the west end of New Street station and terminating by a junction with the BWS at Church Road. The company also had plans for the existing line to Granville Street; this was to be retained and extended to a new goods depot to be built in Suffolk Street, adjacent to Worcester Wharf; powers of compulsory purchase for the land and property required for this development being obtained in the Midland Railway (Additional Powers) Act of 12 July 1882.

Away from Parliament, work was proceeding on the BWS improvements, having a rather unfortunate consequence. The Jewish cemetery in Granville Street, which contained the re-interred bodies of the dead displaced from the Froggery when New Street station was built, now lay in the path of both the goods and passenger extensions of the BWS. Accordingly, these unfortunate remains were removed once more and buried, for a third time, in Witton. Elsewhere along the line, new station buildings were being built to replace the original timber structures with which the line had opened just nine years earlier; those at Selly Oak coming into use first, on 13 April 1885.

Three months later, on 1 July 1885, the extension line between Church Road and New Street station came into use, with a new intermediate station at Five Ways, and on 26 September that year the Stirchley Street & Bournville to Kings Norton deviation line came into use. The latter had a number of consequences. At Lifford, the BWS's former course was by-passed, being designated as Lifford Canal branch; the 1876 station there closing and being replaced by a new Lifford station on the B&G line. Also, at about this time, new station buildings were opened at Stirchley Street & Bournville. Midland Railway expresses first used the new BWS line from New Street on 1 October 1885. The completion of the new goods depot in Suffolk Street took almost another two years. It required additional land on the south side of Swallow Street and the west side of Summer Street, compulsorily purchased under powers contained in the Midland Railway (Additional Powers) Act of 16 July 1885. It opened on 1 July 1887; a doubled connecting line to it from Church Road Junction being opened on 6 December 1892.

Two further improvements remained. The first was a new east facing curve at Lifford, to enable trains working along the BWS from New Street to cross to the B&G line and work back there via Camp Hill. This was authorised by the Midland Railway Act of 24 July 1888 and opened on 1 July 1892. A second and final improvement was the opening of the new engine shed at Bournville on 12 March 1894.

With the opening of the Lifford Curve in 1892 a basic pattern of local services was established on the line which saw around 23 trains in each direction along the BWS on weekdays. Of these, one was an early morning workmen's train to Cadbury's and 11 were New Street circular services, either running on to or coming off the B&G line. This pattern endured until the early 1920s when the suburban service came under threat, and then direct competition, from the extension of the tramway service along the Bristol Road. Until 1923 this had terminated in Selly Oak, but a series of extensions were opened to Northfield, Longbridge and Rednal between 1 October 1923 and 14 April 1924. Church Road station felt the pinch first, closing on 1 January 1925; five years later, on 28 July 1930, Somerset Road was closed. The BWS's passenger service survived though, and continued throughout the war, with only two further station closures: Lifford, on 30 September 1940, and Five Ways, on 2 October 1944; both temporarily at first, but then confirmed on 27 November 1946 and in November 1950 respectively.

The Kingsbury branch

The Midland Railway built a number of mineral branches in the Birmingham area, to particular collieries. One such was the 4 miles 66 chains Kingsbury branch, which served Baxterley Park colliery and left the main B&DJ line between Kingsbury and Wilnecote stations. This was authorised by the Midland Railway Act of 28 July 1873, opening, almost on the expiry of these powers, on 28 February 1878. A 22 chains long branch to Birch Coppice colliery was added, from the mid-point on the line, c1882, and around March 1914 a platform was opened in the colliery sidings at Baxterley Park for the reception of workmen's trains, which operated until 7 December 1928.

Wolverhampton, Walsall & Midland Junction Railway

As the W&W railway neared completion, a second scheme, the Wolverhampton, Walsall & Midland Junction Railway, was proposed to provide it with an indepedent link with Birmingham, partly over Midland metals. The line was to run from a junction with the W&W at Walsall to a junction with the Midland Railway at Castle Bromwich, with an additional Walsall avoiding line, which linked the W&W and WW&MJ directly, via a line from the former, adjoining North Walsall station, to a point on the latter, at Lichfield Road. The scheme was authorised by an Act of 6 August 1872. Given that it connected with the Midland Railway at its Birmingham end, and with a line in which that company was interested at its Walsall end, it was not surprising that the company was approached by the Midland with a view to making some arrangements over its use and working. Discussions were held, resulting in the signing of an agreement, that the Midland Railway would work the line from its opening, on 12 December 1872; confirmed by the Midland Railway (Further Powers) Act of 28 July 1873.

Construction began, and further discussions were held with the Midland Railway, resulting in the latter vesting the WW&MJ in its company under powers contained in its Act of 30 July 1874. Minor delays were encountered with the construction of the line, necessitating an extension of time to complete the work until 6 August 1878, which were granted under the terms of the Midland Railway (Further Powers) Act of 28 June 1877. Even then the opening of

Top:
Cadbury's works at Bournville generated a lot of traffic for the West Suburban line, including occasional passenger specials like the 'Trade Visit' one seen in this view taken on 26 September 1956. The unidentified locomotive would have had to draw up a few times to accommodate this eleven coach rake on Bournville station's platforms. *Michael Walker*

Above:
Bournville shed was opened to serve the BWS line on 12 March 1894 and is seen here on 2 March 1935 with an ex-Midland 2-4-0 locomotive, then numbered 20002 by the LMS.
H. C. Casserley

the line was delayed until 19 May 1879 when goods services began to work along it. Passenger services commenced on 1 July that year, with intermediate stations at Penns, Sutton Coldfield (renamed Sutton Coldfield Town from 2 June 1924), Sutton Park, Streetly and Aldridge. As noted above, passenger services on this line were run jointly with those along the Midland's W&W line. Until the 1930s few changes were made to the pattern of services or facilities provided on the line, apart from the closure of Sutton Coldfield Town station from 1 January 1925.

Following the withdrawal of passenger services along the W&W line in January 1931, those along the former WW&MJ continued to operate, connecting New Street and Walsall via Castle Bromwich. Six trains in each direction operated, on weekdays only; the overall journey time being 43min.

The Walsall Wood branch

As the WW&MJ line was being built, the Midland Railway planned a branch from it to serve the area around Walsall Wood and Brownhills. This was known as the Walsall Wood branch and was authorised by the Midland Railway (New Works, &c.) Act of 13 July 1876 which described it as: 'a 2 miles 3 furlongs line commencing by a junction with the WW&MJ line now being constructed, in field abutting upon the public road from Pelsall to Perry Barr near the Red House, and terminating in Pauls coppice wood (Brownhills)'. Two years later the Midland Railway (Additional Powers) Act of 17 June 1878 authorised a four furlongs or so deviation of this line at its Aldridge end, and the company's 1880 version of the same Act authorised the Walsall Wood Branch Extensions, comprising two railways: No 1 extending the Walsall Wood Branch by one mile or so to a junction with the LNWR's South Staffordshire line at Norton Canes; No 2 extending this line by two miles, to a junction with the Cannock Chase & Wolverhampton Railway. This was passed on 6 August 1880.

The Walsall Wood branch opened for goods between Aldridge and Brownhills on 1 April 1882, the line between Brownhills and Cannock Chase first receiving the same traffic on 1 November that year. Two years elapsed before a passenger service was introduced on the line, working between Aldridge and Brownhills (renamed Brownhills (Watling Street) from 2 June 1924), with an intermediate station at Walsall Wood, from 1 July 1884; five trains in each direction making the 15 minute journey, on weekdays only. The line was always a likely victim of any cutbacks, and succumbed to the LMS's pruning of unprofitable local lines; passenger services being withdrawn from 31 March 1930, Brownhills (Watling Street) closing entirely, Walsall Wood remaining open to goods. This and coal traffic sustained the branch for the next 25 years, but from the late 1950s it was progressively shortened as the collieries went out of use; ¾-mile of it closing from 23 March 1957, a further stretch going from 3 June 1962. Three months later, on 3 September 1962, the remaining facilities at Walsall Wood station were withdrawn and it closed entirely.

The Halesowen Railway

In the mid-1840s, aware that the heart of the Black Country was poorly served by railways, the Midland Railway proposed a branch from its B&G line at Northfield to Halesowen. This was authorised in their Act of 3 August 1846, but not built. Almost 20 years passes. A lot has changed. The GWR is now a major presence in the Black Country. An independent group, the Halesowen & Bromsgrove Branch Railway, revives the idea of building the above line, this time as a link from Halesowen to Northfield. A bill is submitted to Parliament, but opposition is encountered from many sides, including the GWR and Midland Railway, whose intransigence threatens to ruin the whole project. Urgent talks are called, at which, on 27 April 1865, all three parties sign a 'Heads of Agreement' document, detailing who is to do what with regard to the building and use of the line. The Halesowen & Bromsgrove Branch Railway bill is saved, and the company obtains its Act on 5 July 1865, authorising them to build a single line to Bromsgrove, with a branch to join the Midland Railway near Longbridge, including provision for a station at Halesowen, separate from that already authorised for the GWR in the WM Railway Act of 1862.

All seemed well, but difficulties were encountered finding a contractor to undertake the building of the line; and time began to tick away. Two small branches and additional capital borrowing were authorised by a second Halesowen & Bromsgrove Branch Railway Act of 6 August 1866; a third one, of 1 August 1870, abandoning these, and the line to Bromsgrove, but extending the time allowed for land purchase to 1 August 1872 and for construction to 1 August 1873. A new agreement with the GWR and Midland companies over the

Below:
The WW&MJ line opened between Castle Bromwich and Walsall on 1 July 1879. The first station to Walsall was Penns, which is seen here with the 18.44 New Street to Walsall local on 5 September 1959.
Michael Mensing

working of the line was signed on 30 July 1872 and a fourth Halesowen & Bromsgrove Branch Railway Act, of 21 July 1873, authorised minor deviations and extended the construction time allowed for the original lines until 1 August 1876. Away from Parliament, a contractor had also been found and work was progressing, slowly. Despite this, 1874 and 1875 slip by with little to show for them. More Parliamentary acts follow, taking up time and resources that ought to have been directed towards building the line. The first of these, of 13 July 1876, changes the company's name to the plainer and more accurate Halesowen Railway; the second, of 11 August 1879, removes some 'sticking points', defining the junction to be made with the GWR at Halesowen and agreeing the use of their existing station there, thus avoiding the need to build a separate one; a third Act, of 26 August 1880, further altering the junction with the GWR at Halesowen.

Meanwhile, construction had begun in earnest at last and the line's outstanding engineering feature, the 660ft long Dowery Dell viaduct, was substantially completed by Easter 1881, being tested by two 75 ton locomotives on 10 May that year. The viaduct was supported by two stone abutments and eight cast iron trestles which bore it 100ft over a stream and the valley whose name it adopted. Despite this, the line did not open. A dispute had arisen between the GWR, Halesowen and Midland companies over the nature and extent of the works the Halesowen company were supposed to construct at Northfield station. The matter was taken to court, but settled at a meeting held on 20 October 1882 by agreement that the Midland company construct and maintain such platforms and other facilities that would enable Northfield to act as an exchange station between the Halesowen and Midland lines. At the same time, other litigation concerning the cost of alterations at Halesowen station to allow the through running of GWR trains along the Halesowen Railway was settled by the payment of £200 to the GWR to cover the cost work there, plus legal fees. All of these matters were sanctioned by yet another Halesowen Railway Act, of 16 July 1883.

Finally, nearly 40 years after it was first thought of, and almost 20 years after the Halesowen company was established, the seven mile line opened on 10 September 1883, with intermediate stations at Hunnington and Rubery. And, despite all of the hoo-ha that had attended preparation of station facilities at Northfield, the service actually ran through to Kings Norton. Passenger and goods services were provided jointly by the Midland and GWR companies; the former working through to Kings Norton, the latter only as far a Rubery.

Top:
The 660ft long Dowery Dell Viaduct on the Halesowen Railway towered 100ft above Twiland Wood and was completed by Easter 1881, although the line itself did not open until 10 September 1883. Heavily weight restricted, this viaduct was both the line's crowning glory and part of its ultimate downfall. It was dismantled in 1965 but is seen here in an unusual view captured in 1930.
Don Powell

Above:
Rubery station on the Halesowen Railway c1900. This closed to passengers in April 1919 and was only sustained by goods and mineral traffic, such as that from the quarry seen in the foreground.
Don Powell Collection

The initial service was of seven trains in each direction on weekdays only, of which four were provided by the Midland Railway and three by the GWR; the first and last Midland trains of the day working from and to New Street station; the GWR ones being extended Old Hill-Halesowen branch workings. Journey times were unimpressive: GWR, Halesowen to Rubery (4¼ miles), 15 minutes; Midland, Halesowen to Kings Norton (8½ miles) 30 minutes, Halesowen to New Street, 50 minutes. Part of the reason for this 10 mph speed restrictions along the line: over the curves near Halesowen, over Dowery Dell viaduct, through the points at Rubery and over the curves between the branch and the Midland main line.

The Halesowen Railway passed through countryside which was almost the definition of the rural idyll, but for all its charm, hardly anyone used it. Always bad, by the early 1900s, things got much worse, until, in 1904, the company went bankrupt. A Liquidator was appointed and, after much negotiation, the GWR and Midland companies agreed to purchase jointly the Halesowen Railway on 26 October 1905; this was sanctioned by Parliament from 30 June 1906; the Halesowen company

Left:
The Halesowen Railway joined the former B&G line at Halesowen Junction in Longbridge. This is seen on 26 May 1957, the scene dominated by the vast expanse of 'The Austin' works. The junction remains in use to serve this car plant's internal rail system.
Donald Luscombe

being formally wound up on 22 October 1907.

Of course, none of this did anything to improve the line's receipts; but, with the kind of irony which, in retrospect, often seems contrived; moves that would ultimately give it a new lease of life, were afoot near to its junction with the Midland Railway, in the village of Longbridge. In 1894, the Birmingham printers White & Pike Ltd, publishers of the local *ABC Railway Guide,* decided to diversify into the printing and manufacture of tin boxes. For this they built a large new works at Longbridge, but hit financial difficulties and vacated the premises in 1902. Over at Aston, the General Manager of the Wolseley Sheep Shearing Machine Co Ltd, Herbert Austin, who had been experimenting with car manufacture for 10 years, was working out his notice. On 26 June 1905 he formed the Austin Motor Co and began to look for his own premises. On a Sunday picnic trip to Rednal he spied the vacant White & Pike works, made enquiries, and bought them; moving in on 10 November 1905, one day after the formal announcement of the joint GWR/Midland purchase of the Halesowen Railway.

Austin lodged a planning application for a kitchen block at his new Longbridge works with Northfield RUDC on 26 November 1905, the first of many hundreds of alterations and extensions that would transform the works into one of Europe's largest car plants. Austin's workforce expanded tenfold in Longbridge's first 10 years, the Midland Railway local services, including those from Halesowen, being the main beneficiary. With the outbreak of war, Longbridge took on War and Air Ministry work, introducing the first 24-hour working at a British car plant early in 1915. That February, the Midland Railway opened a new station at Longbridge, on the Halesowen branch, close to its junction with the main line, and that summer they introduced workmen's services between there and New Street. A supplementary workmen's service, of early and late trains, to Longbridge was introduced by the GWR on 18 April 1917, the station also having been opened to goods.

Longbridge's war contracts ran until early in 1919, and that April the Midland Railway passenger services between Halesowen and Northfield were withdrawn; Hunnington and Rubery stations closing to passengers. Only the workmen's services remained.

Below:
There have been no fewer than four Longbridge stations; this one being the second. It was opened near the end of the Halesowen Railway in February 1915 to serve the car factory there and was photographed during a quiet moment, of which there were many, on 21 October 1921. The last passengers to use the station were off workers' specials, which ceased to run from Halesowen on 1 September 1958 and from New Street on 1 January 1960.
R. S. Carpenter Collection

Above:
The workmen's services along the Halesowen Railway were worked by an amazing collection of aged locomotives and stock. This was a moment at Rubery captured on 11 September 1947 with Pannier No 1835 passing No 1745 with a workmen's train bound for Halesowen. Note the clerestory stock on the left.
Pat Garland

They continued for almost 40 years and, particularly before the World War 2, were operated by increasingly antiquated stock: four-wheel coaches, clerestory stock, etc. The service dwindled to two workmen's trains in each direction on weekdays only; one of the morning trains working back ECS to Tyseley, via Old Hill, Handsworth and Snow Hill, where the locomotive shunted until it was time to return to Longbridge; the other train would do the same thing on the next day. These were withdrawn from 1 September 1958, a victim of the rising popularity of the product their passengers travelled daily to make. Fifteen months later, on 1 January 1960, the remaining Longbridge workmen's service from New Street was also withdrawn.

From September 1958 the former Halesowen Railway was only sustained by freight traffic: steel pressings for Longbridge and consignments to and from the 'Blue Bird' toffee factory at Hunnington; and when the former ceased around 1961, its closure was inevitable.

The Kingsbury & Water Orton line

One of the last major improvements made by the Midland Railway to its lines in the Birmingham area was the construction of a 3 mile 64 chains cut-off line between Water Orton and Kingsbury. Well aware of the GWR's new route from Birmingham to Bristol, and the threat it implied to their virtual monopoly of traffic between those two places; the Midland Railway set about eliminating instances of operating slack along the route of its north and west expresses. One such instance was the junction at Whitacre between the original B&DJ line and its 1842 extension into Birmingham. The Kingsbury & Water Orton line was designed to bypass this junction and was authorised by the Midland Railway Act of 20 July 1906, opening to goods on 22 March 1909 and to passengers on 3 May that year; there were no intermediate stations.

LMS Birmingham to Bristol line improvements

Shortly after its formation the LMS set about making a number of improvements to its main line from Derby to Bristol via Birmingham. The line south of the junction between the former B&G and BWS lines at Lifford, through Kings Norton station, had been quadrupled by the Midland Railway in an earlier scheme, providing fast lines for express services and slow lines for goods workings; the latter being converted into slow passenger lines in June 1939 under a scheme involving signalling alterations and the provision of new connections at Northfield station. But beyond this, and for the 2¾ miles to Barnt Green, the former B&G main line was only a double track which had to accommodate in excess of 170 trains daily. This section had become a notorious bottle-neck, the greatest barrier to the removal of which was the 440 yard long Cofton Tunnel, whose dimensions did not permit the use of modern coaching stock.

Plans to remove this tunnel had been formulated by the Midland Railway in its last days; the company undertaking geological survey work there in 1922. Under the LMS's scheme, the tunnel was to be removed and replaced by an open cutting, wide enough to take two additional lines on its eastern side. To facilitate this, temporary diversion lines would be constructed for the main lines, to allow the tunnel to be felled without disrupting traffic. The contract for the work was let to Messrs Logan & Hemmingway of Doncaster in September 1925 and they began excavation work in March 1926. Quite quickly, a number of geological faults were encountered which required the whole scheme to be revised. The ground would not maintain the intended 1.5 to 1 slopes on the new cutting's sides, and on the up side there was a massive landslip. Unfortunately, all of the additional land on this side belonged to the Austin Motor Company, who had it earmarked for work's extensions; and so the scheme was revised to include the erection of a 20 chains long, 28ft high, reinforced concrete retaining wall at this point.

Work began on the wall in January 1927, the LMS abandoning its idea of constructing temporary diversion lines and settling for the gradual demolition of the tunnel when occupation of the line permitted. A temporary signal box and special automatic alarm communications were provided to protect the section of line through the tunnel, and, by May 1928, 265yd of it had been exposed from its southern end. Sadly, when demolition began, a cast-iron curbing, forming the eye of one of the ventilation shafts, collapsed, killing four workers. Therefore, with great care, this exposed part of the tunnel was demolished in six stages. Attention then turned to uncovering the remaining 140yd of the tunnel, but quite quickly, in June 1928, there was another landslip and it was decided to extend the concrete wall, bringing its total length to 449yd, nine yards longer that the tunnel.

The extended retaining wall was completed by the end of December 1928 and so work resumed to expose the remainder of the tunnel. This was completed by the middle of the fourth week of January 1929, when it was decided to demolish the tunnel in one go using explosives. Preparation work commenced on Saturday 26 January to drill the 110 holes required, each to receive a charge of ammonal explosive, a detonator and a cap of clay. Then, the peace of an early Sunday morning was shattered

Top right:
A diagram showing the work involved in five of the six stages required in the opening out Cofton Tunnel on the former B&G main line in 1928/9.
Modern Transport/Ian Allan Library

Centre right:
Work progresses on the demolition of the exposed portion of Cofton Tunnel, near Longbridge on the former B&G main line, during April 1928. Sadly, one month later, part of the tunnel collapsed, killing four workers.
R. S. Carpenter Collection

Right:
Gradual demolition, collapses and landslips had left 140 yards of Cofton Tunnel to be demolished somehow. How was by explosives, and this is the moment that 110 charges of ammonal despatched the tunnel to the elements; shattering the peace of an early Sunday morning at Longbridge on 27 January 1929.
R. S. Carpenter Collection

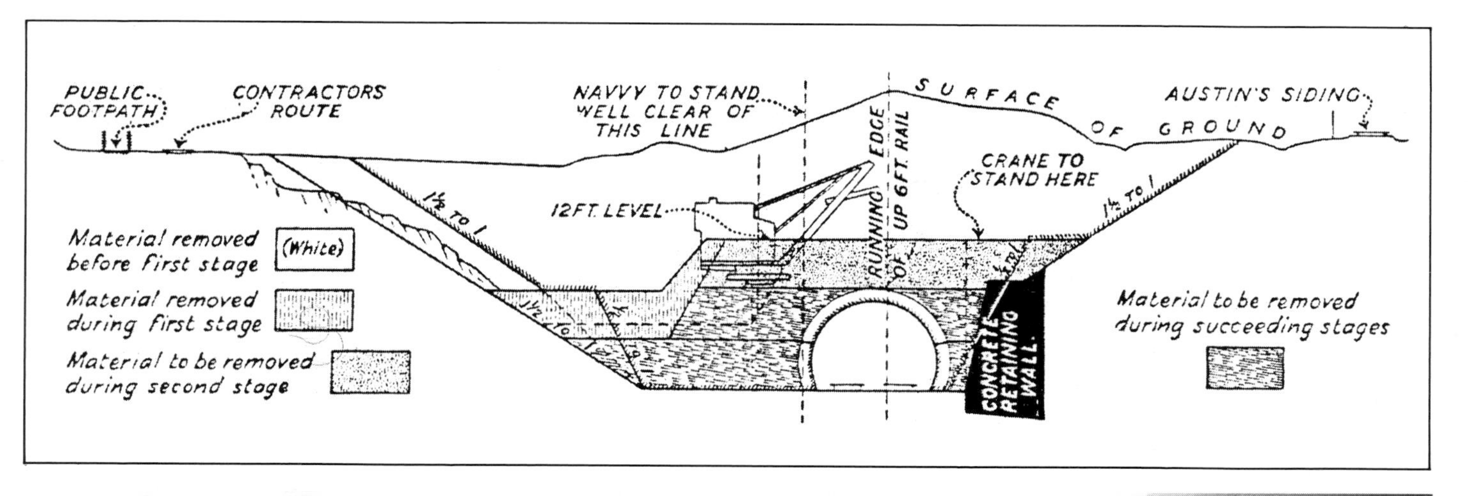
PUBLIC FOOTPATH
CONTRACTORS ROUTE
NAVVY TO STAND WELL CLEAR OF THIS LINE
SURFACE OF GROUND
AUSTIN'S SIDING
EDGE OF UP 6FT. RAIL
RUNNING
CRANE TO STAND HERE
12FT. LEVEL
1½ TO 1
Material removed before first stage
(White)
Material removed during first stage
Material to be removed during second stage
CONCRETE RETAINING WALL
Material to be removed during succeeding stages

Above:
The original timber Stirchley Street station was replaced by these more substantial buildings and was eventually, after a number of name changes, renamed Bournville in April 1904. It is pictured here not long after this last renaming.
Don Powell Collection

by: 'a vivid yellow flash and a roar like that of a land-mine (with which) two hundred tons of brickwork crashed into the base of the tunnel, while the air was filled with flying splinters which landed in fields and on the roofs of buildings 200 yards away. Two more explosions followed, each more deafening than its predecessor, and when the grey clouds of acrid smoke drifted away it was seen that the tunnel had vanished entirely. . . . For some time after the last explosion stray pieces of wall continued to crash at intervals into the depths of the tunnel. . . . Two thousand tons of debris were brought down by the explosions. A small army of workers descended upon the scene immediately, and with the aid of 4 giant cranes, 150 wagons and a fleet of engines they succeeded in clearing the up line soon after daybreak, while traffic over both lines was resumed at 7.45am (Monday 28 January 1929).'

The whole Cofton scheme eventually cost the LMS £250,000; the total amount of spoil removed being 560,000cu yd; some of which was used to build up ground at the Austin works. Completing the work occupied the rest of 1929, and when next travelling the line it is worth remembering that it wasn't only the Lickey incline that was so hard wrought!

The Development of Passenger Services

Although Birmingham is not generally regarded as a stronghold of the Midland Railway, their local and express train services serving the city showed all of the flair for luxury and frequency usually associated with that company. Considerable inventiveness was also shown in the range of services provided to the citizens of Birmingham, as the company made the maximum use possible of the three main and four branch lines at its disposal.

1 – Local passenger services

There were no such things as local trains to the Midland Railway; the company preferring to term them its 'Suburban Services'. Around Birmingham, these were operated within an area described by Whitacre in the east, Barnt Green in the south and Streetly in the northeast; the company not possessing any lines which ran west or northwest of the city. These suburban services were probably at their greatest extent in the early years of this century, in the years up to the outbreak of World War 1, which is the period covered by the following description of them.

The Midland Railway's most dedicated suburban line in the Birmingham area was the former Birmingham West Suburban; a curious hybrid, which had begun as a branch, with its own separate terminus in the city, and had come to usurp the status of the former B&G Camp Hill route as the company's main line south and west. Yet, despite carrying a considerable volume of main line traffic, an intensive suburban service remained. The usual weekday service was of 19 slow trains from (down), and 20 (up) to, New Street; the earliest being the 05.25 workmen's train to Bournville, the latest the 23.03 from there. Individual stations along the route received modifications to this basic pattern, tailored to suit the needs of the people they served. Five Ways and Somerset Road received the basic service, but only 14 down trains called at the intermediate station Church Road, which, despite being situated in the heart of one of the wealthiest parts of the city, was little patronised. Selly Oak, the only station on the line also to have goods facilities, had an augmented service of three semi-fasts daily, plus one other service which only called at Church Road.

Bournville received the most intensive service, having an additional six daily fasts from New Street. Its popularity was due entirely to the presence of the Cadbury Bros factory, and three daily fasts to Birmingham started there. Beyond Bournville is the Lifford Curve, linking the West Suburban and Camp Hill lines. As previously mentioned, this enabled a circular service to

Left:
Brighton Road was the first station after Camp Hill on the former B&G line towards Kings Norton. It was opened by the Midland Railway on 1 November 1875 and is seen here in 1912 with an 0-4-4T locomotive and a seven coach train. Note the clerestory coach fourth from the front. Passenger services were withdrawn from Brighton Road on 27 January 1941 when it closed completely.
Don Powell Collection

Below left:
The original Moseley station on the B&G opened with that section of the line on 17 September 1840. As was the custom, this was later replaced with a more up-to-date station, seen here c1910 with locomotive No 3249 passing through, which opened on 1 November 1867. Unusually though, this new station was so far away from the original that the latter was retained, and renamed 'Kings Heath' the same day. Like Brighton Road, this Moseley station closed completely on 27 January 1941.
Don Powell Collection

be operated from New Street, four such trains starting from there daily, traveling via Kings Heath, the curve and returning along the West Suburban line. A fifth service traversed this route only as far as Selly Oak; five trains making complete runs in the opposite direction, with an additional one starting from Bournville. Saturday services were augmented by two fast trains, but none of the stations to Bournville were open on Sundays. Tram competition took much traffic from the railway along the West Suburban line; the fares being less than half those by rail, but the Midland Railway fought back, trying various experimental fare reductions, which managed to wrest some of this lost traffic back.

Continuing on from Bournville, the next station is Kings Norton, which received no fewer than 43 daily services from New Street, accepting trains from both the West Suburban and Camp Hill lines. Along the latter, there was a basic service of 24 down (to Kings Norton) stopping trains and 25 up ones, this again being modified to suit the needs of individual stations. The first and last down trains ran at 06.35 and 23.20; the corresponding up services being at 06.43 and 22.35. Camp Hill received the basic service and was well used by workers and by pupils attending the nearby King Edward VI Grammar School; whilst Brighton Road only opened to passengers in time for the 08.10 down service. Moseley, Kings Heath and Hazelwell each had the standard down service, but took 24, 25 and 23 of the up trains respectively; Lifford only having 21 down services each day. All but one of the trains in each direction on the line were stopping services and all but five, the ones on the New Street circular route, went on to Kings Norton. A Sunday service of one non-stop and nine stopping trains in each direction was also operated.

Left:
As noted, Kings Heath station on the former B&G line was opened as Moseley on 17 September 1840 and is seen here looking towards Birmingham c1910. There are so many advertisements, it almost looks like a preserved station!
Don Powell Collection

L M S
1014

Left:
A fine view of Kings Norton station on the Midland (former B&G) line just south of Lifford. This was taken in early LMS days in 1925, before the line through the station was quadrupled. Milk churns await collection and one of the station staff attends to one of the platform gas lamps as a train passes through.
R. S. Carpenter

Kings Norton was definitely the place to live for an intensive train service to New Street. During the morning peak there were up departures for New Street at 07.43, 07.58, 08.05, 08.23, 08.30, 08.35, 08.55 09.02, 09.13 and 10.02; and at mid-day up trains left at 13.32, 13.40, 13.46, 1403, 14.28 and 14.39, with eight corresponding services from New Street between 12.00 and 14.00 and nine in the same direction between 16.30 and 19.00; a very liberal service indeed! Kings Norton was also the terminus for services along the jointly owned Halesowen Railway. Five Midland Railway trains worked this on weekdays, three of which were mixed, Kings Norton-Halesowen, two Halesowen-Kings Norton. These were typically worked by an 0-4-4 tank locomotive, three six-wheeled coaches and four or five wagons, plus a goods brake van. The LMS opened a new station at Kings Norton on 14 March 1926; this had extra platforms. Halesowen trains also called at Northfield and were in addition to the 18 down trains it received each day. In Midland days, the village was also free from tramway competition as the extension of the Bristol Road services to this point did not open until 1 October 1923.

All of the Northfield trains went on to serve Barnt Green, and were supplemented by five Camp Hill line fasts, plus another whose only other stop was at Bournville, and extra trains on other days, notably Saturdays. To Birmingham, from Barnt Green, there were 23 trains, three of which were non-stop, taking only 19 or 20min for the 10½ mile journey. From 1 July 1918 there were also platforms at Longbridge, just south of Halesowen Junction. These were added to serve the munitions and aircraft work being undertaken at the Austin Works there; being taken out of use as part of the Midland Railway's preparatory work for the Cofton widening scheme sometime in 1922.

Leaving New Street in a northerly direction, the first station was Saltley, which opened on 1 October 1854 and was heavily used by people with employment in the east end of the city. The next station was Bromford Bridge, which opened on 9 March 1896 and was built to serve the adjacent Birmingham racecourse. Occupying the former site of the B&DJ Bromford Forge station, closed in May 1843, this was only open when race meetings were being held. Castle Bromwich, the next station along the line, was the first of any importance. It had 25 up trains calling on weekdays, of which 11 were slow main line services, bound to and from Derby or Leicester, the balance being suburban workings destined for the Wolverhampton line; the corresponding number of down trains being 10 and 13 respectively. The station increased in importance during the 1920s, as adjoining land became the permanent site for the British Industries Fair (BIF), the first one on this site opening on 12 May 1924. They were suspended during World War 2, but Castle Bromwich's traffic was increased, through the presence there of the main factory building Spitfires.

The BIF's resumed in 1948, the last being held between 6-17 May 1957. Of particular interest was the tendency of the LMS and BR(LMR) to use the fortnight of the BIF as an opportunity to operate experimental main line (see below) and local passenger services. For example, in connection with the BIF opening on 2 May 1955, BR(LMR) ran a 'lightweight diesel' (DMU) service between New Street and Castle Bromwich. These ran nine times a day, starting with the 09.15 ex-New Street and the 09.40 ex-Castle Bromwich; the fares being first-class 1s 6d (7.5p), third-class 1s (5p). This was 10 months *before* DMUs entered regular service anywhere in the Birmingham area, and they were not used regularly on any former Midland routes until 17 November 1958, when they were introduced between Wolverhampton and Burton-on-Trent.

Passenger services along the line to Wolverhampton via Sutton Park and Walsall were operated in accordance with an agreement signed with the LNWR in 1911. This allowed Midland trains to continue to Wolverhampton via the latter's line, to avoid the need to run locomotives round at Walsall; in return for which the LNWR worked most of the Midland's Walsall-Wolverhampton trains via Midland metals. Nonetheless, the Midland Railway ran a service of 13 up and 14 down trains on weekdays, of which the 07.45 from Walsall returned there, after reversing at Penns, and the 18.20 from Walsall was

Far left:
Midland 4-4-0 No 1014 stands in Kings Norton station on 10 March 1938 with the Royal Train, as a lone head peers out of the leading carriage.
W. L. Good

Left:
Saltley station, on the B&DJ's extension line to Lawley Street, was opened by the Midland Railway on 1 October 1854 and is seen here c1900 looking towards Birmingham.
Don Powell Collection

Right:
Ten months before DMUs entered regular service in the Birmingham area they were used to operate a special British Industries Fair shuttle between New Street and Castle Bromwich for two weeks from 2 May 1955. Here, one of these specials is the subject of much curiosity at New Street as a group of passengers ask the 'Guard' the whereabouts of his locomotive.
Michael Walker

a short working to Sutton Park. From 2 May 1955, BR(LMR) introduced 12 extra trains along this route, between Birmingham and Sutton Coldfield, to give an hourly service. The departures were at 33 minutes past the hour from New Street and 48 minutes past the hour from Sutton Coldfield. Leaving this line at Aldridge was the Brownhills branch, which enjoyed a maximum service of three trains in each direction on weekdays. Passenger services along the line ceased on 29 March 1930, but colliery traffic sustained it until the closure of Conduit Colliery in 1949, from when the remaining collieries declined, closing progressively.

Stations beyond Castle Bromwich: Water Orton, Forge Mills and Whitacre, were served by the slow main line workings referred to earlier, the latter being the junction for the Hampton branch. This service has already been described, but not its working, which was usually in the charge of an 0-6-0 goods locomotive, No 3696 being put to this use for a number of years. Its arduous duty was to wrestle a solitary four-compartment composite brake-coach, with a smoking and ordinary compartment of each class, up and down the line; taking about 15min each way.

New suburban services were also introduced, as on 1 July 1896, when the company commenced a passenger working between New Street and Malvern, via Stoke Works and Worcester (Foregate Street). This enjoyed considerable patronage, especially during the summer months, but was withdrawn from 1 January 1917 as a wartime economy measure and not reinstated. The Midland made a number of improvements

Below:
Whiskers and Wymans. A three-car Birmingham RCW DMU waits to leave Platform No 8 at New Street station with the 13.25pm service to Derby on 5 May 1962. In less than two years, all to view, save the unit, would be swept away.
Michael Mensing

Above:
Sutton Park station was almost midway along the WW&MJ line, opening with the line on 1 July 1879. The route was often referred to as the 'Sutton Park line' by drivers, possibly even the one glimpsed here taking the 13.46 local on towards New Street on 19 October 1963.
Michael Mensing

Above:
In the early 1900s Birmingham's suburbs began to be developed very rapidly. One such development was the Priory Housing Estate at Kings Heath and a station, named Hazelwell, was built to serve this on the former B&G Camp Hill line; opening on 1 January 1903 and pictured shortly afterwards.
W. J. Spurrier/Author's Collection

to stations in the Birmingham area in the 10 years between 1893 and 1903. Early in the former year, they opened a new station at Northfield, with a single island platform. The following year they began a programme of work leading to the opening of a new station at Saltley. In May 1895 Saltley level crossing was replaced by a road overbridge, known a Saltley Viaduct, the new station opening four years later, in two stages: the up side of the new island platform there being brought into use on 4 June 1899; the down side on 2 July that year. A new station building was provided at Castle Bromwich towards the end of 1901, and a completely new station was opened at Hazelwell, between Lifford and Moseley on the Camp Hill line, on 1 January 1903, to serve the new Priory housing estate, which was nearing completion there.

2 – Express passenger services

Lacking anyone to compete with on any of their routes to or from Birmingham until 1908, the Midland Railway, here, as elsewhere, sought only to excel through the high standard of comfort and elegance they provided on their express services.

The company had five basic routes over which it could send its express or long distance services. There was the former B&DJ main line from Derby, over which access could be gained to Leeds and Bradford, Manchester (via Buxton), Nottingham, Sheffield and Barnsley, and York. This was worked as a through route with the former B&G main line, as far as Bristol, giving access to Bath and Bournemouth (via the Somerset & Dorset Joint line), Dursley, Nailsworth, Sharpness and Lydney. Then there was a cross-country link line to Leicester, which connected with the Midland's lines in the East Midlands, allowing services to run, through the exercise of running powers, to Kettering and Cambridge, Saxby, Lynn and Lowestoft, Stamford and Peterborough. A fourth route was that to Redditch and Alcester, which left the B&G main line at Barnt Green; providing access to Evesham, plus an alternative way to Ashchurch on the B&G line. Finally, there was yet another route to Ashchurch, built up from two Midland services; one between New Street and Worcester, which ran over GWR metals from Stoke Prior Junction on the B&G line, and another which ran between Malvern Wells and Ashchurch, via Upton-on-Severn and Tewkesbury. The gap between these two was bridged by ordinary GWR services, as the Midland

Right:
The new 'Midland' side of New Street station nearing completion in the summer of 1885. Ahead is the newly created Station Street and the building facing the end of this is the old Market Hall, one of many fine Birmingham buildings destroyed during the redevelopment of the late 1950s, early 1960s. Note the steam tram lines.
Don Powell Collection

Railway was not permitted to run its locomotives over the former's Worcester and Hereford section.

Services along these routes were developed gradually. Between 1 July 1854, when the Midland Railway first gained access to New Street station, and 8 February 1885, when the Midland side platforms there first came into use; the company made less use of the station than is generally thought. This was particularly so after the second half of 1865, when a line linking the B&DJ and B&G lines between Landor Street and St Andrew's junctions first came into use. Authorised by an Act of 30 June 1862, this enabled the Midland Railway to work direct between Derby and Bristol; portions to and from New Street being attached and detached at Saltley and Camp Hill stations. From 1 April 1872 the company also began to carry third-class passengers by all of its trains, and, from 1 January 1875, likewise abolished second-class accommodation.

With the Midland Railway's main line traffic in the Birmingham area concentrated upon the Derby to Bristol route, in December 1872 the company made a belated, half-hearted and, ultimately, ill-fated attempt to poach some of the LNWR's and GWR's London-Birmingham traffic. This was made possible via its newly opened line between Bedford and St Pancras. From this date, some of the expresses on this route stopped at Wigston, where through carriages to (and from) Birmingham were detached (or attached), and conveyed on, via the south curve at Wigston, to be added to (or taken off) Leicester trains at Wigston Central Junction. Coming more under the heading of 'possible' than 'practicable', the Midland persisted with this service, despite the fact that the whole journey took at best 3½ hours. Some improvements were made during the summer of 1875, and from October 1879 the through portion became a slip coach, which was carried by the 15.30 ex-St Pancras express. Subsequently, one or two other expresses began to slip coaches at Wigston, but the practice was discontin-

Right:
The majesty of the Midland side of New Street station forms a backdrop to the departure of ex-LMS Class 5 4-6-0 No 45374 as it departs with the 09.30 SO to Yarmouth on 18 August 1962.
B. J. Ashworth

Left:
Ex-LMS 2P 4-4-0 No 40501 arrives with the 11.30 Gloucester-New Street local on 15 April 1958. Its plate is from the newly denominated 82E shed at Bristol.
Michael Mensing

ued entirely in May 1898, from when the south curve at Wigston was only used by Specials bound for the British Industries Fair and by regular excursions between St Pancras and Birmingham.

The Midland's main line North-and-West through service ran between Bradford and Bristol, and, being both reliable and efficient, was always well patronised. Until 1885 this by-passed Birmingham, in the way noted above, but from 1880 it was improved by a re-routing in the Birmingham area. Two new Bradford-Bristol expresses were introduced, departing at 07.50 and 11.15, which ran direct to Cheltenham from Saltley, via the main B&G line through Dunhampstead, rather than being routed through Worcester, as had been the practice up to that point. This made a useful improvement in running time, the leg between Derby and Bristol being accomplished in just 3¼hr. New stock for this route, and two new services, were introduced on 2 August 1897; the latter being 'Dining Expresses', which started from Bradford at 13.25 and Bristol at 14.05. The new carriages were built at Derby and were 60ft long, having composite underframes of steel and oak, supported on a pair of bogies with three pairs of wheels on each. first-class was panelled in Walnut, third in Mahogany, each being elaborately decorated. Dining carriages were provided for each class of travel, separated by a kitchen car, and could seat 15 first-class and 47 third-class passengers. The new service was sampled by a writer from the newly launched *Railway Magazine*, who was almost overcome in his admiration of the carriages and for the smoothness of the ride, noting that: 'one could have written a letter with pen and ink with the utmost ease and without a sputter, even when clashing over junctions and rounding curves'.

Below:
The 'Pines Express' had just over two weeks left to run into New Street when it was photographed between the sites of Lifford and Hazelwell stations on the Camp Hill line on 25 August 1962. It is headed by BR Standard Class 5 No 73021.
P. J. Shoesmith

As with their suburban trains, the acme of the Midland Railway's express services was achieved in the early years of this century. In the summer of 1903, the company offered the following number of daily each way express and long distance workings from Birmingham: to Derby, 20; Bristol, 13; Leicester, 10; Redditch line, four, and Malvern Wells line, three. The Derby, Bristol and Leicester services offered connections to the places noted above; but these were supplemented by a series of through carriages, which offered single (or multiple) opportunities for each way travel from Birmingham to the following destinations: Aberdeen, Bath (four) and Bournemouth (four), Blackpool, Brecon (two), Cromer (two), Edinburgh (three), Glasgow (two), Harrogate, Harwich, Kingswear, Lowestoft, Lynn (two), Manchester (five), Newcastle-upon-Tyne (three), Norwich, Scarborough (two), Southampton, via Cheltenham (three), Swansea (two), Torquay, Weston-super-Mare, Yarmouth (two) and York (five). New through carriage services were also added, as on 1 October 1910, when the Midland and LNWR offered the first such facility between Manchester and Bournemouth, via Birmingham and Bath, a service which later became a through train.

The one aspect of the Midland Railway's expresses in the Birmingham area which attracts possibly a disproportionate amount of interest is that of working the Lickey incline. This plumb straight, 2 miles 4 chains section of the former B&G main line has a uniform gradient of 1 in 37.7, and for well over 100 years, the activity and near mystique surrounding the working of banking engines over it proved a great draw for railway enthusiasts from all over the country. Most of the early B&G trains worked the incline unassisted, the company having found, through 'experimentation', that trains with loads of 74 tons or less did not require banking and could attain the summit at Blackwell with a residual velocity of 9 mph or thereabouts. But, as loadings increased, the practice of banking trains up the grade was introduced. By the 1900s, the average weight of expresses, less their locomotives, was around 210 tons, and sometimes as high as 240 tons; and with 23 passenger and 30 goods trains booked to ascend the incline daily; some idea of the activity generated by the need to assist these can be gained. Banking was compulsory for most of the trains which stopped at Bromsgrove, but from 2 February 1914, the Midland Railway also introduced this for trains not booked to stop there.

Above:
Blackwell station was at the summit of the Lickey incline and opened on 17 September 1840. It is seen here c1910, as Midland locomotive No 776 calls with a local service. Until 10 November 1941, all down trains had to stop and test their brakes here before descending the incline.
Don Powell Collection

Until 1919, banking duties were in the sole charge of various designs of 0-6-0 tank engines. These waited in sidings in the goods yard to the west of Bromsgrove station, and were 'attached' through buffer contact only, not by direct coupling. The number of banking engines required was decided by the class of the main locomotive and the weight of its train; the general rule being that ones in excess of six passenger coaches or six loaded mineral wagons must be assisted. Drivers signalled the number of banking engines they required through the use of a whistle code whilst approaching Stoke Works

Below:
Lickey bankers were not coupled to their trains, as is demonstrated by WR Pannier No 8409, which, its banking duty done, drops back as its lightly assisted train pulls away over the summit of the incline at Blackwell.
Brush Electrical Engineering Co

Above:
Big Bertha, the Lickey banker, stands, wrong line, in Bromsgrove station on 5 June 1950. She has just reversed down the incline after having worked one of many banking turns along it that day. This shot shows the station to good effect, also emphasising the extreme sharpness of the 1 in 37.7 gradient ahead. *H. C. Casserley*

Left:
What comes up . . . Class 31 No 31271 reaches the top of the Lickey incline at Blackwell with a Washwood Heath class 6 freight working on 17 September 1977; passing a warning board bearing sage advice to goods trains heading in the other direction.
Peter Durham

Junction Signal Box. They would give one short blast followed by a pause and then by either one, two or three short blasts, depending upon whether they needed one, two or three engines to assist them. This information would then be telegraphed to Bromsgrove and appropriate arrangements made. After assisting trains, the banking engines crossed over to the down line, returned to Bromsgrove without steam and crossed back to the up side at the far end of the goods yard, ready to make another trip. The descent of the incline also presented a hazard for most services, and until 10 November 1941 a compulsory brake testing stop was required at Blackwell for all down trains.

In 1919 the ranks of the 0-6-0 banking engines were swelled by the introduction of a purpose-built 0-10-0 banking locomotive. This was superheated and had four cylinders, being built at the Midland Railway works at Derby to designs of Sir Henry Fowler. Numbered 2290, she was christened *Big Emma* when first introduced, but quickly came to be known by the more descriptive tag *Big Bertha*, a name borrowed from the German rail-mounted super gun, which

Above:
Big Bertha freshly out-shopped in LMS livery in the early 1920s, showing its prominent headlight, a unique feature on a British locomotive.
Locomotive Publishing Co / Ian Allan Library

had been used to good effect during World War 1. Equivalent in clout to two tank engines, *Big Bertha* could assist most trains up the Lickey on her own. When new and shiny, a *Railway Magazine* writer noted that she made eight return trips in two hours; each passenger train requiring seven to eight minutes to ascend the incline, each goods train around 15min.

Banking up the Lickey incline became critical because it eventually became the only double track section on the main line for a number of miles; any breakdowns upon it therefore having potentially disastrous 'knock-on' effects on succeeding services. The last link in quadrupling lines either side of the Lickey was completed on 10 February 1933, when new tracks between Bromsgrove and Stoke Works Junction came into use, services being diverted over these whilst the old tracks were improved. In connection with this, various improvements were made to the track and signalling on the incline, in advance of it, to increase its traffic capacity. At Blackwell, the banking engine siding there was moved to in between the up and down lines, so that in the case of any difficulty on either of the latter, the bankers could be stowed out of the way of any main line workings. Changes to the signalling ended the practice of treating the entire incline as one signal block, splitting the up line into the equivalent of two block sections and adding an intermediate automatic signal. Now two trains could work up the incline at the same time, one in each section; regulations to govern the headway the leading one were introduced ensuring that if a slow train was being followed by an express, it would be given a greater headway than if the latter were following another express. These changes had a dramatic effect on the traffic capacity of the incline, increasing this by 40% and reducing delays by 57%.

New regulations were also introduced to govern which trains received banking assistance, and of those that did, how many they required. Trains allowed pass up the incline without assistance were passenger ones not exceeding 90 tons and having a brake van at the rear; and goods trains with either eight mineral, 12 goods or 16 empties behind. Above these limits, one to three banking engines would be required. On passenger trains of 195-270 tons, one Class 3 tank locomotive was required; those of 295-370 tons requiring two such locomo-

Right:
How it worked. Five Lickey bankers wait in a siding by Bromsgrove South signal box to join the quadruple main lines, narrowing to double in the distance, near the station. Duties this day are shared by four WR Panniers and BR Standard Class 9 2-10-0 No 92231, introduced in 1957.
Ivo Peters

Left:
Around 1950 *Big Bertha* was given a fresh paint job and looked very smart when photographed at work assisting a goods train.
P. Ransome-Wallis

Below left:
Bromsgrove early in 1933, just after the quadrupling from Stoke Works was completed on 10 February. The unique Midland Railway banking locomotive, nicknamed *Big Bertha*, and a pair of Jinties wait their turn on banking duty up the Lickey. The 0-10-0 is seeking anonymity by having had her 2290 number painted out, but the driver doesn't seem to mind; he's reading the paper!
Don Powell

Below:
After *Big Bertha*'s final departure on 6 May 1956, banking duties up the Lickey were shared by a variety of locomotives including the familiar 'Jinties' and others on loan, such as Pannier tank No 8402, on loan from Cardiff, seen near Blackwell on 3 September 1956.
John Williams

tives or *Big Bertha*; anything above this needing three tank engines or *Big Bertha* plus one tank engine. Goods trains of 20-31 wagons needed one bank engine; those of 32-43, two, and those of 44-59, three.

The introduction of diesel traction seemed likely to end the need for banking assistance on the Lickey incline. This was brought home forcibly on 2 June 1957, when an eight-car DMU set, working a return excursion from Weston-super-Mare, became the first to ascend the incline; doing this effortlessly in four minutes flat, with a minimum speed of 26 mph as it reached Blackwell. But concern over such matters did not trouble *Big Bertha*, as she was withdrawn on 6 May 1956. In the months beforehand replacements, in the form of ex-LNER Garrett No 69999 and BR Standard Class 9 No 92008, were tried out on the incline; but her immediate successor was BR Standard 2-10-0 No 92079. Thereafter, various classes of locomotives, including ex-GWR pannier tanks, were used on banking duties. The end of such work came in sight on 20 September 1961 following successful tests that day conducted on the Lickey incline with Type 4 diesel No D40 (later No 45133) and a load of 16 coaches, including a dynamometer car, to see if banking was required. Three tests were made: from standing start at south of Bromsgrove station, from standing start at Bromsgrove and from a flying start south of the station. Each assent took six to eight minutes and was accompanied by a banking locomotive, BR Standard 2-10-0 No 92234, which followed 30-50yd behind on each trip. On the following day these tests were successfully repeated using freight stock.

Elsewhere on the 'Midland' main lines, the occasion of the British Industries Fair at Castle Bromwich often gave rise to experimental services. In connection with the Fair which opened on 20 February 1933, the LMS introduced the first main line diesel-electric service in the country between Euston and Birmingham. This left Euston at 11.35, five minutes behind the 'Birmingham Flyer' and 15min in front of 'The Comet'. It was operated by the 'Armstrong-Shell Express', a single carriage vehicle having a 250bhp Armstrong-Whitworth diesel-electric motor, generating its own power from an oil-driven engine and capable of maintaining speeds of 65mph. This conveyed guests of the companies involved direct to the BIF, and on a test run on 14 February 1933, it completed the 113 mile journey in 2hr 7min. Innovations of a different kind were tried on the last BIF specials which ran between 6-17 May 1957. BR(LMR) offered passengers the services of a typist, Miss Rose Holligan, of Hove, who could speak six European languages. The specials, which were worked by diesel electric locomotive No 10203, left Euston at 08.55, returning from Castle Bromwich at 17.10.

Successive changes brought about by the Grouping and Nationalisation were reflected in modifications to the patterns of service along the lines described. Within the period under consideration, two of the lines were also closed. The line between Malvern Wells and Ashchurch was closed as far as Upton-on-Severn on 15 September 1952, the remainder being singled and worked from Ashchurch. Track on the closed section was lifted by 5 October 1956 and the service to Upton saw its last train on 12 August 1961. One year later, on 29 September 1962, the line between Redditch and Ashchurch saw its last passenger working, and from 1 October that year only a daily goods working on the Broom Junction to Evesham section remained.

Below:
The Lickey as a benchmark. Notorious nationwide as a challenge to motive power, climbing the incline with ne'er a falter was *de rigueur* for new designs of locomotive. This view is of a spotless *Lion*, a Class 47 prototype produced by a consortium which included the Birmingham Carriage & Wagon Co, AEI and Sulzer Bros., starting the climb on 23 May 1962 with 16 coaches forming a trailing load of 495 tons.
Sulzer Bros.

The Development of Goods Services and Facilities

Within seven years of its formation, the Midland Railway found itself with two redundant passenger stations occupying prime sites in the heart of Birmingham, both of which were adapted to serve the needs of its goods department. To these, in 1887, was added a third, purpose built goods station on land adjoining New Street station. Together, all three goods stations, plus their satellites, formed the basis of the Midland Railway's extensive goods operations in the Birmingham area.

Above:
Malvern Wells station on 25 September 1952, 10 days after passenger services from Ashchurch were withdrawn. The 13.14 Great Malvern to Ashchurch goods, worked by 0-4-4T locomotive No 58071, passes the closed station, whose nameboards await collection! The line was lifted as far back as Upton-on-Severn by 5 October 1956.
W. T. Baldwin

Right:
The curve, and poor state, of the roof over the Midland side of New Street station is revealed in this 8 July 1961 shot of Class 45 No D94 (later No 45114) departing Platform No 9 with the 12.52 for York.
Michael Mensing

On 17 August 1841 the B&G opened a connecting line between Camp Hill and Gloucester Junction, linking its main line with the L&B and enabling the company to transfer its passenger services to the latter's station at Curzon Street. Rather than disposing of their buildings at Camp Hill, they were retained to serve as the company's Birmingham Goods station. The need to make slight alterations to Camp Hill station delayed the commencement of the carrying of goods traffic on the B&G until October 1841, although the company had conveyed small consignments; packages known as 'van goods', since its opening the previous year. Over the years a number of improvements were made to the facilities at Camp Hill, although its somewhat land-locked site prevented any major expansions and destined the station to always be in the shadow of its sister facilities at Lawley Street and Central. Plans were deposited for new mess rooms and offices on 21 February 1882, followed by ones for platform extensions and a cattle landing dock on 24 June 1883. Additional goods sheds were proposed in plans dated 18 February and 20 October 1898 and 26 January 1899; these being equipped with electric lifts under plans deposited on 9 January 1926 and 29 October and 18 November 1927.

Under depot reorganisations introduced by the LMS, Camp Hill came to specialise in the handling of fruit (imported and home grown), vegetable, timber, coal, tinplate, grain, flour and cattle and livestock. Its total forwarded and received tonnages for 1936 were: Goods & Minerals, 78,658, and Coal & Coke, 116, 241, a total of 194,859 tons; although the station's importance, in comparison to other installations in Birmingham, is shown by figures for the number of cartage units available there on 8 June 1937: just 17 horses and no motorised vehicles; compared with Lawley Street's 257 horses and 57 motor vehicles.

The Midland Railway's second goods station in Birmingham was converted from the former B&DJ passenger station at Lawley Street. This closed to passengers on 1 May 1851 with the transfer of services to Curzon Street over a new spur line between Landor Street and Derby Junctions. From that date the vacated passenger facilities were utilised for all classes of goods, minerals and coal traffic. An extensive reconstruction programme began in 1891, followed by remodelling of the yard and the installation of electric lighting in 1892. These upgraded facilities came into use in 1893; the site then covering over 50 acres, which could additionally handle livestock, and included a 2½ acre ground plan two-storey warehouse and a new goods shed which handled an average of 11 million packages per annum, anything, as the Midland put it, 'from a pin to a piano'.

Many improvements were made to the facilities at Lawley Street, which was the Midland's main goods depot in the city, and were continued under the LMS. The addition of an extra 42 wagon berths, and better facilities for the loading of cartage vehicles, completed in 1935 were amongst the last improvements made there before a disastrous fire on 26 May 1937 which did extensive damage to the station's facilities; totally destroying the two-storey warehouse of 1892. After this fire, although some goods traffic was diverted to other stations and depots in the city, Lawley Street remained open; staff sorting and loading goods in the open. To add to their difficulties, the facilities at the station were further diminished when its main office block, on the corner of Lawley and Viaduct streets, was destroyed in an air raid in November 1940.

Consequent upon the fire of 1937, the LMS planned to replace completely the facilities at Lawley Street. A four stage programme was developed which comprised: a new office block fronting to Lawley Street, with a canteen, drying room and subway to a new goods shed; a single-storey main goods shed; a separate four-storey general warehouse to provide 26,625 square yards of floor space, and a separate single-storey warehouse with a floor space of 3,000 square yards, mainly for the storage of non-ferrous metals. This required the demolition of the original B&DJ buildings on the site, which were eventually removed during 1942. With the outbreak of war it was decided to concentrate efforts on completing the main

Right:
A diagram of the New Goods Shed at Lawley Street, Birmingham, in October 1945. A disastrous fire on 26 May 1937 occasioned this rebuilding, which was delayed by the war and not fully completed until the LMS had become BR(LMR). When opened by the Lord Mayor of Birmingham on 29 October 1945, the new Lawley Street shed was equipped with the most up-to-date goods handling equipment.
British Rail

Left:
Rather cheekily, the Midland and LNWR companies had a joint Parcels & Goods Receiving Office at Snow Hill in Birmingham, right by the GWR's station there. This is how it appeared in 1891, promoting Winter sports in Switzerland!
British Rail

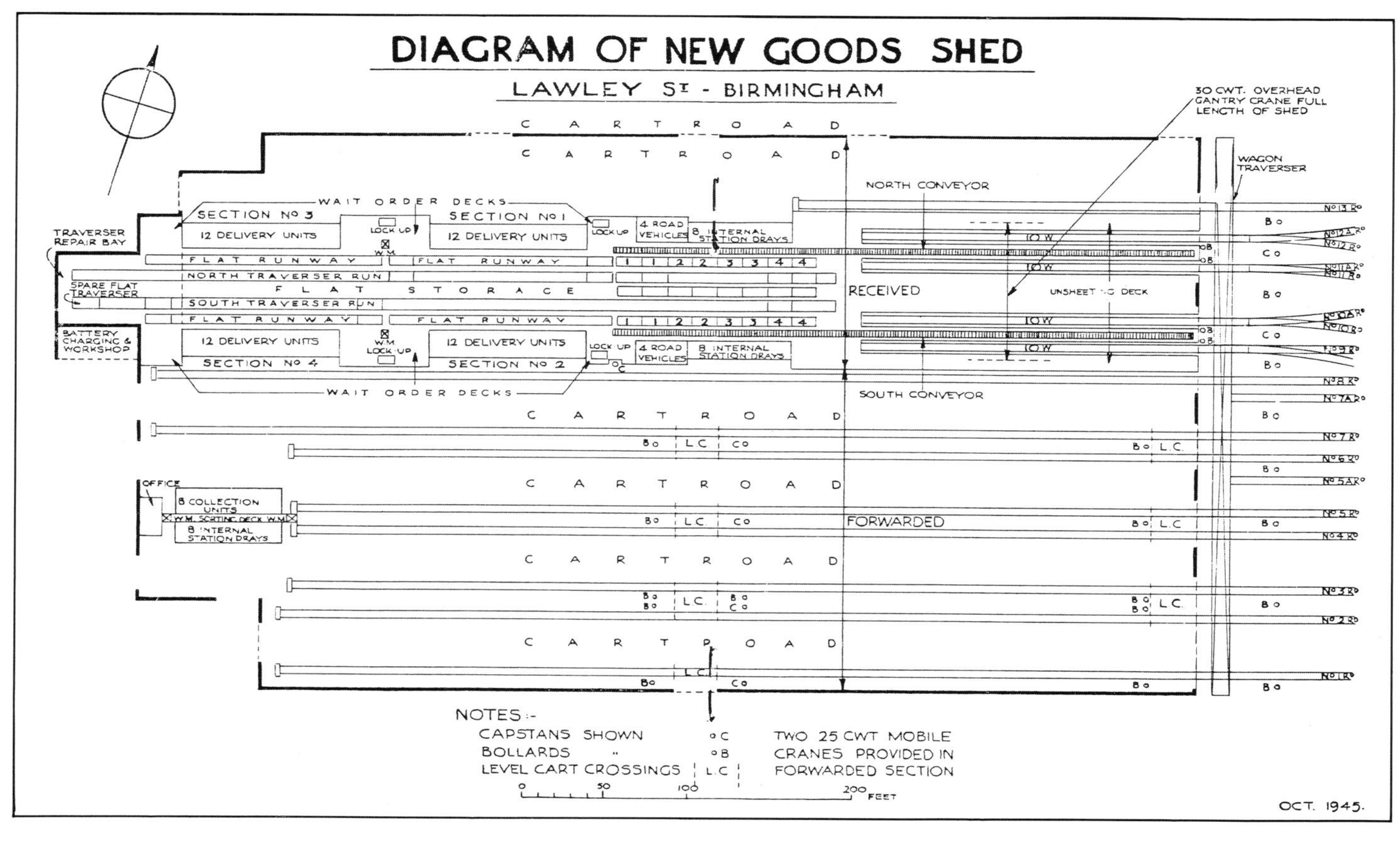

goods shed first, a need made all the more urgent by extensive damage sustained by the Central Goods station during an air raid in 1940. Therefore, as the shed neared completion, in the early part of 1944, it was brought increasingly into use. Work on the rest of the facilities was deferred until after the war, their roles being assumed by temporary pre-cast concrete buildings which served as the station offices and canteen; the majority of the clerical staff remaining in accommodation elsewhere in the city.

The new goods shed at Lawley Street (see diagram) was officially opened by the Lord Mayor of Birmingham on 29 October 1945. It was 650ft long and 350ft wide, covering an area of 5¼ acres. It was equipped with all of the latest mechanical aids, the forwarded section comprising eight roads with a capacity of 203 wagons; the received section having four roads with a capacity of 40 wagons, spanned by an overhead travelling crane; the latter also being fitted with conveyors onto which items were to be place 'label uppermost'.

Below:
The main yard at Camp Hill Goods station, photographed after closure on 7 February 1966. Following the diversion of the B&G's services into Curzon Street, goods traffic was first handled here in October 1841.
Don Powell Collection

Work to complete the rest of the facilities at Lawley Street strayed into BR(LMR) days, being opened fully in the early 1950s. Now its total capacity was 2,470 wagons, of which 320 could be accommodated under cover in sheds and warehouses; 680 could be held in the open yard; 880 in arrival, departure and storage sidings, and 590 in marshalling sidings.

As well as making extensive use of their own metals, which were augmented by the addition of dedicated goods only lines, the Midland Railway's goods services also benefited from the exercising of running powers over other companies lines in the Birmingham area. For instance, from 1 September 1865 they began to use the LNWR's line between Nuneaton and Coventry, and exactly two years later commenced to run over that company's lines between Wichnor Junction and Dudley, and also to and from Wolverhampton, via Bescot. Easier goods workings were also facilitated by the opening of a new down goods loop at Saltley on 31 October 1875 and by the bringing into use of up and down goods lines between Lawley Street and Saltley on 19 November 1876.

Several improvements were made to the Midland Railway's goods facilities in the Birmingham area during the latter half of the 1870s. A new goods station was planned at Walsall; authorised by an Act of 28 June 1877, this came into use on 1 July 1879. Additional siding capacity was added at Washwood Heath, in between Saltley and Bromford Bridge stations on the main line to Derby, these opened on 1 October 1877, and were gradually improved over the next 60 years or so. An additional fan of sidings on down side was brought into use there on 15 November 1891, and new up sidings were opened on 7 January 1918. Down gravitation sidings were brought into use on 5 August 1923 and additional up ones on 24 May 1930. Later that year, an up reception line, No 3, was brought into use, and on 17 February 1935 additional down side sidings came into use. Finally in this period, a set of 'Exchange Sidings', for the transfer of goods traffic between the Midland and LNWR companies, came into use during July 1878. Located in between those companies' lines as they approached New Street station, paralleling Landor and Garrison streets, the first traffic was exchanged there on 2 September 1878. These were used extensively, most traffic being from the south or southwest for the north or vice versa. In their final form, after 1897, the sidings could hold 200 wagons.

Despite all of the improvements made to both Camp Hill and Lawley Street stations, they both suffered from not being originally designed for the handling of goods, and from being limited in the extend to which they could be extended due to their land-locked sites. The company's decision to extend its BWS line into New Street station left the spur to the line's original terminus at Granville Street as surplus to requirements. But under powers granted in the Midland Railway (Additional Powers) Act of 12 July 1882, the company planned to extend this spur to an area of the Birmingham town centre described in this Act as: 'lands, houses and buildings situate between Suffolk Street, Severn Street, Wharf Street and the Worcester Wharf'. On this the company built a new goods station, which took the name of the aforementioned canal basin. The new Worcester Wharf Goods station opened on 1 July 1887, and within a few years was extended, a new goods warehouse being added in 1890, two-storey stables in 1891. On 6 December that year the Midland Railway opened a doubled line between Worcester Wharf and Church Road Junction and on 1 June 1892 they renamed the station as Birmingham Central Goods Depot. Additional stabling was added in 1894 and on 1 April 1897 the company's goods trains began to work to there from Saltley, through New Street station.

Under the LMS reorganisation, Central Goods came to specialise in the handling of metal, grain and flour, general goods, timber, reels of paper, iron and steel, Drikold goods, also having a bonded store which specialised in the handling of wet bonded stores items. It was worked jointly with the goods facilities at Monument Lane and in 1936 handled 164,280 tons of forwarded and received items. During an air raid in 1940, both the goods shed and warehouse there were virtually destroyed, being only partially and temporarily restored by 1945.

Finally in the period under review, on 15 September 1958 BR(LMR) began work on a new road motor engineers workshop for the overhauling of the large fleet of vehicles it operated in and around Birmingham. By the late 1950s, the region's Birmingham cartage fleet comprised 579 motor vehicles and 1,170 trailers, and the new shops were to be in Garrison Street, on the site of some old Midland Railway stables, which were demolished for the scheme.

Below:
Birmingham Central Goods opened as Worcester Wharf on 1 July 1887, being renamed the former on 1 June 1892. Here, members of the SLS crawl all over it as part of a rail tour on 30 May 1959. Following closure, the site was redeveloped and the Headquarters of BR's Midland Region, Stanier House, built upon the site in 1973/74.
R. S. Carpenter Collection

4: The Great Western Lines to 1962

Never exactly modest, the Great Western Railway's (GWR) 'humble' beginnings lay in the building of a line to connect Bristol with London, but contemporaneous events were to determine that this was to be just the first of a whole network of lines owned and controlled by that company. To the north, the success of the country's first main trunk railways: the GJ and L&B, which facilitated travel from London to Liverpool and Manchester only three months after the first section of the GWR opened, ensured that it was not long before proposals were made to continue the GWR northwards. Although these schemes were projected as more or less independent railways, the GWR took an active interest in their progress, acquiring most of them before they were completed.

The company was also the chief proponent of their own Engineer's broad gauge, the use of which gave them exclusive access to certain regions; the spread of which was bitterly opposed by those railway companies operating on the standard or 'narrow' gauge. Conflict was inevitable, and was resolved by the establishment of a Royal Commission directed, during the 1846 Parliamentary session, to consider the benefit to the nation of the adoption of a uniform railway gauge. Coincidentally, also before Parliament that session were no fewer than 11 bills for railways in the Birmingham area; five of which were for lines in which the GWR either had, or would come to have, a controlling interest.

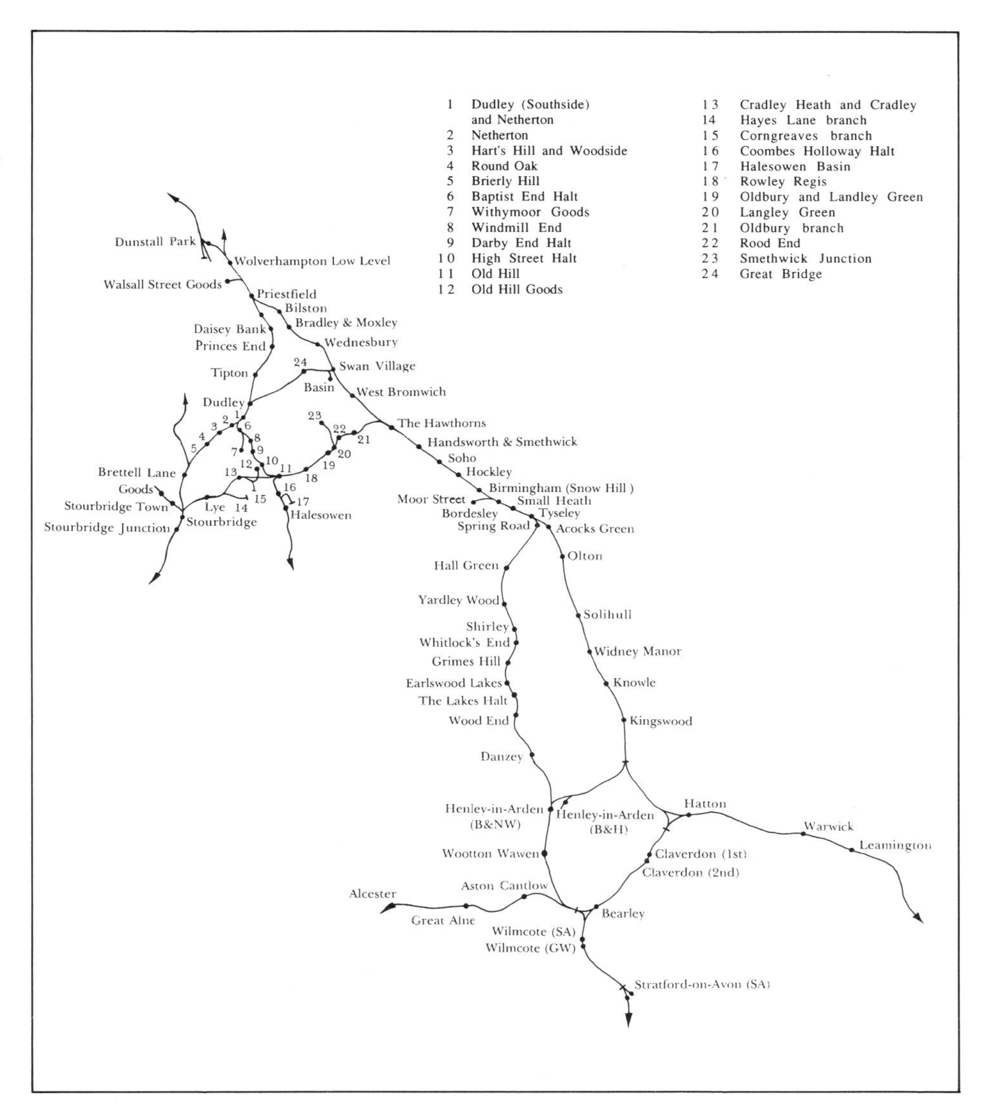

Limiting the spread of the Broad Gauge

On 9 July 1845 the Gauge Commission was established. It was in session for just 30 days, between 6 August and 18 December that year, during which time expert testimony was heard and experiments were conducted. Its 'verdict' was published in a report on 17 February 1846. This recommended that: 'the gauge of 4 feet 8½ inches be declared to be the gauge to be used in all public Railways now under construction or hereafter to be constructed in Great Britain'. Later that year this finding became embodied in the Regulation of Gauges Act, which, whilst passing through Parliament, was influenced by powerful lobbying and by the sheer extent of lines (biased roughly five to one) either open or authorised using the standard gauge.

The Regulation of Gauges Act received the Royal Assent on 18 August 1846. It prohibited the future construction of any passenger railway in Great Britain at any gauge other than stan-

Left:
'Birmingham', a small vignette in the GWR's *Through the Window – Paddington to Birkenhead* book.
Author's Collection

dard gauge. Exempted from this ruling was any future railway act containing a special enactment defining its line's gauge or gauges; in other words, anyone promoting a non-standard gauge railway could build it, if they could prove the need to use the gauge they specified. Nonetheless, history shows that the only broad gauge lines sanctioned by Parliament *after* 1846 were short branches or extensions to lines it had authorised *before* then.

All 11 of the local railway bills before Parliament in 1846 received the Royal Assent on 3 August 1846. These included the bills of the Shrewsbury & Birmingham, Shropshire Union, Birmingham, Wolverhampton & Dudley companies, plus two for the Birmingham & Oxford Railway. These would, in conjunction with three lines authorised by Parliament within the previous three years, bring both the GWR and its broad gauge to Birmingham. The fluke of coincidence whereby these acts were before Parliament at the same time as the Regulation of Gauges Act, would further serve to make the Birmingham area the most northerly limit ever reached by the broad gauge in Britain.

The Oxford Railway

Shown on a map in the original GWR prospectus of 1833 is a branch to Oxford, but efforts to build this were frustrated until the successful promotion of the Oxford Railway Company in 1842. By a Act of 11 April 1843, this company was authorised to build a 10 mile branch from the GWR main line at Didcot to Oxford. This opened on 12 June 1844, just 33 days after it had been amalgamated with the GWR. Seemingly isolated, this line was already common to the proposals of two railway schemes through which the GWR would eventually reach Birmingham.

The Oxford, Worcester & Wolverhampton Railway

A continuation of their proposed Oxford branch to Worcester, to link up with a line then being promoted between there and Wolverhampton, was considered by the GWR's Directors in August 1836. The latter scheme, the Grand Connection Railway, was not built, but eight years later the preliminary work done for it, particularly surveys of expected goods traffic, were to prove invaluable to another railway incorporating both of these earlier proposals.

In August 1844 the Oxford, Worcester & Wolverhampton Railway (OWW), was promoted by local businessmen from the towns along its proposed route, which ran from a junction with the Oxford & Rugby Railway (O&R), a few miles north of Banbury, via Evesham, Pershore, Worcester, Droitwich, Kidderminster, Stourbridge and Dudley, to a branch off the GJ near its station at Wolverhampton. The O&R's proposals had been adopted by the GWR in the spring of 1844. A broad gauge line, its connection at Rugby, where there was a junction between the L&B and Midland Counties lines, would afford access to both the northwest, via the GJR, and to Derbyshire and Yorkshire. The OWW's prospectus also noted that the GWR had agreed to guarantee an annual payment of 3½% on the total estimated capital for the line; something confirmed in a formal agreement between the two companies, signed on 20 September 1844, which also moved the junction with the O&R line much nearer Oxford.

All seemed well; the GWR's guarantee, plus a well produced prospectus, should have given the OWW Bill an easy passage through Parliament. But the Royal Assent it gained on 4 August 1845 was hard won. There were two main areas of difficulty. Firstly, among the powers contained in the Bill were those to lease or sell the OWW to the GWR, who were also empowered to complete the line if the former could not, or if they were called upon so to do by the Board of Trade; thus inheriting the OWW's powers over the line. Secondly, it was to be broad gauge throughout; a point which attracted thunderbolts of opposition to the Bill, much of which came from the L&B and Midland companies. The uproar which followed helped to precipitate the Gauge Commission referred to above. It also proved to be an accurate forecast of the line's fortunes during its first 10 years.

Evidence taken before a House of Commons Select Committee on the OWW and other local railway bills also provides confirmation of the fact that the main purpose behind building these lines was for the revenue to be obtained from the goods traffic they would generate. Consider this example. Richard Smith, the Earl of Dudley's Mining Agent, questioned on the Earl's mining interests in South Staffordshire: 'Lord Ward has 22 blast furnaces, 1 foundry and another Ironworks and requires about 1,4000,000 tons of coal and ironstone per year. There are 145 blast furnaces in full blast in the area, producing 468,000 tons of pig iron; these

require 4,212,000 tons per annum of raw materials. This makes a grand total of 5,062,000 tons of materials on the move, including coal, each year'. All of this was without the benefit of the railways!

The OWW appointed I. K. Brunel as their engineer. Their bill came with strings attached, and almost immediately upon its passing Brunel had to revise his original estimate of the line's cost from £1½ million to £2½ million to take account of extra works these required. The company was already undersubscribed, and so the GWR agreed to increase its guarantee to 4% p.a. on the revised capital estimate of £2½ million; beginning a 10 year period of intense ill-feeling between their Board and the OWW's; a lot of which does not concern railways, or Birmingham, and takes McDermot 37 pages to detail. It is familiar stuff in the period of the railway mania: the OWW's autocratic Chairmen and Directors; their imprudent financial dealings; deception of the shareholders, and attempts to lease the line to other companies. Its interest to us today is not in what dirty deeds were done, but in what was not done; ie. advancing the OWW's rails towards the West Midlands.

Not surprisingly, the OWW became known as the 'Old Worse & Worse'; quite an accurate comment on how things were going. On 1 June 1849 the company's Directors reported that practically all the money was spent, without a mile of workable line to show for it. Independent verification of this comes in a report from one of the Railway Commission's regular inspections of the route. This document, dated 27 November 1849, ends as follows: 'at each end of the the line a great deal of work remains to be done, but from Evesham by Worcester and Stourbridge to near Dudley the works are very far advanced and nearly ready for opening, with the exception of stations and the permanent way not being laid.' Such reports were part of an attempt by the Board of Trade to persuade the GWR to comply with the terms of the OWW Act, to intervene and complete the line. The company declined; were ordered to; refused; and were taken to court, the lengthy proceedings that ensued being dropped on 28 April 1851 when it emerged that the OWW were finally completing the work themselves.

The OWW opened to passenger services in nine stages: Abbotswood Junction (with Midland Railway) to Worcester (5 October 1850); Worcester-Droitwich and branch to Stoke Prior (18 February 1852); Worcester-Evesham (1 May 1852); Droitwich-Stourbridge (3 May 1852); Stourbridge-Dudley (20 December 1852); Evesham-Oxford (4 June 1853); Dudley-Tipton, plus a standard gauge connection with the LNWR's Stour Valley line at Tipton: the 'Tipton Curve' (1 December 1853); and both Tipton-Priestfield, to a junction with the GWR, and Cannock

Below:
Dudley was a joint station between the GW (OWW) and LNW (SS) railways. The latter, to Walsall, can be seen branching off right just above where the column of steam from No 6970 ends. On 27 July 1963, 11 months before closure, the latter is working ECS to Stourbridge and the DMU is working to Snow Hill.
Leslie Sandler

Road Junction-Bushbury (1 July 1854). All but the final section had at least one broad gauge rail laid upon it, although the only recorded use made of this was the running of an inspection train between Oxford and Evesham on 2 June 1853.

The locomotive contractor C. C. Williams, of London, was engaged in April 1852 to work the 36 miles of the OWW to be opened by 1 May that year. He appointed David Joy, of valve gear fame, as his Locomotive Superintendent. Joy was sent off to scour the country for suitable locomotives; he found four: 'Went to Welwyn – Great Northern Railway – and got *Mudlark*, a contractor's engine, to Offord – got a big six-coupled long boiler . . . . Then to Shrewsbury to hire Shrewsbury & Hereford engines; had to see Jeffrey before breakfast, but he could spare none. On to Leeds and Pontefract after a four-coupled *Jenny*, a contractor's engine, just put in fine order at Railway Foundry . . . . Then to Leeds to see a little engine in the shops at Railway Foundry – called *Canary*; she was a little mite. Arranged for all of these to go to Worcester.' The OWW took delivery of the first of its own locomotives in November 1852, and by August 1855 had built up quite an impressive rolling stock. C. C. Williams' contract ran until 1 February 1856; Joy being retained as Locomotive Superintendent for a few months after this date.

David Joy left just as the OWW's fortunes finally took a turn for the better. In June 1856 a new Board was appointed, the quarrelsome element retiring and the all important job of General Manager being given to A. C. Sherriff, late of the North Eastern Railway. Sherriff so took to Worcester that he stayed there, becoming a Town Councillor and its MP. His management made a vital difference. Operating losses declined, and by February 1858 the OWW was talking to the GWR again. Lessons had been learned on both sides and on 1 March 1858 a new accord came into force, confirming an OWW/GWR traffic agreement under which the latter agreed to remove the broad gauge rails south of Priestfield, near Wolverhampton.

The West Midland Railway

After several attempts, a scheme to build a railway between Worcester and Hereford the Worcester & Hereford Railway was incorporated on 15 August 1853, but this seemed in danger of having its powers lapse for want of the capital to proceed with building the line. Late in the day, the W&H Board were approached by the Newport, Abergavenny & Hereford Railway (NA&H) who saw the line as forming a valuable link between their line and the OWW. They took the scheme up and, by means of an Act of August 1858, established funding for the line, jointly with the OWW and Midland companies. This enforced co-operation bore other fruit, and by the time the first section of the W&H opened, in July 1859, the OWW and NA&H Boards saw the sense in amalgamating all three lines into one company. An Act to this effect was passed on 14 June 1860, the new West Midland Railway (WM) coming into being from 1 July that year.

Mindful of the OWW's old nickname, wags soon christened the WM the 'Werry Middlin', witty, but ill deserved. A. C. Sherriff was retained as General Manager, and actively promoted six continuation lines: The Severn Valley Railway; The Witney Railway; The Bourton-on-the-Water Railway; The Much Wenlock & Severn Junction Railway; The Tenbury & Bewdley Railway, and the Stourbridge Railway. The abortive promotion of a seventh line, at the start of 1861, engendered discussions with the GWR, which resulted in two agreements: one, on 4 May 1861, for the latter to lease the OWW section of the WM; another, on 30 May 1861, for the two companies to amalgamate. The leasing arrangement began on 1 June 1861, managed by a joint committee; the amalgamation being sanctioned by an Act of 13 July 1863, becoming effective from 1 August; the new company having 18 GWR Directors and six WM ones, adding a further 281 miles of narrow gauge and two miles of mixed gauge to the former's growing West Midlands network.

The Birmingham & Oxford Junction Railway

On a map, the GWR's other approach to the Birmingham area may seem even more roundabout than that via the OWW; being made up, as it was, of three separate schemes; but this was not so. Taking the Oxford Railway as a common root, the Oxford & Rugby Railway (O&R), already mentioned, was promoted at a Public Meeting in Oxford on 14 May 1844. This was attended by several GWR luminaries, including Brunel. At this stage the route does not appear to have been finalised, as, under questioning, Brunel was of the opinion that it should run to Birmingham; but the 'Rugby' camp won the day. An Act was obtained on 4 August 1845, work commencing soon afterwards. The O&R amalgamated with the GWR on 14 May 1846; the Rugby line being finally abandoned in 1849 in an attempt to reduce general opposition to other bills in which the company had an interest. The broad gauge O&R line opened to Banbury on 2 September 1850, and to Fenny Compton on 1 October 1852.

Next to advance the GWR towards Birmingham by this route was a scheme born of the rivalry between the L&B and GJ railways. In 1845, the latter promoted a line from their Birmingham terminus, via Warwick and Leamington, to join the GWR at Oxford. This offered the prospect of a line to London, independent of the L&B. The Birmingham & Oxford Junction Railway (B&O), as the scheme became known, met fierce opposition in Parliament and was thrown out. Not put off, a meeting of the intended shareholders was held in Birmingham on 13 May 1845, where it was resolved to resubmit a Bill to Parliament, together with another one, the B&O Birmingham Extension Act, to continue the line to a new station site in Birmingham, to be built in the plot of land described by Monmouth Street and Great Charles Street, and Livery Street and Snow Hill.

Also at this meeting, the advisability of extending the line on through to Dudley was discussed; leading to the establishment of a third scheme, to take the line on to Wolverhampton. Called the Birmingham, Wolverhampton & Dudley Railway (BW&D), this was nominally independent, but was essentially the work of the same promoters as the B&O Railway. All three schemes presented Bills before Parliament in 1846, gaining the Royal Assent on that famous day: 3 August 1846. To avoid trouble, each had omitted to specify the gauge to which they would be built, and so by the Gauge Act, passed just 15 days later, they were, by default, to be narrow gauge lines.

On 30 October 1846, the B&O and BW&D companies held their first shareholders' meetings. Here, resolutions were passed, under mutual powers contained in each other's Acts, for the companies to amalgamate and to sell or lease the resultant company to the GWR. The GWR agreed to buy the companies on 12 November 1846, all three Boards meeting to confirm this arrangement on 4 December. Routinely passed by the GWR and BW&D boards; at the B&O meeting it met opposition in the form of a rival offer from the LNWR. This only extended to the B&O line and was to buy it at a much higher price than the GWR were offering. More 'dirty deeds' were done in trying to close this deal, the GWR having to resort to legal action to compel the B&O's compliance with its prior agreement. Matters were resolved in the High Court, whose ruling, on 4 December 1847, the end of a wasted year, was that the BW&D and B&O companies could not be amalgamated and vested in the GWR before the passing of a separate Act to that effect. This was duly done, and it gained the Royal Assent on 31 August 1848. The same Act also allowed the GWR to lay mixed gauge track on the B&O and BW&D lines, a concession which had been hard won during the previous 14 months.

Despite the Regulation of the Gauges Act, which had for all intents and purposes resolved the matter, the GWR continued to lobby for a broad gauge line to Birmingham. Eventually, in June 1847, a House of Lords Select Committee ordered the Railway Commissioners to inquire into the existing railway communication between London and Birmingham and to report back next Session on how the public interest might best be secured and whether it was expedient that the broad gauge should be extended to Birmingham. Written evidence was taken and an inconclusive report produced in May 1848. This recommended that the laying of mixed gauge rails on the B&O 'will prove advantageous to the public interests', but cast serious doubts upon the practicality of achieving this. They had been swayed in their dithering by the proponents of rival means of uniting the gauges. The GWR favoured the use of a three rail mixed gauge track, having a common outer rail to users of both gauges. Opposing this was the LNWR's idea of four rails, essentially separate railways laid on the same trackbed, with horrendously complicated trackwork at points and junctions.

Technical reports favoured the GWR's mixed gauge system, and on 6 June 1848 the House of Lords Select Committee reported to the Commons that they concurred with the Railway Commissioners with regard to the expediency of extending the broad gauge to Birmingham: 'inasmuch as it is only by the use of the mixed gauge that the disadvantages of the route by Oxford can be effectively removed'. Whilst all of this had been going on, as noted above, Parliament had been debating a Bill by the GWR, under which the company was seeking powers to vest the B&O, B&O (Birmingham Extension) and BW&D lines, and to deviate the first of these as it passed through Leamington. Following the 6 June ruling, the LNWR went ominously quiet; until the GWR Bill went back to the Lords for its final reading.

At its Committee stage, they withdrew their opposition to the laying of broad gauge rails in return for 'a few reasonable clauses' to be inserted in the Bill. One related to running powers over the lines' narrow gauge rails, plus those of the O&R line between Fenny Compton and Banbury – reasonable enough. Another related to the terms of the original B&O Act. This had been for a line from the Birmingham terminus of the GJ Railway. These should be complied with said the LNWR, prevailing upon the Lords to insert a clause into the GWR Bill stating that it would be unlawful for the GWR to use the authorised broad gauge rails until they had: 'completed and opened a communication between the line of the said Birmingham & Oxford Junction Railway and the line of the London & North Western Railway in the town of Birmingham, or within one mile on the south side thereof, by means of a double line of narrow gauge rails'. This also sounds reasonable enough, until one stops to consider the changes that had taken place in the intervening period.

Firstly, the GJ was no more, its lines now being part of the LNWR. Secondly, although the LNWR was still using the GJ/L&B terminus at Curzon Street, it was in the course of constructing a new central station, in connection with its Stour Valley line, in Navigation Street; right in the way of the link the GWR were now required to build. But the LNWR still insisted that the connection was to be built to Curzon Street. So the GWR incurred the additional expense of constructing a link, 50 chains in length, completely elevated on a viaduct, from the main line of the B&O, near the present Bordesley station. Work progressed into 1852, until the viaduct reached the LNWR's approach to Navigation Street station. The latter objected to the GWR taking any possession of their property and a new row began. Finally, in February 1853, the viaduct was as complete as it could be without straying on to LNWR land, and then, suddenly, the latter backed down, saying that the GWR needn't bother to build the link after all!

Several portions of this viaduct still stand in the Duddeston part of Birmingham. They are a 'folly' *to* the folly of the disgraceful shenanigans which characterised the period known as the Railway Mania, much of which was played out on the 'Birmingham stage'.

The B&O Railway was finally completed; the line between Moor Street and Monmouth Street, to the site of the Birmingham station, being first used on 6 June 1852. It opened to passengers on 1 October 1852, the same day as the Banbury-Fenny Compton section of the O&R. The opening had been attended, the previous day, by a token, and ultimately ill-fated, ceremony. On 30 September, a Director's train was run from Paddington to Birmingham on the broad gauge. This left at 09.00, hauled by *Lord of the Isles*, then less than three months out of Swindon. Time was lost all along the way and by Aynho it was 30min late. There, a mixed goods service was uncoupling a couple of wagons, its crew unaware of the approaching special. Upon hearing it, the driver attempted to pull away, snapping a coupling and leaving all of his carriages and wagons behind. There was a smash, but not quite in the way intended. Fortunately, no-one was hurt, but pride was badly bruised, and the Directors' party limped sheepishly to Leamington for a late lunch.

Initial express passenger services were timed at 2¾hrs for the full journey. Between Banbury and Birmingham there were intermediate stations at Leamington (Leamington Spa from 26 July 1913), Warwick, Hatton, Kingswood (opened in October 1854; renamed Lapworth from 1 May 1902), Knowle (Knowle & Dorridge from 1 July 1899), Widney Manor (opened on 1 July 1899), Solihull, Olton (opened in January 1869), Acock's Green (Acock's Green & South Yardley from October 1878) Small Heath & Sparkbrook (opened in April 1863; renamed Smallheath & Sparkbrook in April 1864) and Bordesley (opened in June 1855). Services ran into a temporary station at Birmingham, situated on the site described earlier. Far from the grand building, which many remember with great affection, this was very basic; McDermot describing it as: 'a large wooden shed run up in a hurry for the opening'. Limited goods services began over the line to Birmingham in February 1853.

Birmingham Snow Hill station

The GWR's first 'Birmingham Station', as it was designated, opened on 1 October 1852 when the Birmingham & Oxford line opened to passengers between the town and Banbury. In common with other such openings in Birmingham and elsewhere, the station was a temporary affair. It was built on the site of a very large number of old buildings, which had stood in the parcel of land described by Monmouth, Livery and Great Charles streets and Snow Hill. Preparation of the site had begun in January 1852, but descriptions of the station are scant and few. It comprised an overall wooden shed containing or adjoining 'a series of temporary structures – mere sheds – which were improvised with more or less regard to the necessities of a long-suffering public which travelled on the railway'. Fine for an opening, but this temporary station was to serve Birmingham for the next 19 years, from February 1858 becoming the first of three stations on the site to carry the designation Birmingham (Snow Hill).

Palling in comparison with the splendour of New Street, as the 1860s progressed, local people began to agitate for something better: 'The monster wooden shed which has done duty a the Snow Hill station for many years is as great a disgrace to the town as ever the old tumbledown structures could have been that were removed to make way for it', wrote one disgruntled citizen. The sight of the station was at least partly obscured by the building of the Great Western Hotel in front of it in 1867, but it was another two years before the GWR got round to doing anything about providing Birmingham with anything better. Eventually, the principal passenger shed was dismantled and relocated to Didcot, where it served as a very dilapidated carriage shed for a number of years No one was sad to see it go, except the proprietor of a hat shop opposite the station, who for many years had done a good business in sup-

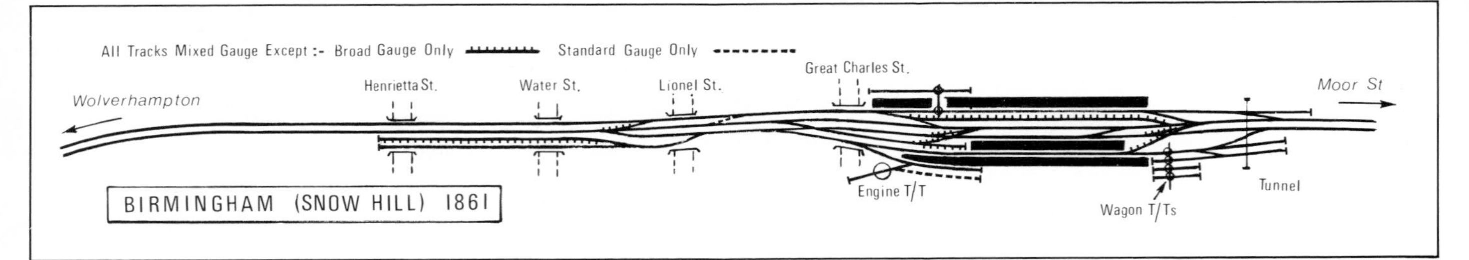

plying hats and umbrellas to the many passengers who tired of being soaked through the old shed's many leaks when it rained.

The Great Western Hotel

Despite its name, the Great Western Hotel was not built by the railway, but by a private company. They acquired the site in front of the 'monster wooden shed' in 1866 and commenced the erection of the hotel the following year. It opened in January 1868 but soon proved inadequate and was therefore enlarged in 1870 to the designs of the eminent Birmingham architect Julius Chatwin (1830-1907). For a time Chatwin had worked for Branson & Gwyther, the builders of New Street station, and he went on to design many churches and commercial buildings in Birmingham; Colmore Row, in particular, bearing his stamp to this day. A master of many idioms, Chatwin chose a French style for his reworking of the four-storey hotel, adding classical detailing to the taller corner blocks. In this, its final form as a hotel, the building now had 126 rooms.

The Great Western Hotel's life as such was quite brief. By the 1900s the GWR were desperately short of office accommodation at Snow Hill and so they approached the proprietors of the hotel with a view to purchasing it. Whether the hotel was doing poor business, or the GWR's offer was either generous (unlikely), or just timely, is not known; but the result is, the hotel proprietors said yes. It closed sometime in 1906 and the GWR set to fitting it out to their requirements. One facility lacking at the the station was a decent restaurant, and so the company converted the ground floor of the former hotel to this purpose. This opened early in 1909 and was known as the 'Birmingham (Snow Hill) Station Restaurant', its name being about the only thing on which expense and imagination had not been spared. It was described as follows to the readers of the *GWR Magazine*: 'Constructed on the most modern and sanitary principles, and equipped with every comfort and convenience, the grill, tea, refreshment, and private dining rooms are capable of seating upwards of 200. Ladies' waiting and cloak rooms are provided; while, as a fitting sequence to the dining-rooms, from a masculine point of view, attention may be directed to the large and comfortable lounge and smoking room. The kitchens are fitted up in such a manner as to enable the food to be prepared under the best hygienic conditions. The whole of the viands provided are of the finest quality, and a carefully selected menu is given daily, both table d'hôte and a la carte. The private dining-room can be reserved for parties of ten and upwards . . . . The grill, tea and

Right:
Following its closure in 1906, the Great Western Hotel was refurbished, the majority of the building going for office accommodation, but the wing on the corner of Snow Hill itself was converted into a very swish restaurant, which opened early in 1909, as this advertisement of the period shows.
Author's Collection

refreshment rooms are open from 08.00 to 23.00 daily. With a view of making these rooms more attractive to ladies, a speciality is made of afternoon tea, with the provision of a large and varied selection of light refreshments. The restaurant, lounge, and private dining rooms, which have been artistically furnished, are available for balls, Cinderellas, concerts, 'at homes', and dinner parties, public or private. The floors are of polished oak, particularly suitable for dancing, and have, as a matter of fact, been specially prepared for that purpose. The entrance to the restaurant is in Colmore Row, or it can be reached from the station platform by means of a covered way'.

The upper floors of the former hotel were used by the GWR as offices for the Superintendent of its Birmingham Division and for the District Goods Manager, in which capacity they served the company and British Railways (Western Region) until 1 July 1963, when they were made redundant by the amalgamation of the former Western and London Midland district offices, following the latter's take-over of the former's lines in the area on 1 January 1963. Just before World War 2 the GWR had plans to demolish the hotel and replace it with a modern building having a large company 'Roundel' device as its main decorative feature. These plans were shelved due to the war and were not revived afterwards.

The second Snow Hill station: 1871-1909

Anyone staying in the Great Western Hotel around 1870 would have had a good vantage point from which to overlook the reconstruction of the station. The abandonment of broad gauge working between Birmingham and Wolverhampton from 1 November 1868, and south of Birmingham from 1 April 1869, gave the GWR an opportunity to reconstruct Snow Hill station. Work began later that year, with the widening of the bridge which carried the line over Great Charles Street. The new station was the

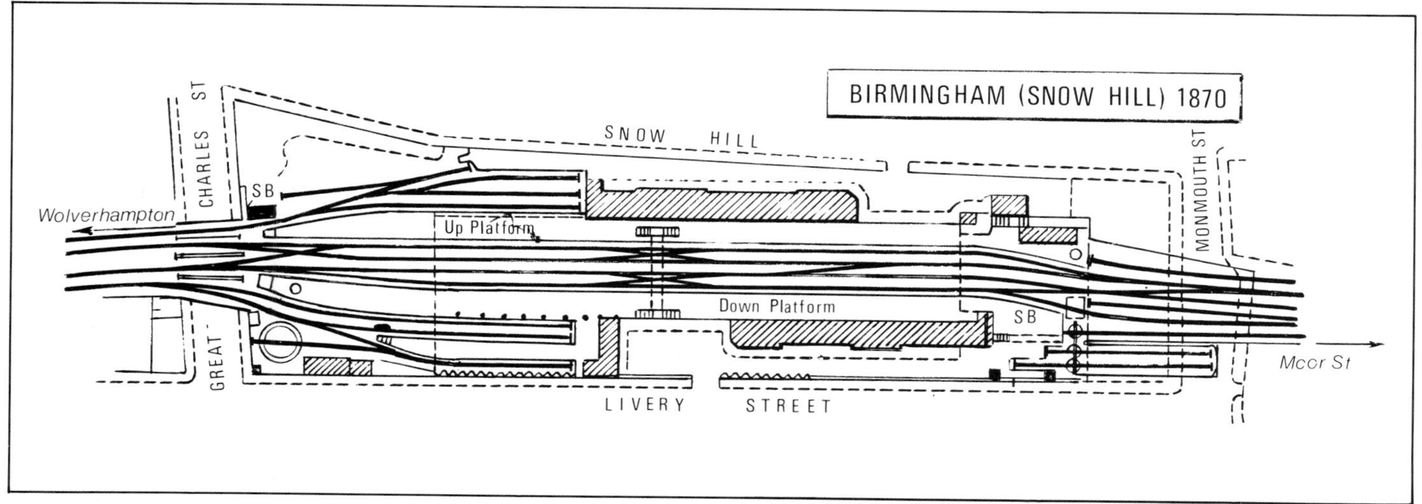

Bottom:
The planned new Great Western Hotel in Birmingham: six floors and a ventilation shaft! Revealed in April 1939, but for the war this would have replaced the familiar frontage of Snow Hill station Mk III and would have been quite an impressive building.
GWR Photographic Department

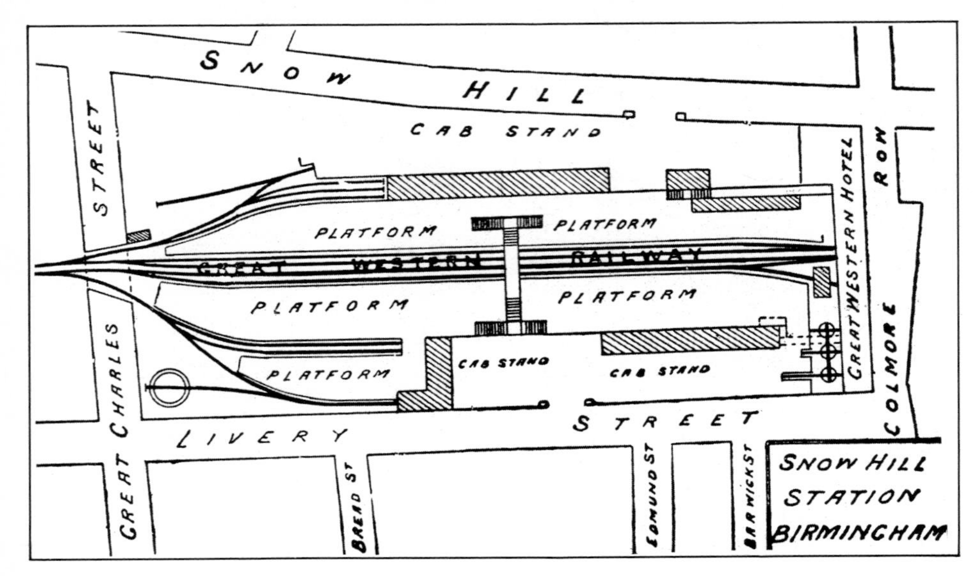

Left:
Snow Hill station Mk II (1871-1909), as shown in James Upton's *Birmingham ABC Railway Guide* of 1904. This shows the internal layout of the station at that time and emphasises the constricting nature of the approach over Great Charles Street.
Author's Collection

work of the company's Engineer, W. G. Owen, being one of the first jobs he undertook since his elevation to that position in March 1868. Owen, like those who preceded and followed him, found that there was not much that could be done with the Snow Hill site. A narrow, elongated scrap of land, hemmed in by streets and buildings, it lent itself to long platforms; which is the solution Owen came up with.

There were two main platform faces, 150yds in length, with bays at their northern (Wolverhampton) ends. Both sides had almost symmetrical platform buildings, those on the up, Snow Hill, side comprising a lavatory, telegraph room, cloak room, dining room, first-class refreshment room, second-class refreshment room, first-class waiting room, first and third-class ladies' rooms, third-class general room, Station Master's office, booking hall, coach parking offices, outward parcels office, and guards and porters' rooms; the buildings on the down, Livery Street, side being very similar. There were also two signal cabins, the main one being at the end of the up platform at the north end and containing 60 levers. Surmounting these were a pair of semi-circular crescent trussed roofs, of a design unique to the GWR. They were designed by T. Vernon, of the Cheltenham firm of Vernon & Evans, who erected them using steelwork supplied by the Patent Shaft & Axletree Co Ltd of Wednesbury. The larger roof covered the majority of the main platforms; it was 506ft long with a span of 92ft, only its central strip was glazed; the smaller, a miniature, covered the down platform bay.

Snow Hill Mk II was completed in 1871, occupying a two acre site. Passenger traffic commenced at 05.00 and ran until midnight; between 350 and 400 trains passing through the station daily. Local ones started from the Livery Street side; the bays and three sidings on the up side being used for stabling reinforcing portions, extra coaches and slip carriages kept in readiness for attachment to up trains. Looking after all of this was a staff of 50-60 officials and 180 or so porters.

The new station was an improvement, but it very soon proved to be inadequate for its purpose. In Birmingham, the GWR enjoyed a massive increase in both goods and passenger traffic, and by the 1890s the company computed that Snow Hill was a busier station even than Paddington. Traffic had become so congested that rolling stock could not be kept there, all trains being formed at Bordesley and Small Heath, five new sidings being added at the former for this purpose. With this move the station could cope with day-to-day running but summer excursion traffic swamped it, as many as 100 additional coaches being required daily. There were staffing problems too. At the start of 1893 the Station Master was taken ill. Unsure of when he would return the GWR did not replace him, a move which displeased some passengers. One, 'SEASON TICKET HOLDER' of Olton, wrote to the *Birmingham Daily Post* on 10 April that year bemoaning the company's lack of action: 'Surely a large station like Snow Hill should not be left in charge of a clerk', he hectored.

The Great Western Arcade

When the GWR first opened to Birmingham in 1852, its southern approach to Snow Hill, between Moor and Monmouth streets, was conducted through a brick lined cutting. Twenty years later that area of the town was being developed at a high rate, and it was agreed between the GWR and the Council that this cutting should be covered over to form a 596yd long tunnel, so that the land above could be built over. This work was completed during 1874. To occupy a part of the line of the newly formed tunnel, a grand arcade of shops and offices was proposed. Construction work began on the 'Great Western Arcade' on 26 April 1875. It necessitated the removal of remains from the old Quaker's Burial Ground, these being re-interred in nearby Bull Street.

The arcade was designed by William Ward (1844-1917), a Scottish architect, new to the town, who was later responsible for both the General Infirmary and Dudley Road Hospital. Its central feature was a barrel vaulted glass roof, from which hung a massive two-tier zinc chandelier bearing no fewer than 42 lights. The scheme cost £100,000 and provided 38 shops, with 56 offices situated in the galleries above. It was first illuminated on 19 August 1876, and opened for public use on 26 August that year. Six years later a second arcade was planned, to link the Temple Row end of the Great Western one with Corporation Street. Called the North Western Arcade, this was designed by the architect W. Jenkins, opening on 5 April 1884 and providing 26 shops, several of which linked directly with properties in Bull Street. A third, less well known, arcade was built facing the station in Snow Hill itself. Called, appropriately enough, 'Snow Hill Arcade', it was designed by the architect C. Ede, and led the short distance to Slaney Street.

The third Snow Hill station (1912)

By the mid-1890s it was apparent that even the second Snow Hill station would have either to be considerably enlarged or replaced. The first moves in this direction came in the GWR Act of 1 August 1899 which authorised the company to enlarge the station over Great Charles, Lionel, Water and Henrietta streets. Funding, to the tune of a staggering £341,693, was allocated to the rebuilding of the station by the GWR Board in October and November 1902; but preparatory work did not commence in earnest until 1906. Once again the first move had to be the widening of the Great Charles Street bridge. On 13 July that year, the *Railway Gazette* announced that the company would shortly commence the reconstruction of the station and that as a preliminary the Public Works Committee of the City Council would lower 250yd of Great Charles Street by 18in at its junction with Livery Street to provide sufficient clearance for the heavier, and thus deeper, steelwork this would require.

Rebuilding proper began in 1909, the *Railway Gazette* for 23 April that year noting that 'steady progress' was being made with the work: 'four new platforms have already been constructed and brought into use as an extension of the northern end of the station, which

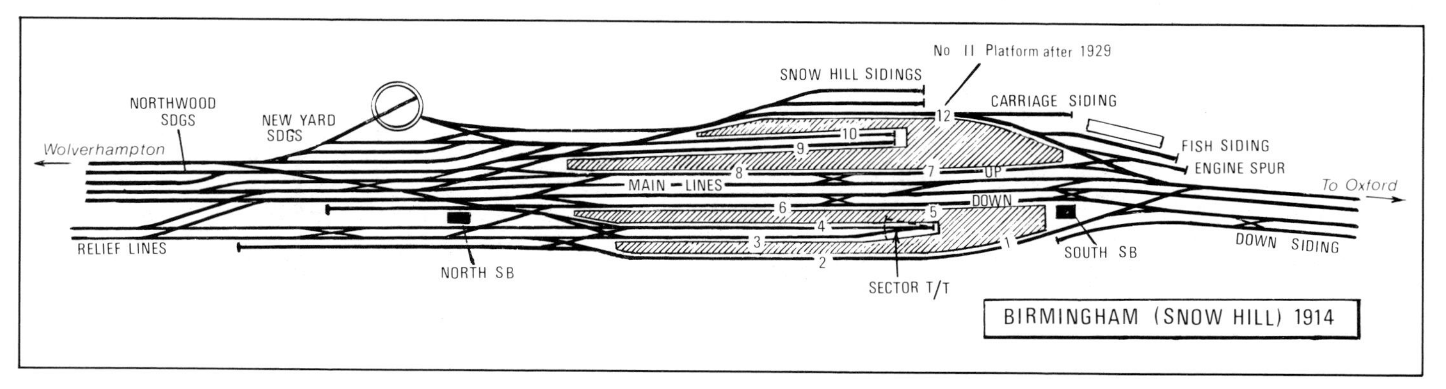

will have a total length of a quarter of a mile on completion of the four new platforms at the south end. Near the old bay platforms on the Livery Street side, which are no longer in use, extensive refreshment rooms are to be erected . . . Work is also in progress for the construction of a large parcel depot and offices, below rail level, and preparations are being made for replacing the existing main roof by one of a more modern type'. Remodelling the north end of the station was completed in October 1909, the new arrangements, together with new relief lines between Birmingham North and Hockley South, coming into use on the 31st of that month.

In overall charge of the rebuilding work was Walter Armstrong, the GWR's New Works Engineer, the day-to-day supervision of the work being delegated to his Resident Engineer, C. E. Shackle. Building work was undertaken by the Wolverhampton firm of Henry Lovatt & Co Ltd, whose engineer was R. P. Mears. Steelwork was supplied and erected by the Darlaston firm of E. C. & J. Keay. The station's main feature was its roofing, which was of three types. Covering the booking hall was a single span arch, consisting of a three-hinged lattice girder of 93ft 9½in span, the centre of which was 54ft above the floor; each end being filled by a wind screen. Sheltering the bay platforms were umbrella-style roofs of a standard GWR pattern, but, most impressive of all, was the ridge-and-furrow main roof. This ran transversely across the main lines and covered almost two thirds of the station, from Great Charles Street, 500ft to the steps of the footbridge, an area of 12,000sq yd. It was carried on girders spaced 35ft 10in apart, which supported roof trusses at 13ft 6in centres, the latter carrying lanterns 8ft 6in wide. One quarter inch rough cast glass and galvanised iron were used to cover the roof, the glazing being of the 'Eclipse' kind, installed by its patentees, Mellowes & Co. A 22ft gap over the main lines through the centre of the station was not roofed over to allow a means of escape for engine smoke and to admit light and fresh air.

Erecting this massive roof whilst keeping the station open was an enormous engineering feat, performed with the aid of a travelling stage which carried a crane capable of raising seven ton loads. The stage consisted of three girders, making one span across two platforms and four lines of rails, and travelling from one wind screen to another, a distance of 500ft. This supported the girders and trusses before they were riveted up and protected the traffic and passengers beneath. Progress on the work was again reported in the *Railway Gazette* on 2 December 1910: 'The construction of the new roof and the widening of both sides of the station has made

Below:
Snow Hill station on a commercial postcard of c1920. The refurbished restaurant of 1909 is featured prominently. Both trams are on different routes to Lozells.
Author's Collection

Haig
Home

Left:
The basic layout of Snow Hill station is seen in this unusual view taken by BR on 28 May 1968, The booking hall is the arched roof section to the rear of the former hotel, and the view highlights the fall in level on the site.
British Rail

Below left:
Snow Hill station looking towards Great Charles Street on 28 May 1968, showing the expanse of the roof and the projecting platform canopies beyond. Its two remaining shuttle services had been reduced to peak hours only and some track lifting has already begun.
British Rail

Top:
A unique, driver's eye view of the approach to Snow Hill station from the tunnel leading from Moor Street.
Ian Allan Library

Above:
Snow Hill had its quiter places too. Platform No 12 was used by Stourbridge local services and, on 11 June 1963, this mixed service hauled by No 5093 *Upton Castle*.
B. J. Ashworth

good progress. Work on the new main platform has already been carried so far that its further extension towards the south cannot be undertaken until the present refreshment rooms and offices have been removed. This . . . will not be undertaken until fresh buildings are available, and these latter will soon be ready, a new telegraph office, third-class, gentlemen's and ladies' waiting rooms and cloak rooms and refreshment rooms being nearly finished. The roof which will cover the new station . . . has been carried over five bays at the north end . . . (and it) will ultimately cover the 14 bays'.

The rebuilt station did not officially open because, as with the one it replaced, the previous one never closed. Pinning-down a precise date for its completion is therefore difficult, although the inclusion of major articles on the station in both the *Railway Gazette* for 12 January 1912 and the *Railway Magazine* for February 1912 indicates that the work must have been substantially complete at the start of January that year. Some details remained to be finished though, and even a year later the *Railway Gazette* for 24 January 1913 noted that 'the work . . . is now practically finished so far as concerns the station buildings'.

At rail level there were two island platforms and, at the north end, two bays, providing 12 faces in all. The main platforms were paved with patent Victoria stone and were extremely long: Nos 1/2 were 1,070ft; Nos 5/6, 1,215ft; Nos 7/8, 1,180ft and Nos 11/12, 970ft, and at their greatest width 80ft; the bay platforms being 500ft long and 20-30ft wide. At the Colmore Row end there was provision for handling horse, fish, milk and general perishable traffic, well away from the passengers. There were four through tracks with a relief line at each side of the station; the lines through Colmore Row tunnel converging into a single pair. Signalling used the Siemens all-electric principle, the whole station being controlled from two boxes: a north box with 224 levers (66 signals, 43 points and bars, 73 discs, three bolts and 39 spares) and a south box with 80 (22 signals, 15 points and bars, 27 discs, one bolt and 15 spares). The main entrance was from Colmore Row, via an archway cut through the former Great Western Hotel (completed in August 1908), into the street-level booking hall, which was 164ft wide and 92ft long, standing about 22ft above rail level. Inclined roads and footways connected this with the platforms. The booking offices were equipped with Regina automatic ticket machines, the first to be installed in the country; these printed the tickets as required and obviated the need to keep vast stocks of preprinted tickets covering all of the different combinations of destination, class, type of journey, etc. A copy of each ticket printed was made for Clearing House records.

Two subsidiary booking offices were provided for passengers entering via a subway off Great Charles and Livery streets; this being 20ft wide, 12 of which were for the use of passengers, the remainder, separated by railings, for use by porters with parcels and luggage. At Great Charles Street the station building was on three levels, the lowest being devoted to parcels traffic, the upper to staff accommodation and stores. On the main down platform buildings were provided for waiting rooms and a large refreshment buffet, handsomely panelled in oak. One curious feature was the provision of a sector table at the buffer stops end of bay Platform No 3/4. This was made by Ransomes & Rapier of Ipswich and was installed towards the end of 1912. It was in lieu of a turntable, for which there was not room in that part of the station, and consisted of a 71ft 6in rail bearing table which was pivoted at the buffer stop end and free to move 8ft 4in at the other, bringing it into connection with a choice of three converging and interlaced roads; allowing a locomotive to be switched between these at the end of the bay. The sector table was out of use by 1929 and removed in 1938.

The whole of the new Snow Hill station was executed in a light and pleasing style, exuding a handsome and cheerful appearance. Sixty years later, following complete closure, it was impressive to the curious trespasser;

brand spanking new, just before Word War 1, it must have been nothing short of magnificent!

Over the years a number of alterations, some major, some minor, were made to Snow Hill. One of the first was the installation of a telephone train control system covering the Birmingham District, from Wolverhampton to Worcester and to Tyseley, which was commissioned on 2 March 1914, the third such to be installed on the GWR. This provided direct telephone links with practically every station, yard, signal box, etc., in the control area. It was worked from four desks by four controllers; each having a unique telephone switchboard, i.e. one which did not duplicate the function of any of the others. These were staffed by four controllers: a Head Controller, responsible for the West Midland Section (ex-West Midland Railway lines); a Second Controller, responsible for the main lines; an Assistant Controller, responsible for assisting the aforementioned controllers and with charting the progress of trains on a large 23ft by 4ft 6in line diagram which dominated the office; and a Relief & Locomotive Controller, who dealt with staff and locomotive matters. Controllers worked eight hour shifts and were responsible to a Chief Controller who had the ultimate responsibility for all matters relating to train movements.

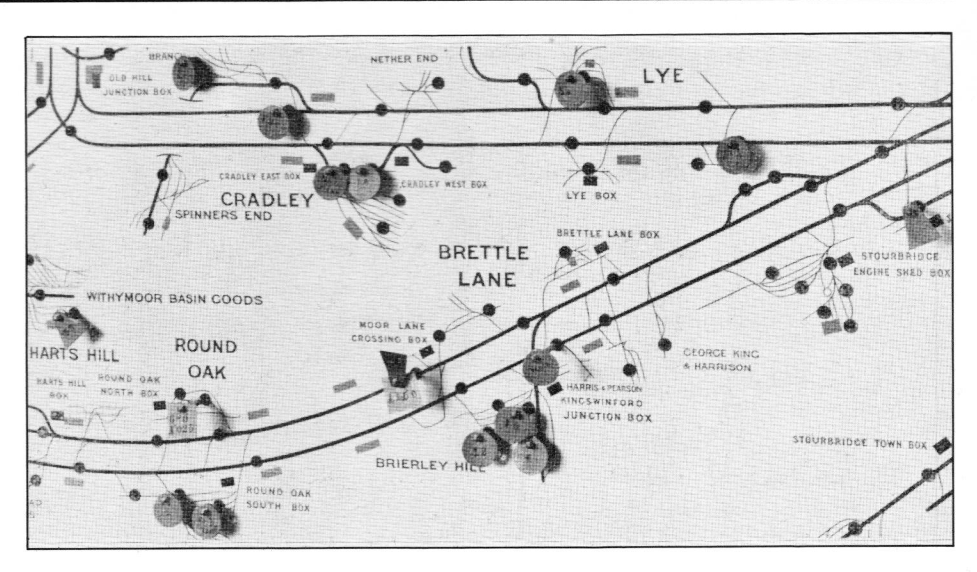

During World War 2, Snow Hill station received considerable air raid damage. On the night of 19/20 November 1940 the roof glazing in the booking hall was shattered and on the night of 8/9 April 1941 the roof to and fabric of Platforms Nos 5 and 11 was also damaged by bombing. The stations biggest enemy was not the Luftwaffe but general wear and tear, most notably on the signalling equipment, whose many 1,000s of pulls a day took their toll. Both boxes were in a poor state by 1956 and so a resig-

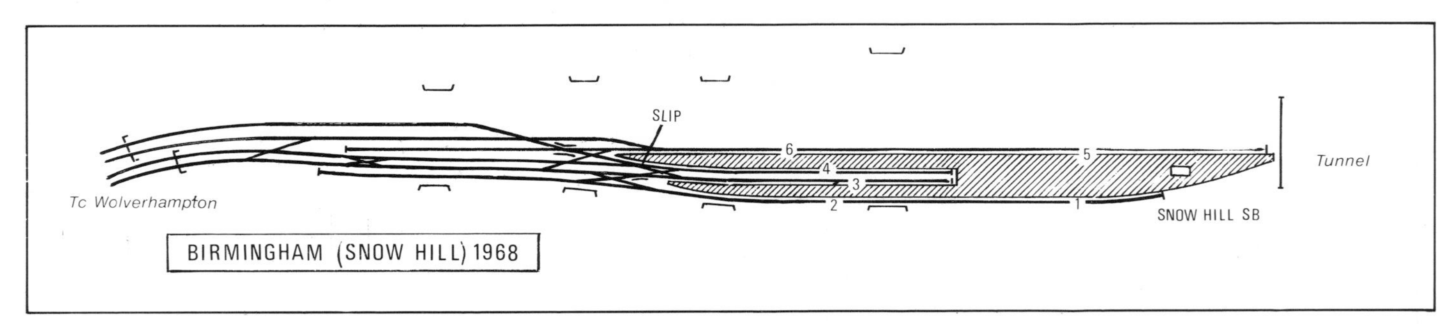

Left:
Another feature of the 9-14 April 1962 'Western Railway Week' special events was a 'Diesel Conducted Tour' which took one direct by rail to Tyseley depot and Herbert Street Goods, in Wolverhampton, all for a fare of 2s 6d (12.5p).
British Rail

Above left:
At the heart of the GWR's new Telephone Train Control system, commissioned on 2 March 1914, was a large, 23ft by 4ft 6in, route diagram, of which this is a portion showing the Stourbridge area.
Author's Collection

Below left:
From 9-14 April 1962 Snow Hill was the centre of a special 'Western Railway Week', highlighting the advantages and career prospects of the railway. One of the attractions was the chance to visit the cab of one of the WR's latest diesel-hydraulic locomotives No D1002 *Western Explorer*, then stabled at Oxley for driver training. The date is 13 April 1962 – anybody recognise themselves?
British Rail

nalling scheme was authorised. This came into use on 11 September 1960. The introduction of DMUs had also reduced the need for many locomotive run rounds and so the track layout through the station was also revised. Multi-aspect colour light signals were installed, controlled from a Swiss designed 'Domino' panel housed in a new building at the south end of the down platform. This panel was 8ft 4in long and operated on the 'entrance-exit' or 'NX' system, a form of electrical interlocking which prevented a route from being entered if its exit was blocked. The illuminated panel showed the chosen route by a series of coloured lights and also featured train describers which displayed each train's reporting number, eg '5A72', etc.

Between 9-14 April 1962, Snow Hill was the centre of BR(W)'s 'Western Railway Week', which was intended to ensure that the public understood why it was necessary for fares to be increased, services reduced, and branch lines and stations closed, and what the railways were doing to improve their present facilities. An exhibition at Snow Hill included displays about railway travel and careers, a look round a 'Western' class diesel-hydraulic locomotive (No D1002 *Western Explorer*) and the station signalling control panel and train control centre there. Twice daily, for a fare of 2s 6d (12.5p), diesel railcars also took parties directly into Tyseley depot, and Herbert Street goods station, in Wolverhampton, to see their work, and displays of track laying and maintenance.

For two years Birmingham was a terminus for the GWR. Work on the BW&D's construction began in 1851, it eventually opening to Priestfield on 14 November 1854, having been delayed by the collapse of a bridge over a road between Soho and Handsworth stations on 23 August, the day *after* it had passed a Board of Trade inspection. At Priestfield, the BW&D joined the OWW, who had been compelled by Parliament to complete their mixed gauge line from there into Wolverhampton. There were intermediate stations at Hockley, Soho (Soho & Winson Green from May 1893), Handsworth & Smethwick, West Bromwich, Swan Village, Wednesbury (Wednesbury Central from 1 July 1950) Bradley & Moxley (opened in June 1862) and Bilston (Bilston Central from 1 July 1950).

The Stourbridge Town branch

During the planing stage of the OWW it was realised that its chosen route passed almost ¾-mile to the east of Stourbridge, and so provision was made for building a short branch into the

Below:
Wednesbury was one of the main stations on the GWR's BW&D line, opening on 14 November 1854. That it was built for and carried mixed gauge lines is emphasised in this 1902 shot of a Dean single passing the station with a southbound express.
R. S. Carpenter Collection

town, to terminate at the Stourbridge Navigation's canal basin in Lower High Street. This was included as part of the original OWW bill, passed on 4 August 1845, but was not built. The following year the Birmingham, Wolverhampton & Stour Valley Railway No 2 bill sought permission for a 20 mile long branch which would leave the scheme's main line at Smethwick and proceed to Stourport via Old Hill, Stourbridge and Kidderminster; in part a route similar to that later adopted by the Stourbridge and Stourbridge Extension lines. Unfortunately, this part of the 'Stour Valley' scheme attracted vigorous opposition from the OWW, whose route it duplicated south of Stourbridge. They won the day, and the bill was withdrawn on 1 July 1846, despite which the 'Stour Valley' tag has stayed with that portion of the line that was eventually built between Birmingham and Wolverhampton.

Other proposals for lines and branches to Stourbridge came and went in the late 1840s and early 1850s, including one in 1852 by the LNWR which partially revived the 'Stour Valley' scheme in the form of an 8½ mile long branch between Smethwick and Stourbridge. Again this aroused OWW opposition, and the bill proposing it was withdrawn on 26 July 1853. By that time the OWW had opened a single line as far as Dudley, having been open as far as Stourbridge since 3 May 1852, and were the company which was in by far the best position to improve the railway service to the town. Accordingly, they included a Stourbridge branch in their bill of 1853, which was intended for both goods and passengers and was planned to leave the main line near Amblecote Hall and descend a 1 in 45 gradient to terminate by the canal basin in Lower High Street. But even as the Royal Assent was being granted for this on 20 August 1853, they were proposing a revised scheme for separate goods and passenger lines, the former of which would parallel the course of the approved branch, the latter of which would branch from this and terminate at a passenger station on Foster Street in Stourbridge town centre.

This revised scheme was authorised on 31 July 1854, but was delayed by a stipulation that work could not proceed on it until the OWW had doubled its main line north of Worcester. Complying with this took so long that the company revised its plans for a Stourbridge town branch again, and in 1857 they proposed a goods only branch which left the main line at the north end of Stambermill viaduct and terminated, as ever, by the Lower High Street canal basin. It was to be worked by a stationary winding engine and the Act authorising it, on 23 July 1858, stated that it had to be open by 31 July 1859. Construction began in April 1859, and it was sufficiently complete by 30 July for an opening ceremony to take place, using a locomotive and four horses in place of the as yet incomplete winding engine and apparatus, which took almost another two years to install and perfect.

Above:
There had been an engine shed at Stourbridge since 1870, but by 1 November 1959, when this view of ex-GWR diesel railcars Nos W15 and W8 was taken, it had been modernised to include a diesel refuelling facility. These railcars had been used on the Stourbridge Town branch, but by this time were stored out of use. *T. J. Farebrother*

Right:
Engineering work on the line, one day late in 1956, has forced streamlined railcar No W14W to wait higher up the platform at Stourbridge Town station than usual as it waits to depart for Stourbridge Junction on the town branch service. Railcar No 8 was the first to be used on the line in March 1936, but their use declined with the introduction of BR single unit railcars in the late 1950s. *Michael Walker*

As useful as this incline was to businesses, it did not offer local people a passenger service, nor was the planned doubling of the line ever carried out, seriously limiting its capacity. Therefore, within a few years of it opening, there were renewed calls for a new branch line into Stourbridge. Proposals came and went until one put forward by the GWR, for a branch of a mile in length, starting at Stourbridge station, descending by a double line at 1 in 400 to a passenger station in Foster Street and dropping steeply at 1 in 27 by a single line to a junction with the existing branch at the foot of its inclined section, was sanctioned by Parliament on 30 June 1874. Construction was delayed until the late spring of 1878, the line opening to passengers on 1 October 1879, with goods services, to a new shed at the canal basin, commencing on 1 January 1880; the original incline closing on the same date. The original OWW station was renamed Stourbridge Junction; the new station in Foster Street inheriting its former name of Stourbridge. A basic service of 17 trains in each direction operated the three minute, weekdays only, journey, plus an additional empty stock working, which formed the first and last train over the line each day. Two branch services were provided by coaches and guards off Birmingham trains: the stock from the 11.40 ex-Birmingham forming the 12.27 service to Stourbridge, returning at 12.33 and continuing through to Snow Hill at 12.50; the same practice being followed with the stock forming the 13.40 departure for Birmingham.

Whilst a commercial success, the new town branch soon presented problems to the GWR. More and more people were encouraged to use the railway, and the inadequacy of the station accommodation at Stourbridge Junction was quickly shown up. An enlarged station was the answer, but the existing site was 'rail-locked' between the curves forming the junctions of the town branch and former Stourbridge Railway lines. And so the original station was endured for 15 years or so until, with increases in passenger traffic showing no sign of abating, the GWR proposed a radical solution, the building of a new Junction station ¼-mile south. This was authorised by the GWR (Additional Powers) Act on 6 August 1897, coming into use, with a realigned town branch, on 1 October 1901.

Since this time the passenger service on the branch has intensified. Between January 1905 and October 1935 it was operated by GWR steam railmotors, these being replaced first by diesel railcars and then, in 1958, by BR single unit railcars. The passenger service on the branch has been withdrawn twice: as a wartime economy, between 29 March 1915 and 3 March 1919, and again, between 7 May and 10 July 1926, due to the General Strike. The double track upper section of the branch was

altered in 1935, to make the down line passengers only and the up one goods only; allowing the removal of a crossover in the town station and the closure of its signal box; these alterations coming into use on 25 August that year.

The Stratford-on-Avon Railway

By the late 1850s, Stratford-on-Avon was already being approached by an OWW branch from Honeybourne which opened on 11 July 1859, but others felt that the town needed a more direct link with Birmingham. Accordingly, the Stratford-on-Avon Railway was promoted to build a 9¼ mile long mixed gauge single line between Hatton, on the GWR, and the town. This was authorised by the Stratford-on-Avon Railway Act on 10 August 1857 and was completed without undue delay, opening formally on 9 October 1860; broad gauge passenger services, operated by the GWR on behalf of the company,

Right:
The Stratford-on-Avon Railway opened on 10 October 1860 and Claverdon was the first station on the line from its junction with the B&O at Hatton. The original station there closed on 2 July 1939 when this replacement, west of the road overbridge, opened. On 20 September 1961 the 12.40 Stratford-on-Avon to Leamington Spa service leaves, formed by railcar No 55018 and a driving trailer.
Michael Mensing

commencing the following day. There were stations at Claverdon, Bearley, Wilmcote, and a temporary station on Birmingham Road, Stratford-on-Avon.

Being so close to the OWW's Stratford-on-Avon branch, the building of a link between these two lines was inevitable, and was undertaken quite quickly, the 29 chains long line opening on 24 July 1861 for the passing of an excursion train conveying passengers to see a military review in Warwick. Possibilities were also opened by this link, and on 1 August 1861 the Stratford-on-Avon and WM Railways introduced a through joint narrow gauge passenger service between Leamington and Honeybourne, and Worcester and Malvern along it. Broad gauge services along the Stratford-on-Avon Railway did not last very long, all regular trains over the line from Hatton running on the narrow gauge from 1 January 1863, although the line was not officially declared narrow gauge only until 1 April 1869. Also on 1 January 1863, the temporary station on the Birmingham Road was closed to passengers but remained open for excursions and goods.

Trains worked from Hatton and continued through to Honeybourne; four trains in each direction making the 45 minute journey on weekdays, supplemented by two 30 minute duration short workings, in each direction, between Hatton and Stratford-on-Avon; the latter also comprising the Sunday service. The Stratford-on-Avon Railway remained nominally independent for over 30 years, finally being vested in GWR on 1 July 1883.

Stourbridge Railway

Whilst the SS Railway was the first line to truly serve some of the Black Country, that part of it to the west of Stourbridge remained isolated from the area's growing railway network. Here lay the nail and hollowware manufacturing district of Lye and the chain and anchor makers of Cradley and Cradley Heath; both heavy consumers of raw materials and energetic producers of finished items, who required vast quantities of iron. The nearest railhead was the OWW line at Stourbridge; the logical starting point for any railway to be built through the area. With the opening of a branch from this line into the town on 30 July 1859 three of Stourbridge's wealthiest Ironmasters: John and Henry Foley and William Orme Foster, were spurred on to promote a railway leading from a junction with the OWW line at Stourbridge, 3 miles 35 chains to Old Hill, via Lye and Cradley Heath. Styled the 'Stourbridge Railway', its proponents presented a bill before the Parliamentary Session of 1860, obtaining an Act on 14 June 1861. This authorised the line described, plus two branches: one to serve collieries at Hayes Lane and Cradley; another to the New British Iron Co's extensive ironworks at the Corngreaves.

Top:
The Stourbridge line extends away into the distance as 2-6-2T No 5109 approaches Stourbridge Junction with the 17.45 local from Snow Hill on 5 June 1957. This portion of the Stourbridge Railway, to Cradley, opened on 1 April 1863, but the next section to Old Hill took another three years to construct due to the extensive earthworks required.
E. J. Dew

Above:
An indication of the gradient (1 in 51) between Cradley and Blackheath tunnel, just north of Old Hill station, is conveyed in this shot of the 09.40 Cardiff-Snow Hill service, formed by a three-car cross-country DMU and a van, just about to enter the tunnel. This section of the line took three years to build due to the height and instability of the earthworks involved.
Michael Mensing

One month earlier, on 20 May 1861, the Stourbridge Railway company signed an agreement with the WM Railway for the latter to work the new line. Close allegiance with the WM also encouraged the line's supporters to promote an extension of it to join the Stour Valley line at Smethwick and a separate bill, the Stourbridge Railway (Extension to Smethwick, &c), was presented to Parliament in November 1860. This proposed a line from the end of the Stourbridge Railway at Old Hill, 4 miles 65 chains to a junction with the Stour Valley line near Galton Bridge, plus a branch from Cradley Heath to a goods depot at Old Hill; obtaining its Act on 1 August 1861. Three months earlier, on 4 May 1861, the WM Railway and the GWR had signed an agreement to lease the former's OWW section in return for reciprocal running powers over each company's system. The significance of the WM supported Stourbridge Railway was not lost on the GWR, who proposed a connecting link between a junction with the Stourbridge Railway (Extension to Smethwick, &c) line at Smethwick and their own BW&D line at Handsworth, allowing trains from Stourbridge to run into Snow Hill as well as New Street. This was authorised on 7 July 1862.

Construction began first on the original Stourbridge Railway portion of the line, which opened to Cradley, with an intermediate station at Lye, on 1 April

Above:
Construction work on the Stourbridge Extension line between Cradley and Galton Junction was delayed by the collapse of the earthworks leading from the former to the 887yd long Old Hill tunnel. Since its opening, on 1 April 1867, this section of the line has repeatedly presented problems, as evinced by this 30 August 1962 view of Class 2800 2-8-0 No 3819 taking an up tanker freight through the tunnel's heavily braced western portal.
Michael Mensing

1863. The Corngreaves branch came into use on the same day, followed in June by the ¾-mile Hayes Lane branch. A basic service of eight trains in each direction per day was operated on week-days, the journey taking just 10min.

On 25 July 1863, shortly after this section of the line opened, the Stourbridge Railway company signed an agreement with WM Railway for the latter to work the Old Hill to Smethwick Extension line from its opening. Less than a week later, the WM company amalgamated with the GWR, who inherited the task of completing the line. Progress to Cradley had been quite rapid, but the next 2¼ miles between Old Hill and Rowley, was hard won. From a little way past Cradley station the line is carried on a steeply graded embankment (1 in 51), of increasing height, which required a considerable amount of earth to construct, the material excavated from Old Hill tunnel providing only a part of this. On more than one occasion during construction the embankment collapsed, setting back the opening of the line to Old Hill, which did not take place until 1 January 1866. Later that year, the GWR obtained powers, under its Further Powers, &c Act of 30 July 1866, to absorb the Stourbridge Railway company at a later date.

Construction of the line to Galton Junction, with the Stour Valley line, was completed by the following spring, and the line opened on 1 April 1867, with intermediate stations at Rowley (Rowley & Blackheath from 1 September 1889, Rowley Regis & Blackheath from May 1891); Oldbury & Langley Green (renamed Langley Green from 7 November 1884, Langley Green & Rood End from January 1904 and Oldbury & Langley Green from 6 January 1936); Rood End and Smethwick Junction. This enabled the LNWR to begin a through passenger service of seven trains each day (four on Sundays), in each direction between New Street and Kidderminster and/or Worcester and Hereford. On the same day the GWR opened its line between Smethwick and Handsworth Junctions, which had no intermediate stations. This was used by the Stourbridge Railway services, which were operated by the GWR, providing a basic service of 14 trains in each direction daily, of which three were semi-fasts, calling only at Cradley and Smethwick Junction; the latter taking only 29min to cover the 11½ miles to Snow Hill, slow trains covering the same distance in 48min. A basic Sunday service, of five up and four down trains, was also provided.

Three years after it opened, the GWR used its powers to absorb the Stourbridge Railway under the terms of an agreement signed on 10 March 1870, which were backdated to 1 February that year and confirmed under the terms of the GWR (Additional Powers, &c) Act of 31 July 1870.

Alcester Railway

In the 1870s, Alcester was, much as it is today, a quite village in Warwickshire, lying along the great Roman south-to-east coast road, Icknield Street. It was served by the Evesham & Redditch

Left:
The Stourbridge Town line is now British Rail's shortest branch, with the most intensive service of any line in the country. To see this eloquent shot of ex-GWR 0-4-2T No 1458 waiting to depart from Stourbridge Town with the 21.22 departure of Stourbridge Junction on 8 September 1956, one would hardly guess that the station served a highly populated town on the edge of the Black Country and Birmingham conurbations. *Michael Walker*

Below:
The line between Smethwick and Handsworth Junctions opened on 1 April 1867. Leaving Smethwick the line rose sharply to pass over the Stour Valley line and the Birmingham Canal. On 22 October 1966, WR diesel parcels car No 55996 has just left Smethwick en route for Snow Hill. Note Smethwick Junction box just visible between the arch of the road bridge at the extreme left, and the Stour Valley line with its electrification seemingly complete five months before the commencement of full electric working. *Michael Mensing*

Above:
Handsworth & Smethwick was one of the very characteristic blue brick stations along the BW&D line, which opened on 14 November 1854. Its proportions and facilities are seen to good advantage in this 28 May 1960 view of a two-car DMU about to depart on the Dudley service, which branched off the line at Swan Village.
R. C. Riley

Railway, which opened a station there on 17 June 1866, and lay just under seven miles west of the Stratford-on-Avon Railway. Quite why anyone should want to built a second line to serve the town is unclear, unless it was to act as a link between these two railways. Nonetheless, such a scheme, styled the Alcester Railway, was promoted around 1871, and on 12 July 1872 its promoters succeeding in obtaining an agreement from the GWR to maintain the line. The Alcester Railway Act was granted on 6 August 1872, authorising the construction of a line between a junction with the Stratford-on-Avon Rly at Bearley and Alcester, a distance of six miles 40 chains.

Construction of the line took four years and it opened on 4 September 1876 with an intermediate station at Great Alne. The GWR worked the line from its opening, formally accepting responsibility for its maintenance on 4 September 1877. Ten months later, on 22 July 1878, the Alcester Railway Company was vested in the GWR by the latter's Act of that date. For the next 38 years the line enjoyed a relatively Spartan passenger service, consisting of five

up and five down trains per day, two of which were mixed goods, and no Sunday service. All of these were withdrawn from 1 January 1917 as a wartime economy measure, and the branch was closed entirely for almost six years.

The line was partially reopened to Great Alne from Bearley on 18 December 1922; the remainder of the line coming back into use on 1 August 1923, together with a new halt, at Aston Cantlow, and Alcester locomotive shed. A basic service of six trains in each direction on weekdays was operated until advertised passenger services were withdrawn again on 25 September 1939, at the end of the 1939 summer

Above:
Alcester station was built by the Evesham & Redditch Railway and opened to passengers on 17 June 1866. The company was taken-over by the Midland Railway on 1 July 1882, producing curious sights, such as this in 1937, of a GWR Autotrailer off the Bearley branch in a Midland station.
Don Powell Collection

Right:
Passenger services on the Alcester Railway from Bearley began on 4 September 1876 but were withdrawn on 1 January 1917 as a wartime economy. Services were reinstated, complete with a new halt at Aston Cantlow, on 18 December 1922. This is pictured c1937, two years before the line was closed to passengers for a second and final time on 25 September 1939.
Don Powell Collection

timetable. Aston Cantlow Halt was closed entirely, but workmen's services, between Birmingham and Great Alne, continued until 3 July 1944. From then the line saw only goods services, and was closed permanently from 1 March 1951; the lines were lifted soon afterwards, with short sections being retained at either end for use as sidings.

The branches from Old Hill

Old Hill was an unlikely place to serve as a railway junction, yet it performed this role for two lines, both of which, at various times, carried services to and from Birmingham. The first such schemes were for lines to Dudley, which were promoted in 1853, 1854 and 1860, several years before the Stourbridge Railway was opened to the town; but the first to secure authority for such a line was the WM Railway. Their Additional Works, &c Act of 17 July 1862 authorised lines between Old Hill and Netherton and Halesowen, with branches to a goods depot at Netherton and a canal basin at Halesowen. But, between the company's amalgamation with the GWR, and the protracted work to complete the Stourbridge and Stourbridge Extension railways, construction did not commence on these lines and the WM company's powers over them were allowed to lapse.

Above right:
The opening of the line to Old Hill gave the citizens of Dudley an even wider range of destinations they could reach by rail as well as, in the case of Snow Hill station, a choice of routes over which they could travel. The station there was operated jointly by the GWR and LNWR, the former's half being to the left in this 1950s view, the latter's to the right. Ex-GWR Class 5700 0-6-0PT No 8742 is waiting in the bay platform on the western side.
R. S. Carpenter Collection

Right:
The Old Hill-Dudley line was opened on 1 March 1878 with just one intermediate station, this one at Windmill End. By c1950, when this photograph was taken, the buildings were showing their age and would be replaced in 1957, even though the line was to close to passengers on 15 June 1964. 57XX Class Pannier No 3778 works an autotrain along the line, the typical motive power along it for many years.

Don Powell Collection

Interest in the schemes was revived in 1870. The Stourbridge Railway was now vested in the GWR, and the company obtained renewed powers to build lines between Old Hill, Dudley and Halesowen, plus a branch to a canal basin at Withymoor (Netherton), in its Act of 18 July 1872. Construction was delayed again and finally began in the mid-1870s. Both railways opened on 1 March 1878, working from a new station at Old Hill, situated in between the junctions of the lines, a little nearer to Stourbridge than the former station there. The double track Dudley line left the Stourbridge Railway west of the new station, veering off sharply northwest. It had an intermediate station at Windmill End, and a new one at Netherton, built at its junction with the ex-OWW line. This was named Dudley (South Side) & Netherton (renamed Blowers Green from 1 August 1921), the original OWW Netherton station, ¼-mile south, closing. The single track Halesowen line left the Stourbridge Railway east of the new station, curving away sharply southeast and terminating at the line's only station at Halesowen, which was situated on Mucklow Hill. One year later, construction of the basin and single line branch at Withymoor was completed, the new facilities coming into use on 10 March 1879.

The arrangement of the junctions at Old Hill did not facilitate through running between both branches. If the WM Railway's proposals of 1862 had been followed, the Dudley line would have had junctions facing both Stourbridge and Birmingham, with an additional line linking it directly with the Halesowen branch. As built, the passage of traffic from one line to the other was possible, but complicated. From the Dudley line, a train would have to pass through Old Hill station on the up line, cross to the down line and then take the Halesowen branch. Without an additional locomotive, waiting on the down line to be attached to this train, it would of course also have to back down the branch. Trains from the latter had to go through the same manoeuvre in reverse to gain the Dudley line. Little surprise therefore that both lines were operated separately.

On the Dudley line, a basic weekdays only service of nine down (to Dudley) and 10 up (to Old Hill) passenger trains worked the 11 minute journey. In addition, there was a weekdays evening goods service, the 20.55 to Banbury (via Birmingham), which began at Withymoor basin and was assisted to Dudley by a bank engine. Quite quickly, the GWR realised that if some of the trains which worked the Old Hill-Dudley route were made to run through, to and from Snow Hill station, this would free capacity on their BW&D main line to Wolverhampton. Accordingly, the service was altered to one of nine trains in each direction, six of which ran between Dudley and Snow Hill, via Old Hill.

On the shorter Halesowen branch, a journey of just six minutes, there was a more intensive service of 13 down (to Halesowen) and 12 up (to Old Hill) trains, on weekdays only. An 'as required' goods service was also provided, worked from Halesowen. At its maximum, this saw four up and three down goods trains on weekdays; the 21.21 Halesowen to Old Hill passenger working also conveying goods for Hockley and Bordesley, again on an 'as required' basis. The timing of services on the Halesowen branch was altered slightly, to suit new working arrangements which followed the opening of the Halesowen Railway on 10 September 1883, to ensure that, wherever possible, the services from Old Hill and to Northfield connected at Halesowen, with a minimum of delay.

A much delayed branch to Halesowen canal basin, which left the line just north of the station there, finally came into use on 2 April 1902; otherwise there were no major changes on either route until the introduction of steam railmotors in 1905. These were first used on both lines that March, without any alteration to the basic timetables, possibly to allow crews to become familiar with their operation and to permit

G. W. R.

CLOSING

BRANCH LINES AND STATIONS

JANUARY 1st, 1917.

The following Lines and Stations will be Closed.

BRANCHES CLOSED.

Alcester and Bearley
Titley and Eardisley
Moorswater and Caradon
Monmouth and Coleford
*Uxbridge (High St.) and Denham
Bridport, East St., and West Bay.

STATIONS AND HALTS CLOSED

WEEK DAYS AND SUNDAYS.

*Alcester
Almeley
Bassaleg (G.W.)
Berwig Halt
Brampford Speke
Cheltenham (Malvern Road)
*Coleford
Daisy Bank
Dawlish Warren
Dunstall Park
*Eardisley
Great Aine
Hart's Hill & Woodside
Ide
Lightmoor Platform
Linley
Llangeinor
*†Llangonoyd
Lyonshall
Newland
Penar Junction Halt
†Pontnewydd (Lower)
Pontrhydyrun
St. Lawrence Platform
†Saltney
Stretton-on-Fosse
Teigngrace
Tidenham
†Uxbridge (High St.)
Vicarage Crossing Halt

* Closed for Great Western Trains only. † Closed for Passenger Traffic only.

SUNDAYS.

In addition to the above, the following Stations will be closed on Sundays.

Ashburton
Bearley
Brixham
Bovey
Bridport
Buckfastleigh
Buttington
Carbis Bay
Causland
Clevedon
Clifton Bridge
Claverdon
Colnbrook
Combe Junction
Daisy Bank
Dunstall Park
Hanwood
Heathfield
Helston
Kingsland
Kington
Lelant
Looe
Lustleigh
Marlborough
Middletown
Moretonhampstead
Nancegollan
Pembridge
Pill
Powerstock
Portbury
Portishead
Sandplace
St. Ives
St. Keyne
Staines
Staverton
Stratford-on-Avon
Titley
Toller
Twerton-on-Avon
Westbury (Salop)
Wilmcote
Yockleton.

Paddington Station,
December 22nd, 1916.

FRANK POTTER, General Manager.

Left:
World War 1 brought shortages of both staff and materials, resulting in the temporary closure of many branch lines and stations. In the Birmingham area the GWR implemented these economies in two phases, the first being early in 1915, the second, as shown here, with effect from 1 January 1917. Amongst the services withdrawn on this occasion were those along the Alcester Railway. Harts Hill & Woodside station, ex-OWW line, was also closed, never to reopen.
Railway Gazette

the upgrading of facilities. The shorter line was the first to be ready for the full introduction of the railmotors, and on 1 July 1905 a new halt, at Coombes Holloway, by Coombes Road, was opened between Old Hill and Halesowen. This was of the standard GWR 'tin pagoda' design, with a plain timber platform. Bearing in mind the 'before' service on this branch, the 'after' one was a little bizarre, consisting of 21 return trips on weekdays and 13 on Sundays!

Three similar halts were erected along the Old Hill-Dudley line, at Old Hill (High Street), Darby End and Baptist End, coming into use on 21 August 1905, with a service of 12 trains in each direction on weekdays, six of which were operated by the railmotors, the balance being the through Dudley-Snow Hill services, which did not call at the new halts. From 1 October 1905, most of the latter trains ceased to run via Old Hill and the line was mainly operated by railmotors. Service cutbacks caused by World War 1 threatened the future of both of Old Hill's branches, but they escaped closure, and only lost their Sunday services from 3 March 1915. After the war these were not restored on the Halesowen branch, which, despite returning to a full weekday service, began to feel the effects of local bus competition. Eventually, on 5 December 1927, the GWR withdrew its public passenger service between Old Hill and Halesowen in favour of a replacement bus service provided by the 'Midland Red', in which it was a major shareholder. Coombes Holloway Halt was closed entirely, but Halesowen station remained open to goods and for workmen's services. For a short time, railmotors continued to ply their way to and from Old Hill to connect with workmen's services from Longbridge, until these too were withdrawn on 31 March 1928; leaving only goods services on the branch.

Things were brighter on the Dudley line. Auto-trains replaced the railmotors in the early 1930s and were themselves partially replaced by GWR diesel railcars from October 1940 onwards. After World War 2, which had seen some service reductions, there were 21 weekday return trips along the line, including one through service between Dudley and Snow Hill. But throughout the 1950s this was steadily reduced. Windmill End, the only full station on the line, was reduced to the status of an unstaffed halt with the introduction of the winter timetable on 15 September 1952. Further cut backs in 1955 reduced the service to 13 return journeys and saw the end of through services to Birmingham. Hopes of a brighter future were raised towards the end of 1957 by the replacement of the ageing halt pagodas by modern pre-cast concrete platforms and bus shelters, but further service reductions, and the closure of Blower's Green station with the withdrawal of the Stourbridge-Wolverhampton passenger service from 30 July 1962, indicated that its days were numbered.

Oldbury Railway

The centre of Oldbury lay almost a mile from the nearest railway, the Stourbridge Extension line, which opened on 1 April 1867. The town was one of great industrial prosperity, having iron and tube works, a railway carriage and wagon factory, and a large chemical manufactory specialising in the production of phosphorous; the last of these being founded in 1851 by Arthur Albright, the inventor of the safety match. With the opening of a line nearby, Oldbury soon became the subject of other railway proposals. One such was the Dudley & Oldbury Junction Railway, which planned a line linking those two towns. The scheme was authorised by an Act of Parliament on 21 July 1873 but did not proceed. Three years later, on 11 August 1876, the proposers obtained a second Act which revised the earlier one, abandoning the majority of the proposed line and substituting a railway of 7 furlongs 2½ chains, commencing with a junction with the Stourbridge Extension line at a point 20yd from the southwest side of the Tat Bank Road bridge, to a junction with their authorised Railway No 2 (of 1873) in land and at a wharf in Oldbury; the Act also including an agreement for the GWR to work the line from when it opened.

Again, these powers were not exercised, and the proposers obtained two further Acts, on 4 July 1878 and 11 August 1881, both of which extended the time they were allowed to purchase the land required by two years and the time to construct the line by three years; the second Act also changing the name of the company to the plainer, and more accurate, Oldbury Railway. Completing the line slightly exceeded even this extension of time, as it did not open, to goods, until 7 November 1884. On the same day, the local station on the Stourbridge Extension line was renamed Langley Green. Passenger services began six months later, being delayed by the building of a new station on the Stourbridge Extension line, around its junction with the Oldbury Railway; this having platform faces on both lines and coming into use, with the commencement of passenger services along the Oldbury Railway, on 1 May 1885. With this station, the former one at Langley Green and Rood End station, this portion of the Stourbridge Extension line now boasted now fewer than three stations within half a mile.

Below:
The exposed nature of much of the Old Hill-Dudley line is shown clearly by this early 1960s view of 0-6-0PT No 6434 working a local service near to Darby End station. *Michael Mensing*

Below right:
Darby End's pre-cast concrete platforms and bus shelter-style waiting rooms are clearly visible at the extreme left of this early 1960s view of an auto-train worked local service. *Michael Mensing*

Accordingly, the latter were closed from 1 May 1885.

The Oldbury Railway had sidings at Albright's chemical works, a station on Halesowen Street in the town, and continued beyond this to terminate at a goods shed situated adjacent to an arm of the Birmingham Canal. There were 15 down (to Oldbury) and 15 up (to Langley Green) passenger trains per day on weekdays only, the first down working being of empty stock. Four goods services also ran daily, one of which, the 07.40 from Oldbury, also collected iron ore traffic from Smethwick Junction as required. An agreement as to the long term working of the line by the GWR was signed on 10 August 1886, which sufficed for eight years until the Oldbury Railway was formally amalgamated with the GWR on 1 July 1894.

Passenger services ran on the branch for just under 30 years, being withdrawn as a wartime economy on 3 March 1915. As with a number of lines and stations closed at this time, local people found they could manage without it, and the service was not reinstated.

Above:
Passenger services along the Oldbury Railway were withdrawn from 3 March 1915 but the line remained open to goods until 7 September 1964 and half of it still serves Albright & Wilson's works. On 23 July 1984, Class 31 No 31189 returns from there pushing three ICI tankers towards Langley Green.
Chris Morrison

Birmingham & Henley-in-Arden Railway

The Birmingham area featured a number of railways on which passenger services ran for but a fraction of the time it had taken to see the lines constructed. One such example was the line to Henley-in-Arden. A scheme to link that town with the rail network was first mooted around 1860, when that part of north Warwickshire was being opened up to the railways. This resulted in the formation of a company, the Henley-in-Arden Railway, which secured authorisation for a line between Rowington, a junction with the GWR, to the town in a Act of 28 June 1861; but despite an extension of time Act of 30 June 1864, and the transfer of the company's powers to the GWR on 30 July 1866, they were allowed to lapse.

In the early 1870s, another attempt to build the line was made by a separate company, styling itself the Henley-in-Arden & Great Western Junction Railway. Their chosen route was the same as the earlier scheme, a 3 mile 8 chains long line to Henley-in-Arden from a junction with the GWR at Rowington. This company also secured additional Acts to extend the time allowed for constructing the line; these were passed on 23 June 1884, 7 August 1888 and 28 July 1891; the first of them also changing its name to the Birmingham & Henley-in-Arden Railway. By the last of these Acts, the company had until the end of July 1894 to complete the line, and it was finally opened to passengers on 6 June that year; goods services beginning on 2 July. The line had no intermediate stations, and was worked between Henley-in-Arden and Kingswood (renamed Lapworth on 1 May 1902), the latter being situated adjacent to Rowington Junction.

There were eight down (to Henley-in-Arden) and seven up trains on weekdays, of which three in each direction were mixed goods and passenger services, plus a Sunday service of two trains in each direction; these were operated by the GWR, under the terms of an agreement signed on 4 August 1888. The Henley-in-Arden Railway was amalgamated with the GWR on 1 July 1900. A few years later, ⅔-mile west of Henley-in-Arden station, the Birmingham, North Warwickshire & Stratford-upon-Avon Railway was built. This also had a station to serve Henley-in-Arden, and when the line opened to passengers on 1 July 1908 it made the rather circuitous route there via Lapworth virtually redundant. A 50 chains long link line was built, connecting the two stations, to enable the existing goods facilities there to be used by both lines, although the older passenger station was closed and branch trains from Lapworth were run through to the new Henley-in-Arden station. The branch services fell victim to the GWR's wartime cutbacks introduced on 1 January 1915; goods services being withdrawn on 1 January 1916. There was never any question of the line coming back into use after the war and it was closed officially on 1 January 1917; all but short sections of track at either end being lifted between May and June that year. One of these permitted the old Henley-in-Arden goods station to remain in use until 31 December 1962.

The GWR's Birmingham 'short cuts'

The GWR's way of acquiring trunk routes had its advantages and its disadvantages. Cobbling together a route from bits and pieces found along the way may have saved time and money in Parliamentary and legal fees, and, in some cases, construction; but it tended to produce meandering lines with awkward junctions which did not facilitate fast running.

The period from the late 1880s has been described as the GWR's 'Great Awakening', when the company finally began to do something about improving its train services. On two routes in particular it was loosing out to its rivals. Between Birmingham and Bristol the Midland Railway had a much shorter and more direct route; similarly the LNWR had a more advantageous line between Birmingham and London. Both of these competitors possessed routes which could take full advantage of the faster running made possible by advances in locomotive design; not so the GWR, until, that is, the turn of the century, when they began to rectify matters.

The GWR's Birmingham to Bristol line

Travelling between Birmingham and Bristol by the GWR in the 19th century was for the adventurous only. Replies as to how this could be accomplished were likely to be either 'Change at Didcot' or 'Don't – go by the Midland'. The latter's route was short, 88¾ miles, and, apart from the Lickey incline, easy. On the GWR, via Didcot, the journey was 146¾ miles and took 5hr and 55min, including the change; the carriage of goods being similarly disadvantaged. Revenue was being lost hand over fist, although some GWR goods services began to use the Midland line between Bristol and Gloucester from 1 August 1871. An alternate route between Birmingham and Bristol was made possible by the opening of the Severn Tunnel to goods on 1 September 1886 and to passengers on 1 December that year. This was only 133 miles, but the line was steeply graded as it wound its way through the tunnel, Pontypool Road, Hereford, Malvern, Worcester, Kidderminster and Smethwick Junction. It was a help, but not the solution; that was to come ten years or so later.

Around the turn of the century, the GWR proposed an ingenious new route between Birmingham and Bristol using a combination of existing running powers and new lines, one of which was already authorised. This would branch off the company's new Badminton route to London (opened to passenger services on 1 July 1903) just after it crossed the Midland line for the second time, gaining the latter by means of a triangular junction at Yate. From there, running powers over the Bristol & Gloucester section of the Midland line would be exercised, the line on to Cheltenham being jointly owned with that company. There, a new 21½ mile long line would be built to connect up with the ex-OWW Stratford-on-Avon branch at Honeybourne, which would be doubled and re-engineered to bring it up to main line standard. At Stratford, the route would adopt the newly authorised Birmingham, North Warwickshire & Stratford-on-Avon Railway's (North Warwickshire line) route, to a junction with the GWR main line at Tyseley near Birmingham; this also being altered to make it suitable for express working. Overall, the line be 95 miles long and would have no gradient steeper than 1:150 and no curve sharper than half a mile radius.

Considering these in turn, the Cheltenham & Honeybourne Railway was authorised by the GWR Act of 1 August 1899. Construction began in November 1902, at the Honeybourne end, the line opening in stages: Honeybourne-Toddington, 1 August 1904; Honeybourne (north loop), 1 October 1904; Toddington-Winchcombe, 1 February 1905; Winchcombe-Bishop's Cleeve, 1 June 1906; Bishop's Cleeve-Cheltenham Spa, 1 August 1906, and Honeybourne Loop (east to south junctions) 28 June 1907. A local service was operated along the line, as it progressed, by steam railmotors. At the same time, the doubling and alteration of 14 miles of the Stratford-on-Avon branch was taking place. This also opened in sections: Honeybourne East Junction to a rebuilt station at Long Marston, with an eased gradient from 1:130 to 1:150, 28 April 1907; Long Marston to a rebuilt station at Milcote, 3 March 1907, and Milcote-Stratford-on-Avon East and West Junction, 9 February 1908; other track at Stratford having been doubled in separate schemes undertaken in 1899 and 1902.

So proud were the GWR of their new line that they ran a special 'Press Train' over it between Gloucester and Stratford-on-Avon on 24 May 1907, gaining a

Right:
Bearley aqueduct on the Alcester branch c1906, before the building of the North Warwickshire line. The contraption on the aqueduct support is to allow passing locomotives to be filled from the canal. Well, they're not going to miss a little drop are they?
G. M. Perkins

Above:
The (slightly reduced) junction between the North Warwickshire and B&O lines, curving away to the left, is shown in this view of a DMU special entering Tyseley station on 6 June 1968. Note the yellow front panel; these were an intermediate stage before the adoption of full yellow fronts.
C. C. Thornburn

very favourable feature in the following Friday's *Railway Gazette* in return!

Meanwhile, work was still in progress on the North Warwickshire line. This had been promoted by a separate company and authorised by an Act of 25 August 1894. As incorporated, the company was to have its own independent line to, and station at, Birmingham; the Act authorising a line between Birmingham, to the east side of Moor Street, and Stratford-on-Avon, with connecting lines to the GWR's Alcester branch at Aston Cantlow and to the Midland Railway's Evesham, Redditch & Stratford-on-Avon Railway, at Stratford-on-Avon. The GWR had originally opposed this scheme, successfully delaying it until the promoter's powers had all but expired. At the last minute, the latter 'relented', obtaining a second Act on 9 August 1899, which altered route to one having a new junction with the GWR at Tyseley, and abandoned the independent route to Birmingham. A year later, knowing when they were beaten, the North Warwickshire company and its powers were transferred to the GWR by the latter's Act of 30 July 1900; this also extending the time to allowed to purchase land to 6 July 1902, and to build the line to 25 August 1903.

Had it not been for the new route to Bristol, these powers would also have been allowed to lapse, as the GWR's motives in taking over the North Warwickshire line were largely protective. Even with the new route, they hardly proceeded with it very quickly. The GWR Act of 26 July 1901 altered the

route between Tyseley and Bearley North Junction, adding a new branch from Henley-in-Arden to the former Birmingham & Henley-in-Arden Railway station there; a new loop between Bearley North Junction and Bearley West Junction; also deviating the junction with the company's Alcester branch at Bearley North Junction. Fresh survey work was also required, together with authorisation for a number of deviations to make the line suitable for the fastest and heaviest traffic. Contacts were finally let in 1905, work commencing on the 17¾-mile railway with the unceremonious cutting of the centre line in a field near Henley-in-Arden station on 5 September 1905.

Having finally decided to build the line, the GWR proceeded with it at a pace. They employed 11 steam navvies (excavators) and 23 contractors locomotives on the work. No fewer than 64 bridges were required, 20 of which were located within the first five miles of Tyseley. Of the bridges 29 were over public roads, seven over rivers and canals, 19 were road accommodation bridges and nine river accommodation ones. The use of steam navvies sped up excavation work on cuttings; that at the Tyseley end being commenced in February 1906 and completed during the first week of July that year. Tunnelling was also accelerated through their use in excavating approach cuttings; work on the 264ft Wood End tunnel's south end commencing on 26 April 1906, the last brick being but into the arch at its north end on 22 November. Tyseley station and large goods shed opened on 1 October 1906, a locomotive shed, fitting and repair shops being built there the following year, opening in late August 1908; replacing sheds at Bordesley and Small Heath. A 600ft x 59ft carriage shed, covering four tracks, was also built at Tyseley, coming into use in December 1908.

The North Warwickshire Railway opened to goods on 9 December 1907, the doubled line between Bearley station and Stratford-on-Avon also coming into use on the same day. Passenger

Left:
Building the North Warwickshire line, c1906. This is the site for Henley-in-Arden station looking north towards Birmingham. To the left, the wooden stages are water tanks for servicing the contractors locomotives, which were sheded at this point. In the middle distance the outline of the navvies' shanty town can be made out.
G. M. Perkins

traffic began on 1 July 1908, with intermediate stations at Spring Road, Hall Green, Yardley Wood, Shirley, Grimes Hill (Grimes Hill & Wythall from July 1914), Earlswood Lakes, Wood End, Danzey for Tanworth, Henley-in-Arden and Wootton Wawen. On the same day the GWR introduced two new express services running via the new Birmingham-Bristol route: one just working between Birmingham and Bristol, the other between Wolverhampton and Penzance, stock off the latter joining an existing Paddington-Penzance express at Bristol, which, strengthened thus, departed at 13.10 and arrived at its destination at 19.08.

Below left:
Supplementing the facilities at Tyseley station was a large goods shed which came into use with the rest of the facilities there on 1 July 1906. It is seen here in 1958, its former owner's name refusing to be covered up, as Class 5700 0-6-0PT No 8700 shunts a train of empties. *Michael Mensing*

Moor Street station

Although the Birmingham, North Warwickshire & Stratford-on-Avon Railway's proposed Birmingham terminus would have been built 'to the east side of Moor Street', plans for a station there appeared to have been dropped when the GWR 'persuaded' that company to drop its plans for an independent line to the city. After assuming responsibility for the North Warwickshire line in 1900, no more was heard of a station at Moor Street and it wasn't until construction of the latter was well under way that the idea of building one there was revived. As the *Railway Gazette* reported on 5 October 1906: 'The building of a new station at Moor Street, Birmingham, to relieve Snow Hill, is also under consideration'. This was agreed upon, the necessary powers being sought in the company's Bill the following November; the GWR Act of 18 June 1908 authorising a branch line to, and a new station at, Moor Street.

Work began very quickly thereafter, evinced by this note in the *Railway Gazette* of 4 September 1908: 'The GWR now has in hand the building of an entirely new station at Moor Street, which will . . . be connected with the main line by a short branch, and will be utilised as a small terminus (and) will have three passenger platforms and a siding for fish and fruit traffic'. The station opened, with a single island platform complete, on 1 July 1909; also having a temporary booking office and waiting rooms. It had a service of 21 railmotors, from the North Warwickshire line, and 12 ordinary main line local trains on weekdays only. The station was closed on Sundays, when the railmotor services worked through to Snow Hill. In 1910, a large expansion plan was announced for Moor Street, which was to have a goods station added to the passenger accommodation. That same year also saw the installation of a pair of electrically driven traversers, one on either side of the central island platform. The site was cramped and short, having neither the room for a turntable nor the length for crossovers, and so these traversers were the only practicable means of transferring engines off incoming trains on to outgoing roads. Each traverser was 60ft long by 32ft 10in wide, had three roads and was capable of moving a load of up to 170 tons at 10ft per minute.

Below:
Upon its opening on 1 July 1908, local services along the North Warwickshire line were maintained by steam railmotors. Here, one of them has halted at a very spruce, and newly opened, Danzey for Tanworth station.
H. W. Burman

Above:
Both Moor Street's passenger and goods stations are clearly shown in this 1959 view, which was only made possible through the efforts of Mr Gallagher's workers in clearing Castle Street and Scotland Passage out of the way. This was not done, needless to say, just for the benefit of our photographer, but also to allow the building of Birmingham's inner ring road.
R. S. Carpenter Collection

Quadrupling of the line between Moor Street and Bordesley, which came into use on 16 November 1913, required the building of a new signal box by the station; this had a 114 lever frame and opened on 7 September 1913. Most sources state that the goods station opened on 7 January 1914, but the *Railway Gazette* for 21 April 1916 carried the following, somewhat contradictory, notice: 'MOOR STREET STATION, BIRMINGHAM – The GWR notify the opening of Moor Street Station, Birmingham, for goods traffic'. It had been built on two levels, the upper one comprising a 420ft long shed with a full-length travelling crane and loading platform; the lower one holding 121 wagons which could be positioned by electric capstans and traversers. All goods traffic formerly handled at Bor-

Right:
Work to widen the GWR main line between Birmingham and Acock's Green was undertaken in association with other works to improve the company's route to London. This is a commercial postcard view from c1905 showing the alterations in progress at Acock's Green. Looking towards Birmingham, the original station can be seen, still in use, over to the right.
R. S. Carpenter Collection

desley Goods Depot, save for livestock, was transferred to Moor Street. Permanent station buildings were finally provided by early 1914, but it was not until 1930 that the single-sided Platform No 1, situated by the lines through to Snow Hill, was built.

The GWR's Birmingham to London line

The GWR's handicap in competing with the LNWR to London was less severe than that formerly existing between the company and the Midland Railway over traffic to Bristol. The LNWR's route from Birmingham to London was 113 miles, and could be covered at best in two hours; whereas the GWR's route was 129¼ miles, which could not be covered in under 2hr 25min.

Ironing out this route was undertaken jointly with the Great Central Railway (GC), who, although newly opened to London, needed an alternate approach to the capital to negate a growing dispute with the Metropolitan Railway over use of their joint line south from Quainton Road. It was divided into four sections, with related widening in the Birmingham area. From London, the Acton & Wycombe Railway was a new line between Old Oak Common and High Wycombe, which had been authorised by a GWR Act of 6 August 1897; the portion of the line between Northolt Junction and High Wycombe becoming the joint property of the GWR and GC companies from 1 August 1899. It opened in stages: Old Oak Common (West Junction)-Greenford Junction (East curve), 3 June 1903; Greenford-Greenford Station, 1 October 1904, and Greenford Station-High Wycombe on 2 April 1906. The second section was formed by doubling the Wycombe Railway, which had opened on 1 August 1854; this involved extensive excavation work at High Wycombe and continued the 'new' line on to Princes Risborough. Advancing the line north of Princes Risborough was effected by a second new line, the Princes Risborough & Grendon Underwood Railway, which was authorised by the GWR and GC Acts of 1 August 1899 and opened on 20 November 1905. At Ashendon Junction, this joined a third new line, the Aynho & Ashendon Railway, or 'Bicester Cut-off ', which was authorised by a GWR Act of 11 July 1905 and connected with the old main line at Aynho. It opened to goods on 4 April 1910 and to passengers on 1 July.

Associated with the above was work to widen the GWR main line between Birmingham and Acock's Green, which would soon have the accelerated services of two main lines concentrated upon it. This began in 1905 and opened in sections: Olton-Acock's Green, 1906; Olton-Tyseley, January 1907; Tyseley-Small Heath, May 1908; Small Heath south-Small Heath north, July 1910; Bordesley-Moor Street, 16 November 1913 and Small Heath north-Bordesley, 1914.

The GWR's new route between Birmingham and London opened on 1 July 1910. It was 110½ miles, 19 less than the old route via Oxford, and two less than the LNWR, enabling expresses to run to Birmingham in two hours; a service of five trains in each direction working to these timings being introduced on the same date.

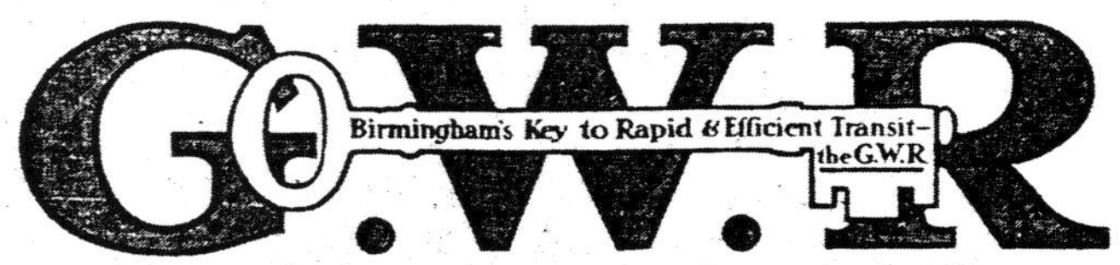

Birmingham's Twentieth-Century Railway

NEW PASSENGER STATION - NEW CENTRAL GOODS STATION—SUPERB EXPRESS SERVICES FROM LONDON, WEST OF ENGLAND, WALES AND SOUTH COAST TOWNS. THROUGH —SERVICES NORTH, WEST AND SOUTH.—

The Railway is a city's great arm of Expansion and progress, and a study of such local railway communications as those afforded to Birmingham by the Great Western Railway is of vital importance to all interested in Birmingham as a progressive city and its people as a progressive community.

Take up the map in any Great Western "Official Time Table" and it will be found that the G.W.R links up Birmingham with all the great sources of supply and with the national seaports. Birmingham is the hub of a great railway system which throws out its lines in all directions, affording access to and from the natural geographical seaports of the Midlands; to and from London (by shortest Route), and communication with the teeming districts of Wales, West of England, etc.

The G.W.R. has been aptly named Birmingham's "Twentieth Century Line." not only because of its new route to and from London and its many improvements, but because a new twentieth century railway station is under construction at Snow Hill, and a finely equipped Central Goods Depôt at Moor Street. The new stations are being completely equipped with modern time and labour-saving machinery, the advantage of which the business people of Birmingham will not be slow to appreciate

The G.W.R. affords an excellent means of communication for both goods and passengers from and to the Birmingham district, it gives Birmingham a service passenger and goods train services of the highest utility from and to all parts of the Kingdom, and opens up for Birmingham residents the best holiday districts in Britain.

ADVANTAGES OF G.W.R. TRAVEL.

The G.W.R is famed for its excellent road-bed and smooth travelling Its locomotives are of the most powerful type. The passenger trains are models of modern travel comfort. There are well-appointed restaurant cars on this Line; ladies' compartments are at ladies' disposal; the Company's servants are noted for courtesy and attention; and the perfection of the G.W.R. permanent way, signalling methods, rolling stock and the general arrangements of the system, all combine to give the Great Western Railway the title of "Britain's Best Equipped Railway."

GREAT WESTERN RAILWAY,

FRANK POTTER. *General Manager.*

Right:
By the time of World War 1, the GWR had ploughed millions into modernising every aspect of its operations in Birmingham; a fact with which they were justifiably proud. It speaks for itself, but note that the company almost uses the term 'rapid transit' – not bad for 1913!
Pete Glews Collection

The Bridgnorth & Wolverhampton Railway

On 7 November 1904, the GWR introduced a bus service between Bridgnorth and Wolverhampton using three paraffin-fired single-deck Clarkson steam buses; but local hills got the better of them, and they were replaced by petrol-driven buses from 10 April 1905. These proved so successful over the 14 mile/90min journey, that the daily service of four buses each way was augmented by two new ones which ran over branch routes opened to Pattingham, in May 1906, and to Claverley, in December 1911.

These services ran in lieu of building of a railway between Bridgnorth and Wolverhampton, a line of that name (B&W), having been authorised on 11 July 1905, by that year's GWR (New Railways) Act. This was to unite two lines near Trysull, a new one, running South from Dunstall Park, Wolverhampton, and an extension of the ex-OWW Kingswinford branch (which had opened on 14 November 1858), with a new line to join the GWR's Severn Valley line at Bridgnorth. This scheme was altered by the GWR Act of June 18th 1908, which diverted the line through Wombourn. Construction was delayed by negotiations with the Earl of Dudley; who had plans to expand his coal mining activities at Pensnett Chase. So, to combine serving these with building the new line, the GWR decided to concentrate its initial construction work on the Kingswinford-Wolverhampton section of the B&W scheme.

The GWR Act of June 1913 revised this scheme further and work on the line to Bridgnorth was officially postponed. That autumn, contractors began work, continuing until sometime in 1916, when wartime shortages of men and materials became acute. Work resumed, in a somewhat piecemeal fashion, after the war, but it was abandoned in the spring of 1920; the contractors plant being auctioned over two days, 12-13 May. Around the middle of 1921, the GWR assumed the task of completing the line, the Board, a little begrudgingly, authorising the additional £173,000 required under an Act of 29 June 1923. Most of the outstanding work was at the line's northern end, its junction with the ex-S&B line at Oxley being opened on 11 January 1925, along with a new signal box to control this: 'Oxley North Box'; the former North box becoming 'Oxley Middle Box'.

Passenger services, between Stourbridge Junction and Wolverhampton Low Level via Wombourn, began on 11 May 1925, and were operated by steam railmotors. The whole journey took between 50 and 54min. Intermediate halts were opened at: Brockmoor, Bromley, Pensnett, Gornal, Himley, Penn and Compton, and stations were provided at Wombourn, between Himley and Penn Halts, and at Tettenhall; these being amongst the last traditional GWR stations to be built in the country. From Tettenhall, the railmotors operated into a bay at the Shrewsbury end of Wolverhampton Low Level station, via a junction with the S&B line at Oxley. A basic basic service of 14 trains (seven up; seven down) was provided on weekdays only, three of which were short workings to and from Wombourn, two of which were in the middle of the day.

The public's use of these services was always less than the GWR had anticipated. There were good reasons for this. Through passengers between Stourbridge and Wolverhampton had the choice of the established ex-OWW route, both nine minutes quicker and serving more populous towns en route; and the majority of those served by the B&W's halts and stations had little need to travel anywhere that it went. The line had probably been completed more for the sake of doing so than to meet any real need, other than for goods services; a branch to serve the large Courtaulds factory at Dunstall Hall opened in August 1927. With little surprise, passenger services were withdrawn on 31 October 1932.

From that time, the B&W line, or 'Wombourn branch' as it became known, saw only occasional passenger services, other than non-stopping diversions and specials. From 6-10 July 1937, Tettenhall station was reopened to serve passenger to the Royal Agricultural Society's 'Royal Show', which was being held that year in Wrottesley Park Wolverhampton; an additional platform and siding being added for the occasion. In World War 2, D-Day wounded were brought by 40 or so trains to be off-loaded at Tettenhall and Wombourn stations en route to Wolverhampton's New Cross Hospital. Perhaps the real measure of the public's perceived need for the line can be seen in the response to a public meeting held in Wombourn on 30 June 1961 to discuss the prospects of reopening it to passengers; only 25 people attended !

The Hatton to Bearley widening

By the mid-1930s, the section of single line between Hatton and Bearley was carrying an increasing load passenger and freight traffic between the Midlands and South Wales, Bristol and the West of England, in particular the 07.40 and 18.30 West of England departures from Birmingham, which were so routed through overcrowding on the more accustomed express route. And so the GWR decided to upgrade the line; a scheme to this effect being announced in early December 1936. This included the doubling of about 4½ miles of track, the widening of five road bridges and the removal of over 27,000cu yds of earth. At Bearley, the up platform was to be extended to 440ft and the down one to 550ft; Claverdon, the only intermediate station, was to be rebuilt about 150yds nearer Bearley, providing a new booking office at road level and electric platform lighting. Work commenced in the spring of 1937 and was completed by the end of that year.

The Development of Passenger Services

When the GWR's Traffic Department was reorganised in 1865/6, a new Birmingham Division was created; final recognition from the company that the town had a greater importance than that of a mere 'northern extension'. From that time onwards the GWR developed a range of local and express services to serve the ever growing needs of the emerging city of Birmingham.

1 – The Development of Local Passenger Services

The task of converting the GWR's Birmingham local services to run on the narrow gauge began in late 1868; a comparatively simple matter where mixed gauge lines existed, more administration than engineering. All of the local trains between Birmingham and Wolverhampton ceased running on the broad gauge from 1 November 1868, although the pattern of services remained very similar, despite the more generous timings the GWR typically allowed its narrow gauge trains. The mixed gauge lines between Oxford and Stafford Road Wolverhampton; on the Bordesley link to the Midland Railway in Birmingham (opened 1 November 1861); on the spur to LNWR at Wednesbury (opened 1 June 1859), and between Hatton and the Stratford-on-Avon Railway station, on the Birmingham Road, were all converted to the narrow gauge on 1 April 1869.

Almost 40 years later, in October 1908, the GWR began to withdraw second-class accommodation on trains in the Birmingham area, beginning with services on the West Midland lines. In doing this they were way behind the Midland Railway, who abolished it in January 1875, but ahead of the LNWR by four years. This said, the GWR took a long time over the change. Both of its rivals managed it at a stroke, and nationally to boot; but by 1 May 1909 the elimination of second-class was said to be 'virtually complete', but was not actually so until 1 July 1910!

As with the other railway companies serving Birmingham, the period leading up to the outbreak of World War 1 was the heyday for local rail services. Tram competition had done most of its damage; motor buses were still in their spluttering infancy, and, down the road at Longbridge, Mr Austin had yet to

Left:
The oldest new stations in the area. Long after passenger services ceased on 31 October 1932, and not long before final closure, the Wombourn line is used by the 17.00 Oxley-Worcester freight service, hauled by ex-GWR 2-8-0 No 2865.
Geoffrey F Bannister

popularise private motoring. And so Birmingham enjoyed an unrivalled local service, especially from the GWR. The stations immediately adjoining Snow Hill were particularly favoured by intensive services. Along the BW&D line to Wolverhampton, the stations between Snow Hill and Swan Village received a triple service, having calls from trains on the Wolverhampton, Dudley and Stourbridge routes. On weekdays, Hockley had 58 up (to Snow Hill) and 49 down trains; Soho & Winson Green 35 up and 33 down, and Handsworth and Smethwick 56 up and 57 down.

The line to Dudley branched off the BW&D at Swan Village. It had been authorised by a GWR Act of 13 July 1863 and opened, with a single intermediate station at Great Bridge and a branch to Swan Village Basin, on 1 September 1866. The average passenger service along the line consisted of 11 trains in each direction on weekdays with six on Sundays. This was withdrawn from 29 November 1915 as a wartime economy measure, and not reinstated until 5 January 1920. Later, under BR(WR), Great Bridge gained the suffix 'South' to distinguish it from the former LNWR station nearby. Along the Stourbridge Extension line there was a particularly intensive service of 23 stopping trains and eight semi-fasts on weekdays, with 11 and four of these respectively on Sundays. In addition, on weekdays there was a morning short working between Snow Hill and Langley Green, and one evening peak hours Stourbridge service which started at Hockley; both with corresponding return workings each evening and morning respectively.

As noted earlier, a number of GWR services to the south of Birmingham terminated at Moor Street station. On weekdays there were four each way workings to Shirley, five to Earlswood , 12 to Henley-in-Arden and five to Stratford-on-Avon; some of the shorter runs being worked by steam railmotors. These destinations were also served directly from Snow Hill on weekdays, with one each way service running to Shirley, one to Earlswood, two to Hen-

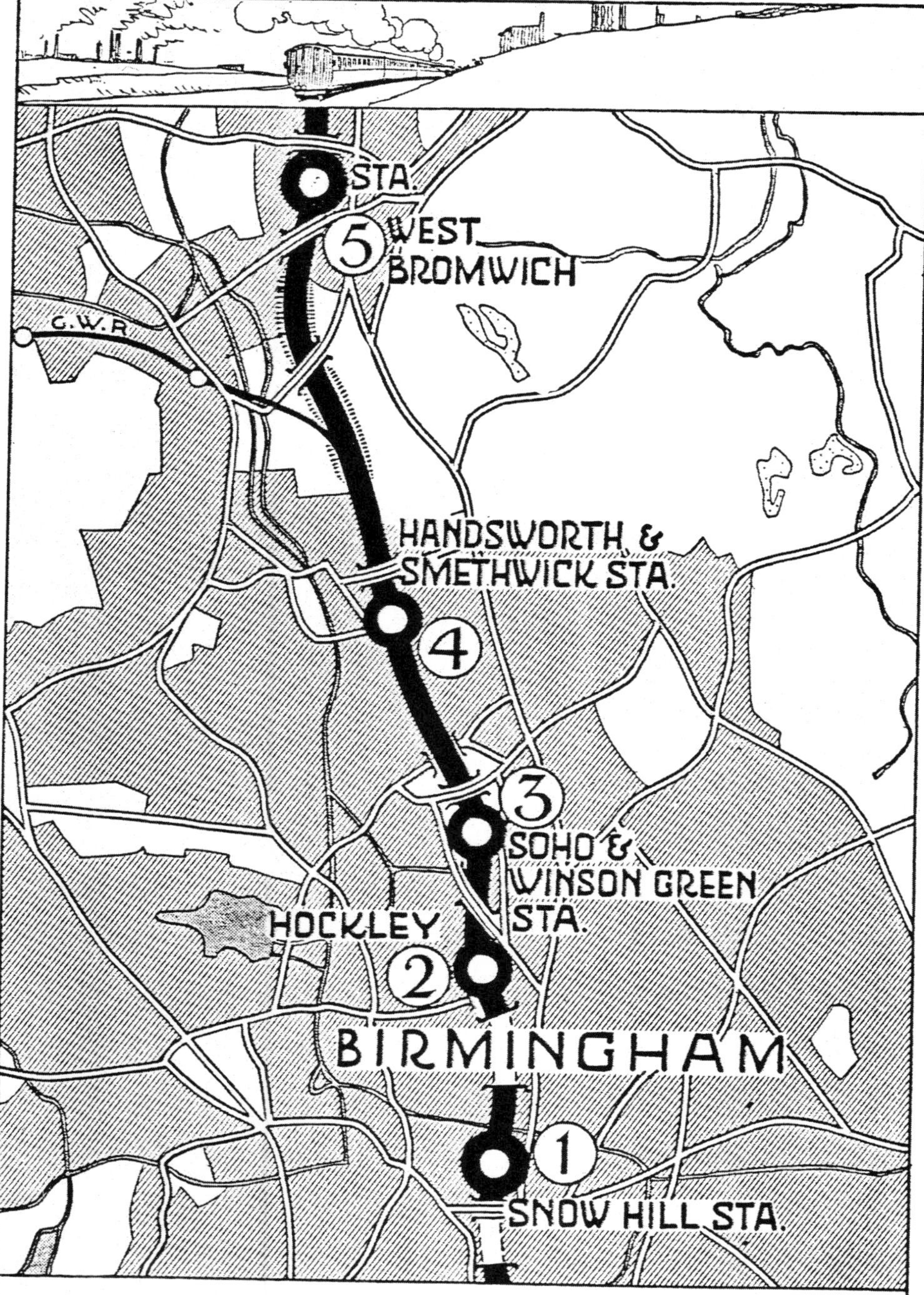

Left:
How the GWR saw Birmingham: an illustration from *Through the Window – Paddington to Birkenhead*, one of a series of lineside guides published by the company in the 1920s.
Author's Collection

Left:
Spring Road Platform is the first station from Tyseley on the North Warwickshire line and opened with the route on 1 July 1908. It is seen here as a six-car DMU (Suburban/Cross-Country) passes with the 11.36 Moor Street to Stratford-on-Avon service on 31 July 1961.
Michael Mensing

Below left:
This three-car multi-unit railbus was produced by ACV Sales Ltd in 1952. Each unit was just over 40ft long and the outer units were each powered by an AEC six-cylinder diesel engine delivering 125hp. Despite their sleek appearance, in a grey and red livery, they gave an awful ride; and this driver 'having a minute' at Solihull station, might have hoped no passengers had spotted him.
Ian Allan Library

ley and 10 to Stratford; a slightly reduced form of this being operated on Sundays, when Moor Street was closed. Also, like the stations to Handsworth & Smethwick, those to Tyseley received an intensive service from local trains working the B&O and North Warwickshire lines; Bordesley, Small Heath and Tyseley having an average of 60 trains calling on weekdays and about 30 on Sundays.

Services to Leamington Spa ran from Snow Hill, there being 17 slow and three semi-fast trains each way on weekdays, plus one morning working which ran through from Wolverhampton. On Sundays this was reduced to four slow trains each way from Snow Hill with no fewer than five each way trains to and from Wolverhampton and beyond; including the 16.15 stopping service from Liverpool Central (Low Level).

A number of branch lines and stations were closed in the Birmingham area on 1 January 1917 through staff shortages due to the war; some of which did not reopen when the hostilities were over. In October 1924, the GWR placing new trains in service for its Birmingham suburban services. These had a special feature of centre couplings, which dispensed with the need for buffers and minimised oscillation. Each train was capable of accommodating 80 first-class and 220 third-class passengers.

During the 1930s, to compete more fairly with increasing competition from motor buses, the GWR invested heavily in the building of new quickly erected stations. Usually unstaffed and situated adjacent to new housing developments, these were given the status of halts; the idea being that if they generated a good deal of new traffic their somewhat basic facilities could be improved; and if they failed to do so they could be closed and removed at little cost. The first such station in the Birmingham area was at The Hawthorns, situated between the Handsworth & Smethwick and West Bromwich stations on the BW&D line, which opened on 25 December 1931. This was for occasion use only, timetables noting that it was; 'opened when

Top right:
Local services between Snow Hill and Dudley were worked by diesel railcars for many years. This service became known as the 'Dudley Dodger' and on 18 February 1958, railcar No W14 had dodged its last for the day, and was waiting to cross to the down-side of the station.
Michael Mensing

Above right:
The Hawthorns Halt was opened on 25 December 1931, an unusual date for an unusual station. More of an excursion platform, it was only open when there was a football match at The Hawthorns, the nearby ground of West Bromwich Albion. Here, on 25 March 1961, there is a match against Everton, and ex-LMS Class 5 No 44907 is pulling away after disgorging its passengers on a special working from Liverpool Lime Street. Behind, through the bridge, Handsworth Junction signal box, controlling the line to Stourbridge, can be glimpsed.
Michael Mensing

Right:
One of the first runs of the GWR diesel railcars is creating quite a lot of interest at Snow Hill. This is probably a demonstration run, spot the white uniformed driver, and pictured in c1935.
Ian Allan Library

Football Matches are being played on the West Bromwich Albion Football Ground which is adjacent. See local announcements'. A second halt, The Lakes, situated between Earlswood Lakes and Wood End stations on the North Warwickshire line, was opened on 3 June 1935; a third, Whitlock's End Halt, between Shirley and Grimes Hill & Wythall stations, also on the North Warwickshire line, being opened on 6 July 1936. Both of the latter proved their worth and remain open to this day.

World War 2 brought slight service reductions on all of the GWR's local Birmingham lines, which did not return to their prewar service levels by the time of Nationalisation. There were some slight improvements though, such

Above:
The introduction of DMUs on most WR services in the Birmingham area changed the face of Snow Hill station. On 26 September 1959, two three-car sets forming the 12.10 Cardiff-Stratford-on-Avon service has just arrived, coming to rest under the station's perfect natural lighting.
Michael Mensing

Left:
Smethwick Junction was once much more complicated than the present arrangement. This shot of the 11.50 Snow Hill-Cardiff service, formed by two three-car Swindon 'Cross-Country' DMU sets, entering Smethwick station on 25 September 1960, shows the link to Galton Junction curving away to the right and two curious little sidings. The former was taken out of use four months later. *Michael Mensing*

Right:
In preparation for the take-over of local WR services by DMUs on 17 June 1957, driver instruction was given along the lines affected. Here, on 4 May that year, a unit returns from such an exercise along the Leamington and Stratford lines, pulling out of Tyseley station into the specially adapted carriage sidings there.
Michael Mensing

as the introduction of an express diesel railcar service from Malvern Wells (08.21) to Malvern and Snow Hill, calling at principal stations, and returning at 11.20 to Worcester, where it arrived at 12.24. There were few changes to the pre-Nationalisation service pattern prior to the introduction of DMUs on local Western Region services from 17 June 1957. These worked services from both Snow Hill and Moor Street, serving stations to Wolverhampton, Wellington, Kidderminster, Dudley, Bewdley, Leamington Spa and Stratford-on-Avon. With their quick turnaround ability, these units allowed some increases in passenger services, although 10 lightly loaded Birmingham Western Region local services, including some to Wolverhampton, were cut-out in the first major reorganisation these had received since Nationalisation; which took effect from 5 March 1962.

Towards the end of the period under consideration, local passenger services were withdrawn on the Cheltenham & Honeybourne line on 7 March 1960; and, in a move that was soon both regretted and revoked, the curve between Smethwick West and Galton Junction taken out of use in January 1961. The following year, BR(WR) withdrew the passenger service between Stourbridge Junction and Wolverhampton Low Level on 30 July 1962; all of the intermediate stations, except Dudley, being closed to passengers.

2 – *Express Passenger Services*

Birmingham's first GWR expresses were those over the BW&D; B&O, and O&R lines to Paddington via Didcot, which began running to there on 1 October 1852. On the broad gauge, they were initially scheduled to do the trip in 2hr 45mins, but this was a little ambitious, and they were rescheduled to three hours dead, to match the corresponding LNWR Euston-Birmingham expresses.

The key element in the development of this express service was rivalry with the LNWR. In spite of the disadvantage, until 1910, of a longer route; the GWR was quite capable of matching the LNWR almost minute for minute on any improvements they introduced. Occasionally though, one company took a small lead, such as when the GWR reduced its time to Birmingham to 2hr 50mins from 1 March 1859, whilst the LNWR's remained at three hours. As the GWR opened more narrow gauge routes, such as that to South Wales, via Worcester and Hereford, on 18 April 1864, its broad gauge services became increasingly isolated; restricting the planning of through services. They were also resented by passengers, who had to change trains in order to continue their journeys. More and more broad gauge duties were changed over to the narrow gauge, until, from 1 November 1868, only the 19.30 Birmingham-Paddington and the 18.15 Paddington-Birmingham services were run over the broad gauge; these finally ceasing from 1 April 1869.

The 1870s was a difficult decade for the GWR. Its attention was diverted away from the West Midlands by a massive programme of gauge conversion in the West and South Wales, but

North of Oxford no improvements were made. Only one train a day offered travel to Birmingham in under three hours, the others taking between 3hr 20mins and four hours. There were many problems, not the least of which was the state of the track. Much of this was the older style 'baulk road'; broad gauge 'bridge' rail, laid on longitudinal sleepers, which many drivers said was 'stiff' and harder to work. Some reckoned it to be like hauling an extra two carriages compared to a train on the more conventional transverse sleepered track.

The first signs of improvement came on 1 June 1880, with the introduction of the 16.45 Paddington-Birkenhead express, which reached Birmingham in 2hr 42min, and Birkenhead in 5hr 17min. This became known as the 'Zulu', or sometimes the 'Afghan' or 'Northern Zulu', to distinguish it from the Paddington-Penzance service which had been given this quite unofficial name when it had been introduced one year earlier; being introduced at the height of the Zulu War, whose warriors were reputed for their speed. For most of this time, the burden of working the Birmingham-Paddington expresses fell on the GWR 7ft single locomotives from the '999' or '157' classes, the Wolverhampton pool of Nos 999; 1000; 1116; 1121; 1127, and Nos 157; 160; 161; 164, being the nine engines mainly responsible; typically being called upon to work the four daily turns to London.

It took nearly a decade for Birmingham's expresses to improve. In 1889, an extra Paddington express was introduced to supplement the six daily 'fasts' that worked through to Shrewsbury, but it was not until July 1891 that three additional expresses were introduced to Paddington, in response to LNWR competition. From then onwards, improvements came more rapidly. A corridor train, the first on the GWR, was introduced on 1 March 1892 on the 13.30 Paddington-Birkenhead service, and on 1 July 1896 the company introduced the first express to run non-stop between Paddington and Leamington, via Didcot, which took 2hr 27min to reach Birmingham. On 1 July 1898 a new service commenced to Liverpool Central (Low Level) via the Mersey Tunnel. Journey times began to fall too. Although a non-stop Paddington-Birmingham express, inaugurated

Above:
'The Inter City', a name that never really caught on, began to run between Paddington and Wolverhampton on 25 September 1950. On 20 April 1956, the 09.00 working of this service, hauled by No 6015 *King Richard III*, waits to make the final leg of its journey to Low Level station.
Michael Walker

for the summer timetable on 1 July 1898, first completed the run in the familiar 2hr 27min, it took two minutes off this in 1899, including slipping a coach at Leamington, and reduced it by four more in 1901. Water troughs had been installed to remove stops en route to Birmingham, but other improvements brought new problems. The GWR's new 70ft 'Dreadnought' coaches, introduced on 1 July 1904, were too wide, at 9ft 6in, to work north of Wolverhampton, limiting them to the Paddington expresses.

Two hour timings between Paddington and Birmingham were only finally achieved on 1 July 1910, with the complete opening of the GWR's new joint route to London, described earlier. The year also heralded a major step forward in the range of GWR's services from Birmingham. A number of joint services were introduced on 1 October 1910. Three joint services were arranged with the Midland Railway: Weston-super-Mare-Birkenhead; Torquay-Wolverhampton, and Penzance-Wolverhampton; with one train in each direction per day. Jointly with the London & South Western Railway (L&SW) and the LNWR, a service was introduced between Bournemouth West, Manchester and Birkenhead. This was worked by the L&SW to Oxford, the GWR working it on through Birmingham to Wolverhampton where it was split; one portion going non-stop to Crewe via Wellington, to be attached to an LNWR train to Manchester; the other being taken on by the GWR, stopping at major stations to Birkenhead. Returning, the two portions would be united at Wolverhampton.

Finally, two joint services with the South Eastern & Chatham Railway (SE&C) also began that day. 'The Continental Express' ran between Wolverhampton-Birmingham-London (Victoria)-Dover and Paris, in 11¾hr, the inaugural run being taken by 'Atbara' class No 3384 *Omdurman*, which worked the stock, of three carriages plus a restaurant car, through to Kensington (Addison Road), where an SE&C locomotive took over. The other joint through service with the latter ran from Deal and Dover to Birkenhead. To supplement these, a service of Sunday Paddington expresses began the following day, 2 October 1910.

One year later, on 2 October 1911, the company introduced a new two hour luncheon car service to Birmingham, the 13.00 ex-Paddington. This became the 10th two hour train by the new route, there now being six down and four up. The luncheon train stopped at Leamington and returned on the same schedule from Birmingham at 16.50. It was sampled by a writer for the *Railway Gazette* on its inaugural day, who commented that it would become: 'very popular with businessmen as it would enable them to perform the journey between tea and dinner time'. How convenient! They could therefore arrive at Birmingham, sated and refreshed, and step into the building site which Snow Hill station represented at that time.

The 1915 GWR summer timetable boasted 13 Birmingham-Paddington expresses, nine of which had restaurant or tea cars, but these services and facilities were cut-back as the war progressed and staff shortages increased. Timings and service improved gradually after the war, and on 2 July 1923 the company introduced new carriage stock on its Paddington to Birkenhead route. These consisted of seven vehicles, varying in length between 70 and 71ft 8¼in and a uniform width of nine feet, formed as follows: Brake Third, Third, First & Third Composite, Dining Car, First & Third Composite, Third, and Brake Third. They were painted in the then new company livery, with waists and bottom panels in chocolate, and top panels, above the waist, in cream; the whole surmounted by a white roof and lined in black edged with yellow. One unusual feature was the use of automatic 'Buckeye' couplers, and drop-down buffers. The latter were stowed out of the way when the stock was coupled by the Buckeyes, but locked into place if it had to be joined to conventional screw-coupled carriages.

By the early 1930s, with almost every improvement possible made on the rails, the GWR introduced its own air service between Birmingham and Plymouth on 22 May 1933. This flew out of Castle Bromwich Aerodrome,

Below:
With a journey time of just 2hr 5min to Paddington, the 'Birmingham Pullman' proved very popular and quickly became an established feature of the scene at Snow Hill. In this 1961 view, whilst his owner seems interested in the sleek lines of the new units, the dog has other things on its mind. *Michael Mensing*

Below right:
The 'Birmingham Pullman' brought a new standard of luxury to the Paddington-Wolverhampton service upon its introduction on 12 September 1960. The Pullman set is seen here in Snow Hill on 26 April 1965 whilst a Stanier Class 8F passes with a southbound freight.
Ian M. Slater

which, to the company's embarrassment, was well situated on the LMS; and so passengers were taken from Snow Hill by bus. The aircraft made a number of calls, and a good day out could be spent doing the whole trip. Take-off at Castle Bromwich was a 09.30, landing at Cardiff at 10.40, taking off again at 11.00 and arriving at Haldon Aerodrome at 11.50. The final leg left Haldon at 11.55 and landed at Roborough Aerodrome at 12.20, where a bus conveyed passengers to Plymouth North Road station for 12.40. Returning from there at 15.20, the whole journey was repeated in reverse, arriving back at Snow Hill at 19.20. From 7 May 1934, a northern leg was added to Speke Aerodrome, near Liverpool, taking 45min. Return fares from Birmingham were: to Plymouth, £4 10s (£4.50); Cardiff, £2 10s (£2.50); and Liverpool, £2 5s (£2.25).

More service reductions followed the outbreak of World War 2; the express passenger service between Birmingham and Bristol, for example, being withdrawn quite quickly, on 25 September 1939, not being reinstated until 1 October 1945. After the war important additions were made to the GWR's express service between London and Birmingham on 4 March 1946. An express restaurant car left Paddington at 09.00, arriving at Snow Hill at 11.15, after a call at High Wycombe. This was booked for a 52mph start to stop run between the latter and Birmingham, and was then the fastest service on the route. After Nationalisation, the basic pattern of former GWR services was retained, with additions. 'The Inter City' Paddington-Birmingham-Wolverhampton express was introduced on 25 September 1950, and between 18 June and 23 September 1951 'The William Shakespeare' ran to Paddington via Stratford-on-Avon, in connection with The Festival of Britain; this being one of five Festival trains, the first to be formed of the new BR Standard Mk 1 corridor coaches and dining cars.

British Railways' Modernisation Plan, published in January 1955, heralded the adoption of diesel traction, and in April 1957 it was announced that they intended to build 'diesel-electric multi-car deluxe trains to operate at high speed between London, Birmingham and Wolverhampton (WR)'. These were the Blue Pullmans, which were introduced on 12 September 1960. They could maintain speeds of 90mph, and regularly arrived ahead of schedule. Each eight-car train could seat 108 first-class passengers and 120 second-class ones; all of the seats being bookable.

Further changes were made in 1962. On 24 July it was announced that the service to Penzance, named 'The Cornishman' from 18 June 1951 onwards, would, from 10 September, no longer run through Snow Hill, but would start from Sheffield Midland, running via Derby and Birmingham New Street to Bristol and Penzance. In later years this would be extended to run from Bradford Forster Square. It was also announced that from 10 September 1962 an existing Wolverhampton-Birmingham-Bournemouth service would be given the name of the LMR's famed 'Pines Express', and be rescheduled to start from Manchester, as part of the West Coast main line electrification scheme.

On 14 August 1962, it was also announced that new 'Western' diesel-hydraulics would replace the ex-GWR 'King' class locomotives, the mainstay of the Paddington-Birmingham expresses for 35 years, on 10 September. Crew training on the hydraulics had taken place throughout the period of the summer timetable (11 June – 16 September), when No D1004 *Western Crusader* had been used on the 06.50 and 10.15 Wolverhampton-Stourbridge local services and their 07.55 and 11.50 returns, until 30 July. A fortnight later No D1000 *Western Enterprise*; No D1002 *Western Explorer*, and No D1005 *Western Venturer*, together with No D1004, were allocated to Oxley shed and began to run regularly on the

Top:
The essence of Snow Hill: 'Kings', sunlight, wide platforms and expectant crowds. No 6002 *King William IV* pulls into Platform No 7 on 18 August 1962 with the 06.30 Birkenhead-Paddington express. A pity then that just three weeks later the 'Kings' would be withdrawn, and the station would be catapulted into its decline.
B. J. Ashworth

Above:
The through roads at Snow Hill were necessary as, in addition to a vast number of passenger services, the station also saw a lot of freight traffic. Here, No 7810 *Draycott Manor* takes the up through road with an up class H freight on Sunday 13 September 1953.
E. D. Bruton

Wolverhampton-Birmingham-Paddington service, working the 10.35 up and 16.10 down services on Mondays to Thursdays, and taking an earlier turn on Fridays and Saturdays.

'Last King' specials were run on 8-9 September, the first regular run of No D1000 on the 10.35 Wolverhampton Low Level-Paddington service on 10 September being marred only by a faulty signal at Wednesbury, which made it 20mins late arriving at Paddington. This was possibly an omen of things to come, for, despite BR(WR)'s hopes for these, they presented reliability and availability problems during their early months of service, resulting in a number of steam substitutions, including, on at least three occasions, turns by officially withdrawn 'King' class locomotives. On 30 October 1962 No 6011 King James I worked the 09.35 up service, deputising for a failed Western; that 17 November No 6000 *King George V* worked the up 16.35 'Inter City', and on 21 December *King James I* worked the Paddington-Birmingham-Wolverhampton leg of the 10.50 down service to Shrewsbury.

The Development of Goods Services and Facilities

The GWR's goods operations in Birmingham were based around four major installations which were arrayed along its B&O/BW&D main line, to either side of Snow Hill station. The company had extensive sidings at Bordesley. These were developed over the years, coming to have a total wagon capacity of 1,291. They were grouped into six sections, each adapted to receive/despatch specialised traffic. A seven line 'Baltic Yard' had a capacity of 241 wagons and handled traffic for Gloucester, Bristol and the west. Adjoining this was a seven line Sorting Sidings, which was for up and down traffic shunted off the LNWR/LMS and had a total wagon capacity of 214; four Reception Roads serving as reception lines for up to 136 wagons of inbound traffic from these. Local passenger trains were made up, and cripples stored, on a seven line Baulks Yard which had a capacity of 313 wagons. Completing the facilities at Bordesley were a three line, 161 wagon capacity, Pilot Lines Siding, for traffic bound for the Midland/LMS at Washwood Heath and Lawley Street, and a five line Old Yard, for marshaling up to 226 wagons worth of down traffic.

At Hockley, the GWR had its major goods depot. It came to comprise two large sheds, one for outwards goods, one for inwards goods, plus a bonded store; all of which were situated on the up side of the BW&D main line opposite the passenger station. Work to quadruple the lines through Hockley began in 1907, an opportunity being taken to improve the rail connections to, and interconnections within, the goods depot, which was also considerably increased. The completed scheme came into use on 3 May 1909. Hockley was linked to a goods yard at Soho & Winson Green by means of a ¾-mile long pilot line, which ran alongside the down goods line. It also had a canal basin, which was closed in January 1958; all BTC boatage services in the area having been discontinued from 1 April 1954.

A second large goods shed was built at Small Heath. This was eventually 442ft long, providing berthing for 21 wagons, and was served by an extensive yard with a Metals Shed and a total wagon capacity of 1,366. The latter comprised seven groups of sidings. A six line Caledonia Yard dealt with up to 480 wagons worth of traffic for the LNWR/LMS lines and for its sister depot at Hockley and those on the way to Wolverhampton. An eight line Small Heath Goods Yard specialised in timber and other heavy items, plus transhipments, from up to 306 wagons, and a four line Field Traffic Siding marshalled up to 138 wagons worth of LNWR/LMS traffic. The oddly named Empty Shed Sidings held 152 wagons on four lines, and another four line North End Traffic Siding held up to 150 wagons of rough traffic off the Caledonia Sidings to be marshalled. Completing the yard was a two line North End Mileage Yard, handling up to 70 wagons for the Metals Shed and traffic bound for Bordesley; plus a 70 wagon, three line, Metal Shed Roads siding for inbound metals traffic.

Small Heath was modernised extensively after World War 2 and on 14 February 1957 a new Universal Chain Conveyor was ceremonially inaugurated there. This consisted of three parallel endless chains which ran in channels around the whole shed, enabling returned empties to be handles direct from truck to cartage front. It moved at 40ft per minute and eliminated the need for the unnecessary handling of items as all of the wagons kept circulating. Using this conveyor, an average of 42 wagons, or two shed loads, were discharged during an average working day.

A large goods warehouse was built alongside the existing yard at Soho & Winson Green in the early 1930s. This was five-storeys tall and had a reinforced concrete frame, being 300ft long, 74ft wide and 60ft high. A pair of symmetrical canopies, cantilevered 17 feet, ran along the entire length of the warehouse at first floor level. It cost £23, 000 to build and came into use in December 1932. Shortly after opening, the local brewery firm of Mitchells & Butlers negotiated to take almost the whole of the top floor and part of the second to store hops, barley and sugar. They had previously brought this by road from London, but from October 1933 brought it all by rail; a considerable coup for the GWR.

Below:
Snow Hill did handle a great deal of parcels traffic, with most of the underground parts of the station being set aside for this business. On 17 April 1961, Gloucester RCW built parcels unit No W55994 stands on the up through road, waiting for the clear.
Michael Mensing

5: Birmingham's Railways from 1963 to the present

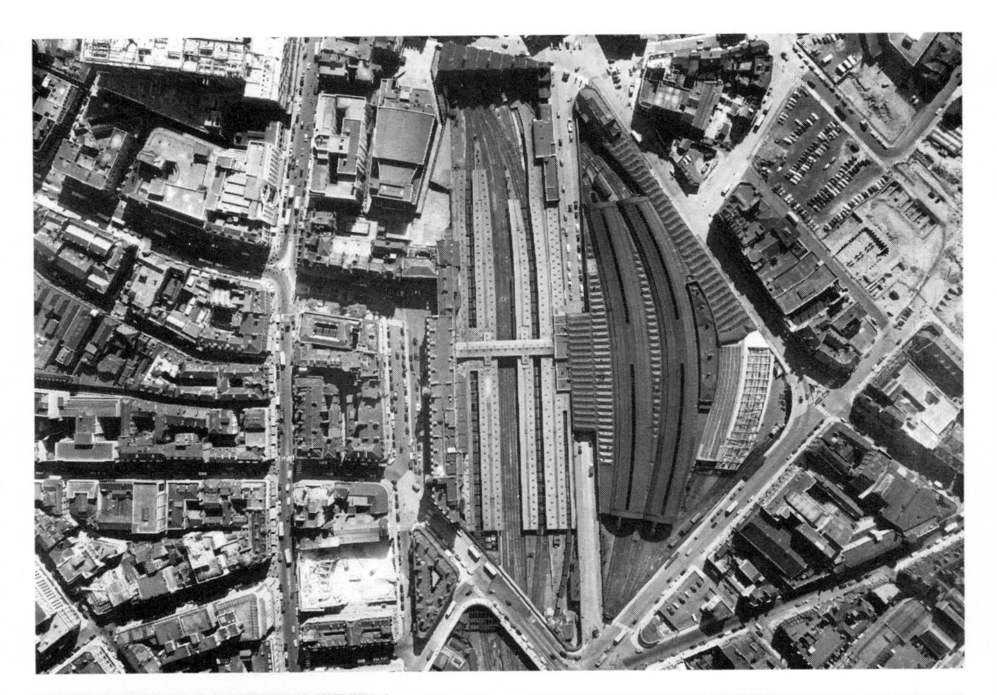

The latter part of 1962 was a period of great reorganisation for Britain's railways. Under provisions of a new Transport Act (1962), which came into force on 1 September, the BTC was dissolved, and railway control was placed under a new 'British Railways Board'. This delegated many managerial and operational functions to Regional Railway Boards. Following Nationalisation, ex-LMS lines in the Birmingham area had been controlled by the London Midland Region (LMR), and ex-GWR lines by Western Region (WR). But, under inter-regional boundary changes, also announced that September, the latter relinquished control of an area to the LMR stretching from near Bicester through Barnt Green to the Welsh Coast, from Aberystwyth northwards. This included the line through Birmingham, Wolverhampton and Shrewsbury to Chester. Later, on 1 July 1963, the LMR's 'Western lines' were divided in to four divisions, based at Euston, Birmingham, Stoke-on-Trent and Chester; all responsible to a Western Line Manager based at Crewe.

Although nominally only administrative, this regional transfer was to have the most profound effect upon the railways serving Birmingham, as millions of pounds was spent modernising them.

Electrification and resignalling

Paragraph 43 of the BTC's *Modernisation and Re-equipment of British Railways* report, published in January 1955, identified two major trunk routes for electrification; one of which was the LMR main line from Euston to Birmingham, Crewe, Liverpool and Manchester. Little more was heard of this scheme until March 1957, when Lord Rusholme, Chairman of the London Midland Area Board, announced further modernisation plans whilst on a visit to Birmingham. Beginning that

Below left:
One of a series of aerial photographs commissioned by BICC in preparation for the electrification of the line from Euston to Liverpool and Manchester. New Street station c1962, showing the clear division between the 'North Western' and 'Midland' sides and emphasising the monumental task that was about to be embarked upon with its complete rebuilding whilst remaining open.
BICC

Bottom left:
Electrification work south of Birmingham at Hampton-in-Arden in October 1965. Work has commenced on the extension of the platforms by 500ft to a total length of 892ft and the overhead gantries are in place. The station can be glimpsed through the bridge.
British Rail

month, he said, a team of railway experts would reconnoitre stations, depots and lines on the Birmingham-Crewe line to enable detailed plans to be drawn up for its electrification. Their findings were incorporated into the BTC's revised modernisation plan, published on 23 July 1957, which accorded priority to electrification of the Euston-Birmingham-Wolverhampton-Liverpool-Manchester line, using a 25kV overhead collection system which had been pioneered by French railways. This was supported by the LMR's announcement that 13 December of a £5.5 million electrification scheme for West Midlands lines using the same system.

Work on the trunk route electrification began immediately, at its northern end; the first 9½ miles, between Wilmslow and Mauldeth Road stations, opening on 26 November 1959; the first train being hauled by No E1000, a converted ex-GWR gas turbine locomotive. The whole scheme was divided into 44 stages covering 412 route miles and over 1,500 miles of track, and was to be spread over 10 years. In addition to the laying in of 12 power feeder stations, 58 track section cabins and 109 relay rooms, it required clearance work under 649 bridges and through 27 tunnels, also encompassing the remodelling or reconstruction of 89 stations. Stages 1 through to 21 focused upon the line south from Crewe to Euston via the Trent Valley line and both routes between Rugby and Wolverton, via Northampton and Blisworth. Work progressed so well that its scheduling was revised in February 1964, bringing the completion date forward to March 1967. The stages serv-

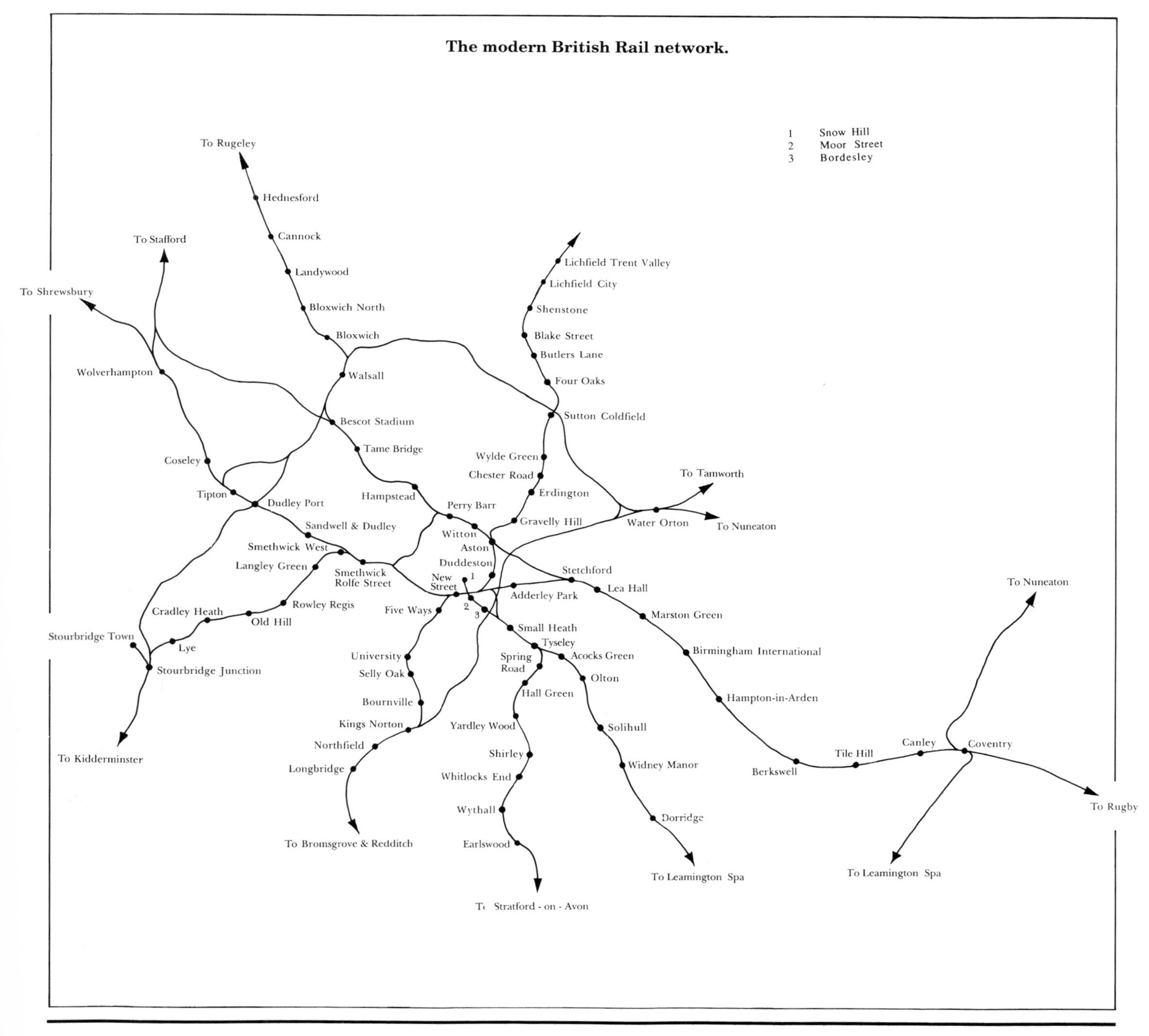

ing the Birmingham area are shown in the table, right.

As can be seen from this, the electrification scheme included both the Grand Junction and Stour Valley lines to Birmingham, plus the line to Walsall and ex-LNWR 'Soho loop line'; thus preserving the operating flexibility enjoyed under steam with regard to the choice of route available, and to the approach made to New Street station. Until electrified passenger services began on 6 March 1967, electric trains only used these lines for clearance tests or for freight workings.

This electrification scheme made increased speeds and service frequencies possible, but also required modernisation of the lines' signalling. The dozens of older signal boxes were unevenly spaced, because their siting had originally depended on the position of stations, junctions and level crossings; and this had an irregular effect upon line capacity. Therefore, in tandem with electrification, the manually-worked semaphore signalling, with the exception of that around Stockport, was replaced with high beam-intensity colour light signals, backed up by the Automatic Warning System of train control, a development from the GWR's Automatic Train Control.

Instead of the many signal boxes formerly controlling main line train movements between Stafford and Coventry, four large power boxes were built at

Stage No.	Section of line	Energised	First used
3	South of Stafford – North of Colwich Junction	7 Jan. 1963	7 Jan. 1963
4	North of Colwich Junction – North of Tamworth	31 Aug 1963	31 Aug 1963
5	North of Tamworth – North of Nuneaton	4 Jan 1964	2 Mar 1964
6	North of Nuneaton – South of Nuneaton	4 Jan 1964	2 Mar 1964
7	South of Nuneaton – North of Rugby	Oct 1964	Jan 1965
8	Lines North and South of Rugby	Oct 1964	Jan 1965
22	South of Stafford – North of High Level Station; Bushbury – Wednesfield Heath	Jan 1966	Mar 1966
23	Monmore Green – North of High Level Station; Crane St. Junction – South of Portobello Junction	Sept 1966	Dec 1966
24(1)	Wednesfield Heath – Bescot	Jan 1966	Mar 1966
24(2)	Bescot – South of Aston; Perry Barr North & South Juns. – Handsworth Wood; Aston – Duddeston	July 1966	Oct 1966
24(3)	South of Portobello Junction – Walsall	Apr 1966	June 1966
25	Oldbury – Monmore Green	Oct 1966	Dec 1966
26	Monument Lane – Oldbury; Soho North & South Junctions – Soho	Oct 1966	Dec 1966
27	Monument Lane – Adderley Park & Duddeston	Oct 1966	Dec 1966
28	South of Aston & Adderley Park – South of Stechford	July 1966	Oct 1966
29	South of Stetchford – North of Coventry	July 1966	Oct 1966
30	Lines through Coventry station	July 1966	Oct 1966
31	South of Coventry to North of Rugby (to Section 8)	July 1966	Oct 1966
36	Soho – Handsworth Wood	Oct 1966	Dec 1966

Birmingham New Street, Walsall, Wolverhampton and Coventry. Resignalling work began during 1963, the engineers involved taking the former Wolverhampton District Goods Managers office as their base. Wolverhampton's power signal box was completed first, early in July 1965, and commissioned on 18 August. It controlled 23 route miles, from a boundary with Stafford box at Littleton Colliery, to a boundary with New Street box at Tipton station on the Stour Valley line, and a boundary with Walsall box at Willenhall station on the Grand Junction line.

The New Street power signal box was built on the site of the former station's turntable, on its western side, adjoining the mouth of the tunnel taking the West Suburban lines south to

Below:
An historic moment. On 11 October 1966 the last length of contact wire is being paid out from the drum carrying vehicle at the end of the wiring train in Birmingham New Street. In a few minutes the electrification of the station will be completed, and someone is in position to record the event for posterity.
British Rail

Right:
In tandem with electrification was a complete resignalling scheme, with the replacement of 64 manually operated signal boxes by four power boxes at Wolverhampton, Walsall, Coventry and, seen here under construction on 1 January 1965, at New Street. This was fully commissioned by 4 July 1966.
British Rail

Lifford and backing on to Navigation Street. Structurally complete by late 1965 it came into use in three stages, between 8/9 January and 2/4 July 1966. Its panel controlled 347 signals and 223 points located on 36 route miles, mainly on former LNWR lines, from boundaries with Wolverhampton power box at Dudley Port, Walsall box at Great Barr and Coventry box at Hampton-in-Arden. Together, New Street, Wolverhampton, Walsall and Coventry power signal boxes controlled 85 route miles, the equivalent of 192 single track miles, and assumed the roles of no fewer than 64 manually operated signal boxes.

With the run down of Snow Hill station, and the transfer of many of its former services to New Street station, a further power signal box was built at Saltley, to control these and the former Midland Railway lines in the Birmingham area. Designated 'Washwood Heath Power Box' at its planning stage, this was built 'over the tracks' from the motive power depot at Saltley, by the junction of the lines serving Lawley Street Freightliner Depot. Its fabric was completed by the summer of 1969 and it was commissioned in four stages: 9-11 August 1969, lines from Tamworth, Abbey Junction, Sutton Park to Bromford Bridge; 23-25 August 1969, lines from Bromford Bridge to Kings Heath and to Bordesley South; 30 August-1 September 1969, lines from Moor Street station to Leamington, Hall Green and Hatton to Bearley Junction; 6-8 September 1969, lines from Kings Heath, Church Road Junction to Barnt Green main line Junction and from there to Redditch.

Below:
The electrification of the Stour Valley line meant more than just erecting some overhead gantries. Here at Dudley Port, the station was remodelled, the former island platform being rebuilt and enlarged, and the one on the left, plus its buildings, being removed. Elsewhere along the line, stations were closed and removed.
British Rail

The rebuilding of Birmingham New Street station

The announcement that New Street station was to be reconstructed was made by Lord Rusholme, Chairman of the BR(LMR) Board, following its monthly meeting, held in Birmingham on 15 March 1957; this, he said, would be in connection with the electrification of the Western Division main line and would be completed in some 10 years time. An exploratory meeting with a deputation from the Birmingham Corporation followed in October 1957, at which the station modernisation and the City's Inner Ring Road schemes were discussed. Both sides then went their separate ways, to draw up more definite plans, meeting again on 6 February 1959, where an exchange of information took place on the respective schemes and further joint meetings were scheduled. Details of the rebuilding were announced, along with other improvements in Birmingham area, by Sir Brian Robertson, Chairman of the BTC, at the annual banquet of the Birmingham Chamber of Commerce on 1 May 1959; the scheme would be 'harmonised with the plans of the City Council for the redevelopment of the central area of the city', he said.

So far, no public reference had been made to the design of the new station, but a hint at things to come was made by Sir Herbert Manzoni, the Birmingham City Engineer & Surveyor, in his presidential address to the Institution of Civil Engineers on 1 November 1960: 'Two schemes for erecting buildings over the platforms and tracks of Birmingham New Street station had been prepared but had not been proceeded with, principally because of problems connected with ventilation; but in the past 20 years it had become more apparent that the expansion of the city centre was of growing importance and that the covering over the station would be highly advantageous'. Sir Herbert was in fact being very cagey, because in March 1960, W. R. Headley, the Regional Architect for BR(LMR), had completed a series of drawings and a model which showed, in fine detail, the design and layout of the proposed new station. These depicted, almost exactly, the station that would eventually be built; with some exceptions. For instance, it was intended to replace the Queen's Hotel with a modern building in the same place and for the LMR Western Division to have its offices in the block above the station.

Three years passed, then, at the start of June 1963, a joint company was formed, between Railway Sites Ltd and City Centre Properties Ltd, to carry out a comprehensive redevelopment in conjunction with the rebuilding of New Street station, ie the buildings above, which were to comprise a shopping precinct, entertainments centre, restaurants and car park. Details of the station itself were announced in March 1964, accompanied by a new model, which showed the changes of recent years. Gone was the new hotel, and so would be almost all of the original structure, which was to be razed to its platforms. The layout comprised 12 through platforms, of 12-14 coach capacity, erasing Queen's Drive, the whole to be covered by a 7½ acre concrete slab which would carry all of the offices and passenger amenities. Platform access would be via escalators from a dispersal bridge, the provision of luggage and mail subways to be continued, as would the public right of way, which would now pass through the shopping centre to the city's new Bull Ring development.

Top:
One of the early designs for the new New Street station. The view is from the southeast and the model car is in a representation of Station Street. To the right is the intended replacement for the Queen's Hotel, and the tower block in the centre is sitting where the shopping centre eventually went.
British Rail

Above:
Work had begun, on 19 October 1963, on driving through the division between the two bay platforms Nos 1 and 2 at New Street. This was to create extra through roads in lieu of those to be lost when reconstruction of the station began on the far side opposite.
Michael Mensing

Preliminary work on the £4½ million rebuilding scheme began at the end of 1963, the bay platforms Nos 1-1a and 2-2a being joined to provide more through running lines on the 'LNWR' side. Formal reconstruction work began on 27 April 1964 when the contractors, C. Bryant & Son, began demolition of the 'Midland' side, by Station Street – last in, first out! Platforms Nos 10 and 11 were closed, some Bristol-Derby expresses being handled at platforms Nos 8 and 9, others using No 5 on the 'LNWR' side; Leicester and Derby locals using platform No 7. Over the weekend

15-17 August 1964, a 55yd, 250 ton, concrete box beam was erected, in 4 x 57ft sections, as a preliminary to the replacement of the Hill and Navigation street road bridges; forming a new carriageway which allowed the old structure to be demolished and replaced.

Right:
Five months later, on 15 March 1964, inroads, literally, have been made into the fabric of the 'North Western' side of New Street station and Queen's Drive is beginning to disappear in this view looking towards Worcester Street.
British Rail

Below:
By 28 June 1964, a good part of Queen's Drive has been obliterated, if not to say submerged, and one half of the 'Midland' side of the old New Street station has been demolished. A temporary footbridge has been erected to maintain the public right of way through the station, and the cleared site over by Station Street, on the far right, is being prepared for rebuilding.
British Rail

BULL RING CENTRE
The Mayfair Banqueting & Party Catering Mecca Ltd
RICHARDS &
WALLINGTON
RICHARDS &
WALLINGTON

Left:
23 March 1965: rebuilding work has progressed well on the former 'Midland' side of New Street station but the 'North Western' side is relatively untouched and the Queen's Hotel has just over nine months worth of guests to check in and out. Meanwhile, cautious DMUs pick their way through the contractor's materials and debris.
British Rail

Below left:
Over the weekend 7-8 August 1965, the main girders left from Queen's Drive at its Worcester Street end were removed. This view over the parapet from St Martin's Circus is looking towards Station Street and shows the offending girders plus the emerging Platforms Nos 9/8 and 7/6. At newly completed Platform No 10, Brush Type 4 No D1735 (later No 47142) waits to depart.
British Rail

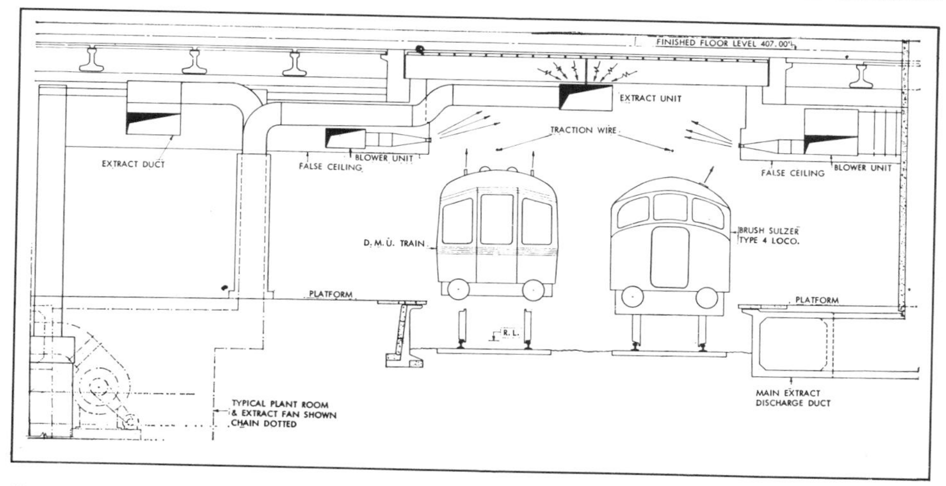

Top:
To combat the problems created by operating diesel locomotives under cover, the new New Street station was equipped with sophisticated extraction equipment, which can be seen being installed on 15 September 1965.
British Rail

Above:
This diagram offers an explanation of the principle behind the New Street fume extraction system, which worked by a combination of forcing air in to direct fumes up towards the ceiling mounted extraction units.
Modern Railways/Ian Allan Library

To speed work up, on Sundays in April and May 1965, a number of services were diverted to Snow Hill; northbound trains regaining the LM route at Bushbury. By the end of December that year, the new platforms Nos 6 to 12 were in use, old platforms Nos 1, 4 and 5 on the 'LNWR' side being closed for rebuilding, with only Nos 2 and 3 remaining open. The new platforms Nos 4 and 5 came into use over the weekend 12/13 February 1966, completing reconstruction over platforms Nos 4 to 12, taking in Queen's Drive, the line of which was taken by the tracks in between platforms Nos 7 and 8 in the new station. By May 1966, 60% of the station rebuilding was complete and work on the remaining three platforms, Nos 1 to 3, was in progress. Fitting out of the concourse had begun that February, and four of the platform escalators, the first on any station in the country, were in use; as was a new parcels depot in Station Street.

The Queen's Hotel was retained as long as possible, partly to maintain an income from it and partly because it acted as a very efficient screen between the station rebuilding work and the city centre; it did not finally close its doors until 31 December 1965, toppling into Stephenson Place early in 1966. Solid progress was made throughout the year. On 9 October the new station concourse, including an eight-window booking office and a temporary refreshment room, came into use; together with a new vehicle entrance off Smallbrook Queensway, opposite the Bull Ring. Two days later the last lengths of contact wire needed to complete the whole LMR electrification scheme were secured into position between platforms Nos 1 and 2, the wires in the New Street area being energized on 31 October.

Despite this work, some 300-400 diesel trains would be using the new station each day. To remove their exhaust fumes an elaborate ventilation system was devised by the LMR's Chief Engineer. This was under timer control, so that it was on continuously during peak periods, but was also triggered by a train entering a platform circuit, and could be over-ridden by hand controls. It comprised 24 centrifugal fans and three axial-flow ones which could remove 510,000cu ft of air per minute, a further 35 fans supplying 402,400cu ft of air to replace this; leaving 107,600cu ft to be drawn in from outside; which explains why the station is always so draughty!

Electric working into New Street station began on 5 December 1966, and by the end of the year most of the loco-hauled services on the electrified lines were worked by electric locomotives. A shortage of 'AM10' EMU's resulted in some local services being worked by green liveried 'AM4s', whilst the majority were still in the hands of DMUs; Birmingham-Rugby stopping services being worked by heady combinations of 'AM4s' and 'AM10s'. The opening of the full electric service on 6 March 1967 was marred by a serious collision at Stetchford on 28 February, when the 'AM4'-worked 13.15 Manchester-Coventry semi-fast ran into the locomotive of a ballast train at Stetchford, overturning, killing its driver and nine passengers. The line was closed for repairs until 3 March.

Like its predecessor, the New Street station that was brought into use in March 1967 was incomplete. Complaints were soon heard, and three months later questions were even asked in the House. On 12 June 1967 Victor Yates, MP for Birmingham Ladywood, commented: 'to get to the station one has to walk up 30 temporary wooden stairs, a long way over the roof, walk down 36 steps to the next level and to reach the station, down another 36 steps. . . . This is temporary, and there has been such an outcry that the railway authorities have put a temporary entrance at the front (but) this is limited to between 8am and 9.30am and

Above:
An official party, including (Left to Right), John Morris, MP; Sir Stanley Raymond; A G Ellis, Project Manager; George Smith, the Station Manager and H C Johnson, General Manager of BR(LMR), inspect the nearly completed New Street station on the first day of full electric operation, 6 March 1967.
British Rail

4.30am to 6pm, so that other people traveling have to suffer this inconvenience. . . . This entrance from New Street – the main centre of Birmingham – is called 'the hole in the wall'. There are (also) no down escalators, which is extraordinary for a modern station, . . . a tiny refreshment room . . . (and) no proper accommodation for the 253 drivers except in the old huts left by Bryants the builders.' His colleague Christopher Price, MP for Perry Barr, added: 'it is one of the worst station designs I have seen in Europe. It is in what I would call the British public lavatory architecture tradition – and it is a very bad example of that. But the worst feature is the . . . crossing of what some people have described as the Siberian waste of the vast plateau on top of the station, . . . what this will be like during the coming mid-winter is impossible to imagine.' Six months later, a deputation of five Labour MPs complained about the dearth of amenities on New Street's platforms at a session of the West Midlands TUCC, whose Chairman welcomed their comments as 'most helpful' and forwarded them to the Central TUCC for attention; which is presumably where they still are!

Work to rectify these omissions was already in hand. A range of shops, buffets and bars opened on 23 August 1967. Amongst these was the 104-seater 'Toreador' quick-service licensed restaurant, which boasted some bizarre hi-tech features, including separate table-mounted bell-pushes for food and wine service and waitress-only service runways along which the staff manoeuvred side-rail guided serving trolleys. Even their uniforms were the first to be produced using computer guided cutting tables! Complementing the Toreador was the the 'Taurus' Bar, the 'Pieman' light refreshment counter and a walk-round gift shop, a sweet and cosmetic shop and an off-licence wine and spirit shop; the first in a BR station.

Surmounting the station; in November 1965 work had started on the construction of 'Exchange Buildings', a 10-storey shops and office development which took its name from the 100-year old Exchange Buildings which had been demolished for their construction. This was designed by the architects Cotton, Ballard & Blow and built by a partnership formed between the Capital & Counties Property Co, Norwich Union Insurance Society and Taylor Woodrow Estates Ltd. The scheme included nine shops at ground level, with shop storage areas above at first floor level, and eight floor of offices, giving 47,500sq ft of accommodation, plus a basement car park, for 49 cars, and a caretaker's flat on the 10th floor; all built over the podium formed by the second floor roof of the station. A topping-out ceremony was held for the building work on 21 November 1967 and the works were finished in April 1968; concluding the first stage of a project, the second stage of which was the building of the 94 unit Birmingham Shopping Centre, which opened in February 1970.

New Street station has been revamped and redecorated a number of times since 1967, and since the late 1980s has seemed like a perpetual building site. Much of this work has been part of a £13 million improvement programme, which has embraced both redecoration and alterations. This was under way when, under new fire regulations brought into effect following the tragic fire at Kings Cross, New Street was classed as an underground station; requiring the addition of fire safety equipment in an extra work programme, which began in the summer of 1989. The latter has included the installation of fire and smoke detection apparatus, sprinkler systems and back-up wiring; all of which has been tucked away in the ducting and roof voids above the platforms. To the customers using the station, the most noticeable change has been the addition of smoke lobbies at the foot of each stairway/escalator access on each platform. These are designed both to restrict the spread of fire and smoke, and to act as a refuge in the case of an incident. All of the fire regulation work was completed at the end of July 1991. Attention has also been turned to ways of leaving the station in an emergency, and an alternative route has been provided, in the form of an additional footbridge at the station's Wolverhampton/Bristol end. This serves platforms Nos 2-11 and exits on Navigation Street, by its junction with Pinfold Street, coming into use at the end of 1991, having taken a number of months to erect; work upon it only being possible for a few hours on Sundays.

The closure of Snow Hill Station

The future of Snow Hill station was in doubt from the time that the electrification of the Euston-North West alternative was announced, but not everyone agreed. 'A Correspondent', writing in the *Railway Gazette* for 30 November 1962, proposed the use of Western Region lines and Snow Hill as the principal Birmingham station. In a carefully reasoned argument, our anonymous writer commented that LMR traffic could be channeled into Snow Hill far easier than WR traffic into New Street; and that the former GWR route, having been built to broad gauge dimensions, offered a far more generous loading gauge for both electrification and future traffic demands. Calmly and skillfully, he built up a powerful case for Snow Hill which makes all the more interesting reading in the light of subsequent, and inevitable, events.

The lack of any direct reference to Snow Hill's closure in *The Reshaping of British Railways* or 'Beeching Report' gave some cause for optimism, but not for long. In April 1963, Mr J. Royston, North Western Line Manager of BR(LMR), confirmed that the station would close 'on completion of the electrification'. People still had their doubts, with good cause. Just six weeks later, work started on an £400,000

Above right:
The rundown of the former GWR main line through Birmingham to Wolverhampton was done, some argued, in the face of engineering advantages such as the generous loading gauge the former mixed gauge line offered. Considerable sums had also been spent on it, such as the rebuilding of Swan Village station, seen here in 1966 with a passing pannier-hauled coal train.
R. S. Carpenter Collection

Right:
Six weeks after its closure was officially announced for 1967, BR began a £400,000 widening scheme on the bridge carrying the line over Great Charles Street. This was the progress made by 8 June 1963, as the 13.10 Paddington-Birkenhead service arrives at Platform No 1 hauled by a 'Western' class diesel-hydraulic.
Patrick Kingston

STATION

PLATFORM
4
AVON
1M13

Above:
Dying it might have been, but Snow Hill station was still capable of producing memorable images, such as this study of a quiet Sunday morning on 20 March 1966.
A. J. Dewis

scheme to widen Snow Hill station's engineering equivalent of an Achilles heel, the Great Charles Street bridge, by the addition of an extra span on the Wolverhampton side of the existing structure; the work to be completed in July 1965. Now surely, many thought, no-one would be spending . . . if? Well, BR would, and, on 21 April 1964, before the Great Charles Street bridge work was even half finished, Mr H. C. Johnson, Chairman & General Manager of BR(LMR) confirmed that Snow Hill station would close when the rebuilding of New Street station was completed, in 1967.

Although Snow Hill had enjoyed an increase in traffic since work began on the Euston-North West electrification, as this drew nearer to completion its services began to decline. Perhaps the most noticeable day upon which this could be noted was the second Saturday in August, by tradition Snow Hill's busiest day as its usual services were swelled with holiday specials and reliefs. That day in 1964 had seemed as usual, but 14 August 1965 was described as 'but a pale shadow of former years' even though steam haulage proliferated, with 'Halls', 'Granges' and 'Britannias' working most services except the Paddington ones, which were in the charge of Brush Type 4s (Class 47s). Things were even more pronounced on 13 August 1966, when the only way of distinguishing the day from an ordinary Saturday was the running of three relief trains.

Earlier that year, work had begun to link up the former LMS and GWR routes in the Birmingham area. Five areas were affected: at Wolverhampton, to connect the Shrewsbury line to High Level station; at Galton Junction, to reinstate the Stourbridge Extension line to Stour Valley line link; at Bordesley, to link the lines between Bordesley South (ex-GWR) and Bordesley Junction (ex-LMS); between St Andrews Junction and Grand Junction the lines were to be brought up to passenger standards, and at Leamington, a new junction was made between the ex-GWR main line and the ex-LMS line to

Right:
Snow Hill's last Saturday as a main line station, 4 March 1967, was a busy day: six soccer specials, plus two Ian Allan Last Steam Specials, augmented the usual service. Meanwhile, in a quieter moment that day, a Brush Type 4 passes with a freight on the down through road.
J. H. Cooper-Smith

Right:
Where once had stood 'Kings', now rested Brush Type 4s. The driver of No D1595 (later No 47469) and a station hand pause to exchange pleasantries and to decide to just which of their colleagues the term 'Rivet Heads' applies.
Author's Collection

Berkswell. First to be completed was the line at Galton Junction, which was laid in on 6 February 1966; reopening to freight and ECS workings on 27 May, and being first used by a passenger train, a special, on 4 August.

On 4 March 1967, Snow Hill's last Saturday as a main line station, it was busier than usual. The usual services were augmented by eight extra trains, six to convey West Bromwich Albion supporters to Wembley, where their team was playing QPR in the League Cup, and two 'Last Steam Specials'specials, organized by the publishers Ian Allan to commemorate the last day of the former GWR Paddington-Birkenhead through route. These were worked by a pair of 'Castles', *Pendennis* and *Clun*, ensuring that steam played a role in Snow Hill's send-off. Strictly speaking, the station's last full day was Sunday 5 March 1967, but the 21.40 from Birkenhead Woodside cheated a little, having the dubious distinction of being Snow Hill's last main line departure as it left for Paddington at 01.00 on 6 March! Later that day, the station assumed the mantle of an empty echoing vault as 107 of its 'usual' complement of services didn't turn up, leaving just 74 locals, worked by DMUs.

Gone were all main line services, and local ones off the Stourbridge line. Of the remainder, the bulk were locals, working through Snow Hill to and from Wolverhampton Low Level and stations to Leamington Spa; with the exception of 10 trains which comprised a new service from Langley Green (working from a former Oldbury Railway platform), inaugurated to maintain a Snow Hill service for passengers on the Stourbridge line, and eight others to and from Wellington, also retained to pro-

vide a link whilst the majority of S&B line workings had been transferred to New Street. Operationally, the station layout was drastically reduced, with only the up side, platforms Nos 1 to 6, being used.

For a few hours on the morning of 31 May 1967, Stourbridge services returned to Snow Hill as a derailment at Smethwick West blocked the line into New Street, but such excitement was limited. With so little use being made of the station, in December 1967 BR appealed to Barbara Castle, the Minister of Transport, for permission to close it completely. They were refused, Mrs Castle regarding the Wolverhampton Low Level-Snow Hill service as important, as well as the link to Langley Green. These should be retained she said, but BR could sell off most of the Snow Hill site for redevelopment, and passenger services south of Birmingham to Moor Street Junction and north of Wolverhampton to Wellington, could be diverted to New Street. Further reductions in activity at Snow Hill came following the closure of the traffic control office there at the end of 1967. This, and a similar office at Smallbrook, were replaced by a new Birmingham Division Traffic Control office at Rail House in Broad Street.

Snow Hill was now operated by a minimum number of staff, who were both surprised and over stretched when main line services returned there for a few hours on 9 January 1968; heavy overnight snow having closed New Street. These trains worked through Wolverhampton Low Level and on to Shrewsbury, but such operational flexibility was not possible for much longer. On 4 March 1968 the line through Snow Hill tunnel was closed to traffic; services which had used it being switched either to New Street or to operating as short workings from Moor Street. Only the Wolverhampton and Langley Green shuttle services remained, and from 6 May 1968 these were cut back to peak hours only, between 06.30 and 08.00, and 16.30 and 17.45. A new entrance was also created off Livery Street, the former

Above:
The frontage of Snow Hill station on 28 May 1969, one of a series of photographs taken by BR to record the building before demolition work began.
British Rail

Below:
How the trackwork at Snow Hill station was rationalised immediately following the withdrawal of main line services in March 1967.
Modern Railways/Ian Allan Library

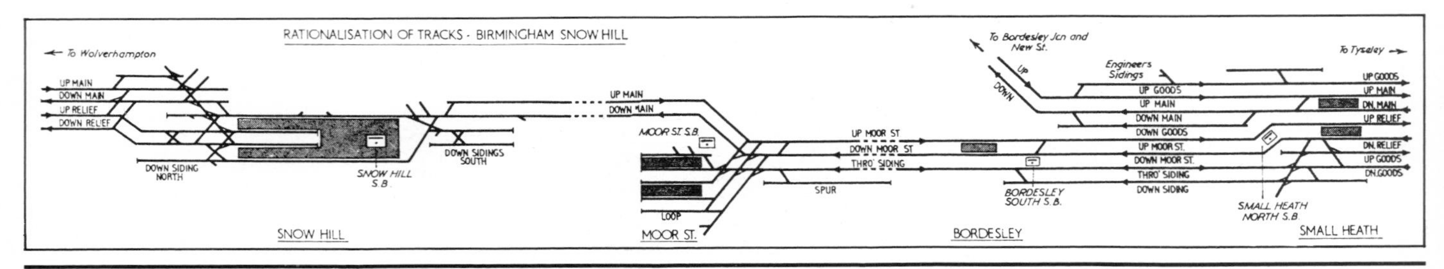

Above:
The main platforms at a deserted Snow Hill station on 28 May 1969. Closed to main line traffic, and to services through the tunnel to Moor Street, and despite the fact that demolition was to begin five months later, one half expects a train to emerge form the tunnel at any moment!
British Rail

one there, plus the one off Great Charles Street, being closed.

On 5 August 1968, Snow Hill was further reduced by line and platform closures; only platforms Nos 3 & 4 and the up and down relief lines being used regularly after this date. The Wolverhampton shuttle service was initially operated by three-Car DMU sets, but showed poor passenger loadings and so Class 122 single-units were substituted, also from 5 August. That same month, BR signed a £12 million agreement with City Wall Properties for the redevelopment of the station site. Provision was made in the proposed exhibition hall, hotel, cinema, dance hall, sports centre, shops and office complex for the retention of the two tracks needed to maintain the Wolverhampton passenger service. One year later this plan was formally accepted. Work was to begin immediately upon the demolition of the frontage, the redundant parts of the station to be pressed into temporary use as a car park. With a late pang of conscience, on 28 May 1969 BR(LMR) dispatched a photographer to record the station, but on 23 October that year, after having received many mortal blows, Snow Hill's fabric received the first of many thousands of physical ones, as demolition work began on the former Great Western Hotel.

Meanwhile, the Wolverhampton and Langley Green shuttle services continued. On 5 May 1969 Conductor/Guards

Right:
In 1970, the gap between the main platforms at Snow Hill was filled in and the station was used as a car park for seven years until the main demolition work began on 17 May 1977.
Ian Allan Library

Right:
Bilston Central station in 1976, four years after the withdrawal of the Snow Hill shuttle service on 4 March 1972. At that time the line saw occasional freight trips between Wolverhampton and Wednesbury, but has since been lifted. Preserved by the late West Midlands County Council, it will form part of the *midland metro*'s first route.
Ian Allan Library

were introduced on these, thereby allowing *all* of the stations served by the Wolverhampton one to become unstaffed from that day. The mighty Snow Hill station was now an unstaffed halt! Track in the station was further rationalised from 15 February 1970 by taking platforms Nos 5 & 6 out of use. The shuttle services continued throughout the year, during which time the regular passengers and train crews established a very friendly relationship. And so when, on 31 March 1971, British Rail announced the line for closure that 4 October, claiming the saving of £90,000pa, plus £22,000 in signalling costs, the passengers organised a protest in the form of a leaflet campaign. Their stance was supported by local councils, but to no avail; closure only being deferred until 4 March 1972.

Local people ensured that the old station went out in some style that Saturday. A special last train, the 'Champagne Special', organised jointly by the Standard Gauge Steam Trust and 7029 Clun Castle Ltd., departed Snow Hill at 18.05, hauled by No D1543 (later No 47014), to the sound of detonators, making a special, possibly unique, 20 mile round trip from Snow Hill to New Street stations, via Stourbridge Junction; its first-class passengers, in Pullman coaches, each being served a glass of champagne en route. On the Monday, 6 March, the former BW&D line to Wolverhampton was formally closed and work to rationalise and take it out of use was carried out between 17-22 September that year. Portions of the line remained in use for a few years, but the section between Handsworth Junction and Winson Green was taken out of use on 23 September 1979; the up and down freight lines between Handsworth and Smethwick Junctions were singled during March 1983; and lifting work between Wednesbury and Swan Village was completed on 27 July 1985.

From 1972, Snow Hill's carcass quietly decayed, prey to vagrants and amateur demolition workers, who 'practised' their skills upon it. Something of its forlorn and brooding presence was captured by the BBC in 1976; their 13 part drama series 'Gangsters' making extensive use of station as a backdrop to the main action. That December the demolition of the remainder of the station began at the north end. This completed, on 19 May 1977 work began on the demolition of the main structural steelwork. By the end of the year, the main station had gone, leaving only the parcels station, tucked away below Great Charles Street, and the original Livery Street entrance, as reminders of what once had been.

Above:
Little could any of these passengers on the 08.04 Coventry-Stoke-on-Trent working on 20 August 1963 realise that, in a little over 10 years time, the fields to either side of them would become the site of the National Exhibition Centre and Birmingham International Airport and station. *Michael Mensing*

The West Midlands Passenger Transport Authority

Under the terms of the Transport Act of 1968, the West Midlands Passenger Transport Authority (WMPTA) was formed on 1 October 1969; taking over responsibility for local authority bus services which were operated on its behalf by the West Midlands Passenger Transport Executive (WMPTE). Local rail services came under the latter's control under an agreement signed with British Rail on 12 January 1973, which was backdated to 1 January 1972. Under this, the Executive paid British Rail a grant, calculated on the same basis as the Government's current grant to BR for these services. In practice, the Government's grant was transferred from BR to the PTE, and reduced by 10% each year, the difference being raised through a corresponding annually increased precept on the domestic rates levied by the newly formed West Midlands County Council. This arrangement brought greater co-ordination of train and bus services; and joint bus and rail prepaid 'Travel-Card' tickets, which offered maximum flexibility in the use of public transport.

Birmingham International

The 1970s were to see great changes in and around the village of Bickenhill, just eight miles southwest of Birmingham. Its peace had already been disturbed in the late 1930s with the building of Birmingham Municipal Airport at neighbouring Elmdon. Planned since 1924, this finally opened on 8 July 1939, coming under Air Ministry control almost immediately and remaining in Government hands, through the Ministry of Civil Aviation, until 1 April 1960; when it reverted to the city council who gradually began to develop it throughout the decade.

Another key issue of the period was a proposed exhibition centre to serve the nation. London, already having Earls Court and Olympia, naturally assumed that this would be somewhere in the Capital, and much time was wasted in squabbling over where it would be sited. In 1969, sensing a wasting opportunity, Birmingham City Council and the Chamber of Commerce proposed an alternative site, in fields at Bickenhill, alongside Birmingham Airport. This proposal was formally adopted in 1970 and within hours the 400 acres of land required were purchased. Separating the airport and the site for the newly christened 'National Exhibition Centre' (NEC) was the L&B main line, and one of the factors that had swayed the Government in favour siting the centre at Bickenhill had been the unique combination of motorway, air and rail links which already existed there. To link the airport and NEC a new main line railway station was planned, to be known as Birmingham International.

The station was designed by Mr J. S. Wyatt, Regional Architect of BR(LMR). It occupies a 20 acre site, having five platforms of 1,000 ft length, each capable of accommodating a 13-coach train, space being provided to extend this capacity to 16-coaches, and to add an extra two platforms, if traffic demands. A four-level main building straddles the lines, with, at the lowest of these, 200ft platform canopies covering adjoining portions of the four main platforms, on which waiting rooms and toilets are provided, plus a parcels office. At a second, mezzanine, level, the British Transport Police have their offices, and above them is the main station concourse, which is divided by ticket barriers. To the outside of these are a range of passenger facilities, including the ticket office, travel centre, a bookstall, bank, car hire office, refreshment kiosks and telephones. Passing through the ticket barriers gains access to a cafe and bar, lost property office, left luggage lockers, toilets and more telephones. The fourth level contains the station's administrative offices, plus the plant for the heating and air-conditioning systems.

Below:
Work progresses on the construction of the NEC as a Euston electric heads towards New Street through the site of Birmingham International station at Bickenhill, eight miles south west of the city.
British Rail

Leading off from the main station concourse level is a fully enclosed footbridge which links it directly with the NEC. In mid-1985 a second link between the station and an expanded International Airport finally came into use. Due to open with the new airport in April 1984, this is provided by a 650yd long rapid transit link, which works on the linear induction motor principle. The 'Maglev', as it is known, runs along an elevated concrete track; a pair of cars, each capable of carrying up to 32 people, being born 15mm above this by magnetism and propelled along by 'waves' of electric current, which enable them to cover the full distance in just 90sec.

Birmingham International station was built by A. Monk & Co of Warrington, construction starting in March 1974. It was opened, incomplete, on 26 January 1976; in time for the official opening of the NEC by HM The Queen on 2 February, and was finished by May 1976.

The Cross-City Line

Sections 5.4.3 and 5.4.4 of the *Transport Development Plan*, published by the West Midlands Passenger Transport Executive (WMPTE) on 29 November 1972, dealt with the present and future potential of the railway lines between Birmingham and Redditch and Lichfield. At that time, the PTE's namesake Metropolitan County Council was 18 months away and its boundaries were still not finalised. Both Redditch and Lichfield had been included within the planned West Midlands County at preliminary stages, as had reinstating part of the former Halesowen line as far as Frankley, and it occurred to some that the development of a through commuter route between these places would both maximise the benefit gained by those living adjacent to the lines and make more efficient use of the rolling stock which worked them. Unfortunately, the final boundary of the West Midlands County did not conform to these expectations, and Lichfield, Redditch and Frankley remained outside it. Redditch, in particular, felt left out of things; its original station being closed on 7 February 1972, and replaced by a single platform.

Undaunted, the PTA continued with its plans for the line, which was now confined to the most northerly and southerly stations within the Metropolitan County's boundary: Four Oaks and Longbridge. The £6.3 million 'Cross-City Line' project was announced early in 1975. On the Longbridge side it included the improvement of the existing stations at Northfield, Kings Norton, Bournville and Selly Oak, and the building of new ones at Longbridge (on the site of the 1841-1849 one there), University (to serve the University of Birmingham and the Queen Elizabeth Medical Centre), Five Ways (reinstating the station closed in 1944) and Erdington. Each new station would have canopies and heated waiting areas, plus facilities for easy interchange between buses and cars; the scheme also allowing for track upgrading and signalling improvements, and the construction of a nine-car long turnback siding south of Halesowen Junction. On the Four Oaks side, Sutton Coldfield station would be remodelled to provide better access from the town centre and a new station would be built at Erdington.

Construction began with a formal ceremony at the site of University station on 5 January 1976 when Sidney Weighell, the then General Secretary of the NUR, cut the first sod using a traditional shovel and wheelbarrow. Apart from the station rebuilding, preparation for the line included major work at New Street, where alterations were needed to the track, installing three electrified crossovers, and to the signalling. At Kings Norton, the freight only lines on the section to Longbridge required upgrading to passenger standard; the

Above right:
The final section of steelwork is lowered into position for the bridge linking Birmingham International station with the NEC during its construction in 1975.
British Rail

Right:
'Birmingham International to Birmingham International please?' No wonder the MAGLEV is unstaffed! It could get confusing. Engineers fiddle with the new airport to station automatic link on 21 July 1984. This was already three months late entering service and did not come into full use until the middle of the following year.
J. G. Glover

Left:
Five Ways station on the BWS line had been closed on 2 October 1944 but was to be reopened as part of the Cross-City line. This view of Class 46 No 46004 passing through the closed station with the 10.50 Paignton to Leeds service shows the progress of the refurbishment work on 6 September 1977.
Les Bertram

junction with the Camp Hill line there needed remodelling, and the freight link from the car terminal to the Longbridge car plant had to be completely recast. The redundant junction with Cadbury's internal railway at Bournville was taken out of use on 9 June 1977, and a new layout at Halesowen Junction came into use on 23 April 1978.

North of Birmingham, two stabling sidings were laid in at Four Oaks and colour light signalling was installed between there and Aston. An additional £1.1 million was spent upgrading Tyseley depot, whose maintenance and servicing facilities were extended to refurbish and maintain the DMU fleet scheduled to operate the new line, up to a maximum of 76 three-car sets; the carriage stock servicing work formerly undertaken there being transferred to the depots at Duddeston and Oxley. As a final stage in completing the project, the former Longbridge station on the Halesowen line was closed to parcels traffic on 2 May 1978.

The Cross-City line opened on schedule on 8 May 1978, when the then Minister of Transport, William Rodgers, unveiled a plaque at University station. All of the new stations were complete, but planning delays had delayed the completion of work at Northfield (opened 24 February 1980) and Longbridge (opened 2 November 1980), which had to use Portakabins for a while. Between Four Oaks and Longbridge a basic Monday to Friday service of four trains an hour was provided between 06.30 and 23.15, increasing to six per hour at peak times. Saturdays had a basic daily off-peak service all

Above left:
Here at the new University station on 5 January 1976, Sidney Weighell, the then General Secretary of the NUR, had cut the first sod on the Cross-City line project. By the summer of 1977, this was the progress there. The main building had still to go in; this would be built at road level, where the University's power station chimney is projecting up from.
British Rail

Left:
Selly Oak was another station undergoing a major refurbishment as part of the Cross-City line scheme; this included rebuilding and lengthening the platforms to take nine-car DMUs, and providing a new booking hall, ticket office and toilets. This was the work during the summer of 1977.
British Rail

Above:
As part of the Cross-City line project, £1.1 million was spent upgrading the DMU servicing and maintenance facilities at Tyseley. The refuelling portion of these is seen in May 1978, with three of the units in the new Cross-City line livery of white with a blue band bearing the PTE's logo.
British Rail

Above right:
The work on the building of the new Cross-City line station at Longbridge over-ran the opening of the line on 8 May 1978. As shown three days later, Class 45 No 45055 passes with a train of empty bolster wagons, mobile buildings doubling for the as yet unfinished main station ones.
Les Bertram

day, and Sunday services consisted of two trains per hour between 08.00 and 23.00. At New Street, northbound trains used platform No 5 and southbound ones platform No 12. Three-car Class 116 DMU sets were used on the line; refurbished with reupholstered seats and repanelled interiors, fluorescent lighting, improved heating and quieter exhausts. Each was emblazoned with a new livery of all over white with a blue stripe bearing the PTE's logo; the cars being used in sixes at busy times.

An instant success, calls were soon heard to extend the Cross-City line, especially to Redditch. The latter was a burgeoning New Town, linked to Birmingham by a single line which joined the B&G main line at Barnt Green. It had retained a tenuous rail link to Birmingham, consisting of two trains each way per day, since 1964. With the opening of the Cross-City line this was increased to three trains each way per day, but local people felt they needed more. An augmented service was sponsored for an experimental period of one year jointly by the Redditch Development Corporation and Hereford & Worcester County Council, and a Redditch and Alvechurch Rail Users Association was formed in January 1980 to ensure that this was promoted as well as possible. The new service, consisting of three 15min interval trains to New Street in a morning, an hourly service during the day, and three 30min interval trains to Redditch in an evening, began on 12 May 1980. It was so successful that limited station improvements were made, the service being retained for 1981 and made permanent from May 1982. Most of the additional Redditch services were formed from extended regular Cross-City line services, some of which were also extended at the northern end to provide an improved hourly service to Lichfield. The payment and level of fares on these trains was simplified from September 1981, when new cross boundary fare regulations came into force, allowing for add-on portions to be purchased for the PTE's prepaid Travelcard and other season tickets.

Cross-City line passengers soon became a very unshockable lot, and Tyseley's attempts to confuse them, by testing recently overhauled DMU stock from other regions along it, fooled no-one; hardened commuters boarding the occasional Strathclyde 'Jaffa-Cake' unit with scarcely a blink. Steady growth in passengers led to the use of four-car DMUs on the line in the mid-1980s; these were formed by the addition of a non-powered trailer car in the middle of conventional three-car units. Overloaded and underpowered, these hybrids were very unpopular, and caused such an escalation in passenger

Right:
Redditch people fought hard for a decent train service, eventually winning a 30 minute frequency service, which is about as much as the single line from Barnt Green can stand. Unfortunately, the 'Train Service Alteration' notice seen in this 23 February 1980 shot does not announce a service improvement, but the temporary withdrawal of the 22.59 train from Longbridge for six months.
Chris Morrison

Above:
The placing of track alignment pegs in position on the eastern entrance of Snow Hill tunnel alerted local people to the fact that the much rumoured reopening of Snow Hill station was about to begin. These were photographed on 20 December 1983. The Snow Hill project also involved the rebuilding of Moor Street station on this alignment; the station now occupying part of the foreground shown here.
John B. Gosling

complaints about the service on the Cross-City line that their introduction can claim some direct responsibility for the decision to electrify it. A number of service changes have been made on the line in recent years, including the introduction of semi-fast trains, which miss-out all of the stations between New Street and Kings Norton with the summer timetable on 12 May 1986. The northern terminus of the line was also extended from Lichfield City to Lichfield Trent Valley High Level from 28 November 1988; the city also becoming part of the 15min interval service enjoyed by most of the rest of the line.

The Snow Hill station project

Plans to reopen Snow Hill station had been formulated whilst the last remnants of the old station were still open, let alone before its main fabric was demolished in 1976/77. Rumours of its reopening also circulated periodically for the next few years or so, but first took definite form in 1982. A two stage project was conceived, at whose heart was the relief of that section of the Stour Valley line between New Street and Galton Junction by diverting some or all of the Stourbridge line services back to a rebuilt Snow Hill station; thereby creating a second Cross-City line. Stage 1 envisaged the rebuilding of a station on the Snow Hill site, with the extension of the services currently terminating at Moor Street to it; Stage 2 encompassing the reinstatement of the lines to Smethwick West, to complete the link with the Stourbridge line.

In 1983, initial attempts to secure Ministerial support and Government backing for the project were unsuccessful, but the area around the station site was greatly improved that year by the restoration of the Great Western Arcade; its owners, Prudential Assurance, engaging the John Madin Design Group to direct the work. The Arcade reopened in April 1986 and, significant or not, it at least showed that someone had confidence in what had become a decaying part of the city. Another attempt at securing funding for the project was made, this time concentrating on Stage 1 only. Detailed plans were prepared; and in January 1984, rows of brightly painted pegs, marking out the alignment of the tracks between Moor Street and the entrance to Snow Hill tunnel, alerted everyone to the fact that something was actually happening this time.

In July 1984, Government support, to the tune of £10million, was pledged to what had become dubbed the 'Snow Hill Project'. Both Moor Street and Snow Hill stations were to be rebuilt, the latter also including an 800-space car park, to be built by the City Council,

Right:
Rebuilding Snow Hill station could not proceed before the completion of this car park above it. Work on both projects is well advanced in this view of the scheme taken from Livery Street on 10 August 1987. Sadly, much of what remained from the old station, notably the subterranean parcels station, was demolished at this time.
R. M. Clayton

Below right:
Moor Streets old and new. With the old station still in use for another six months, the new Moor Street station takes shape on 13 April 1987.
M. E. Haddon

and an office development, to be built by a private company. The new Moor Street station would be built alongside the relaid tracks through Snow Hill tunnel; with two platforms each bearing canopies and waiting rooms, plus a ticket hall and ramps for disabled passengers. Snow Hill would be a much grander affair, consisting of four platforms formed into two islands, each capable of accommodating nine-coach long trains, with waiting rooms, toilets, staff facilities, public address and electronic passenger information systems. Access to the station would be direct from Colmore Row, through the office development above the station. Here would be a street level booking hall plus a number of small shop units; a covered walkway leading passengers on to stairs descending to the platforms.

Overall, the Snow Hill Project cost £8 million and was funded by the PTA, with £2.1 million coming through a Government grant and a further £3.2 million coming from the EEC's Economic Regional Development Fund. For practical reasons, the car park had to be built first, and, on 8 May 1985, as this proceeded, work began to clean the tons of soot and dust which had accumulated in Snow Hill tunnel since it had been enclosed in 1874. Once completed, the track could be relaid within the tunnel, each wooden sleeper, recycled from the Woodhead route, being laid on a special all-enclosing rubber pad which, together with extra ballast, significantly reduced the noise and vibration transmitted to the offices, then being built, above. The main contractors were Shand Northern Ltd, the redevelopment requiring demolition of most of the remaining portions of the former Snow Hill station, including the Parcels Depot. During this, whilst removing the old platform No 2 in January 1987, some lengths of original Barlow rail were discovered. Work to relay the new track was completed by 13 July 1987, when the last length was ceremonially bolted in place. Then it was time for one of the most intensive and highly orchestrated railway promotions of recent years to begin, one which would leave no doubt that Snow Hill station had returned.

Events began on 12 September 1987, with an invitation to walk through the newly refurbished Snow Hill tunnel. Always possible, but never advisable; 14,057 people leapt at the chance to do this 'legally', each making a voluntary donation to charity, which raised £8,171.57, and receiving a certificate for their efforts. Next came a grand send off for the old Moor Street station on its last day of operation: 26 September 1987. A series of steam specials was operated to and from Dorridge, an hourly service between 10.07 and 15.07 being worked by ex-LMS 2-6-0 No 46443 and BR(WR) No 7029 *Clun Castle* on alternating turns. At 16.07, No 46443 worked a special to Stratford via Solihull, then, at 21.00, *Clun Castle* performed the last rites at Moor Street, as it had done 20 years before at the old Snow Hill, this time taking a train to Dorridge and returning to Tyseley. How many of the party of enthusiasts and invited guests on board, reminiscing and studying their souvenir tickets, noticed the Engineering Train they passed at Small Heath?

Left:
Contrasts at the old Moor Street station on its last day of operation: 26 September 1987 – 1. In this shot the routine life of the station for the last 30 years continues as a three-car DMU waits to depart with the 12.55 to Leamington Spa.
D. S. Lindsey

Below:
Contrasts at the old Moor Street station on its last day of operation: 26 September 1987 – 2. Ex-LMS 2-6-0 No 46443 works one of an hourly service of steam specials out of the station. These ran to Dorridge, and the task of hauling them was shared with BR(WR) No 7029 *Clun Castle*. The specials ran from 10.07 to 15.07; the honour of taking the last one out of the station, a special Special, falling to *Clun Castle*, which, 20 years ago, had performed the same rite at the old Snow Hill.
British Rail

TUNNEL
400 YARDS
TO GO
Evening Mail
HC 13

MIDLINE
MIDLINE
SNOW HILL

Left:
As part of the publicity drive leading up to the opening of the new Snow Hill station, the public were invited to walk through the tunnel from Moor Street on 12 September 1987. 14,057 leapt at the opportunity, and the photograph shows the Lord Mayor of Birmingham leading the first party through. From voluntary donations made that day, £8,171.57 was raised for local charities.
British Rail

Below left:
11.00 on 2 October 1987, the opening moment of the new Snow Hill station captured as an immaculate Class 47 No 47484 *Isambard Kingdom Brunel* emerges from the tunnel, setting off detonators and breaking a banner.
Brian Morrison

Waiting its chance, this moved to Moor Street, where its engineering crews immediately began the task of slewing the old station's approach lines over to join up with the new track through Snow Hill tunnel. This was completed the following day, and on Monday 28 September 1987 the new Moor Street station opened for business. Trains worked through ECS to the new Snow Hill station to test the new track and signals, controlled from Saltley, for operational ease; both lines through the tunnel being bi-directional and affording access to all four platforms. Snow Hill station was officially opened at 11.00 on 2 October 1987, when No 47484 I*sambard Kingdom Brunel* emerged from the tunnel setting off detonators and breaking a banner which displayed the station's name. The occasion was marked by the joint unveiling of a plaque, depicting scenes from the old and new stations, by Councillor Peter Lister, Chairman of the PTA, and Sir Robert Reid, Chairman of BR; the former taking the opportunity to chastise the BR for using the West Midlands as 'a dumping ground for scrap stock'. Public services began on 4 October 1987, with a shuttle service to an Enthusiasts' Special Day at Tyseley Traction Depot, regular services commencing the following day.

A point of detail in connection with the Snow Hill project is that neither of the two new stations carry the designation 'Birmingham', being plain 'Snow Hill' and 'Moor Street'. For a while it also seemed that the cost of gaining a new station at Snow Hill would be the loss of the last remaining GWR glory in Birmingham: the old Moor Street station. Happily, through the intervention of the City Council, this has been mothballed; although something needs to be done with it soon, before the ravages of the climate and vandals achieve what the Council's enlightenment has so far prevented. Attempts to secure funding for Stage 2 of the project have so far been unsuccessful. Estimated to cost £30 million, and to require the relaying of 2½ miles of track and the rebuilding of a number of stations, it is certain to go ahead sometime. But, with a curious twist of history, vehement opposition has been raised to the scheme by rail users in Stourbridge, who have become so used to having a direct connection with a busy InterCity station that they do not want to lose this in return for a total return to a new, but emasculated, Snow Hill station.

Cross-City line electrification

The Cross-City line was a victim of its own success; the more passengers it attracted the worse the service became, as overstretched and life-expired DMUs were ground into the track. Success stories shouldn't end in failure, and solutions were actively sought. Similar problems around London had been solved by electrification before World War 1, but this was rarely an option in the West Midlands, the region's only electric suburban services being operated along electrified main lines.

A number of proposals to electrify parts of the Cross-City line had been made over the years; the earliest, for electrification between Rugby, Birmingham and Lichfield, being part of the detailed planning which followed publication of the BTC's Modernisation Plan in 1955; which was still included in BR's Electrification Review of 1971. South of Birmingham, the main line between New Street and Barnt Green was considered as a lower order electrification priority in an overall review of main lines carried out in 1974/75.

Facing a costly bill to replace aged DMU stock, the PTE commissioned an electrification feasibility study in 1979 for all of the remaining diesel worked routes radiating from Birmingham, including Lichfield-Redditch. This was completed in 1982 and, following a period of discussion and review, the PTA requested BR to develop a full 25kV electrification scheme for the route between Blake Street and Longbridge. To these BR added alternative proposals for the tail-end PSO supported portions to Lichfield and Redditch, which included diesel shuttles, full 'under-the-wire' diesel working and even bus substitution. From this emerged a fully developed proposal to electrify between Lichfield and Redditch, which was endorsed and jointly funded by WMPTE (Centro) and BR (Provincial), on a roughly 30/70 basis, and formally presented for Ministerial approval in November 1988. Further negotiations took another 15 months, but on 7 February 1990, approval for a £64.5million scheme to electrify the entire Cross-City line was announced.

The scheme's costs break down into £34 million for new rolling stock, £18 million for electrification fixed works, £4 million for rolling stock fixed works, £4.5 million for signalling between Aston and Lichfield and £4 million for station improvements. An electrification depot was established on the site of old freight sidings south of Kings Norton station from where the main contractor, Pirelli, operated. Three main kinds of work were required: track lowering, by four to six inches, installation of overhead line equipment and signalling. To facilitate these, engineering occupations of the line were granted on weekends (between 20.00 on Saturdays and 05.00 on Mondays), on weekdays, on the northern section (between 20.00 and 05.00), and during the middle of the day on the line south of Barnt Green (09.30 to 15.30). From 5 August to 25 October 1991, services on the latter section were replaced by buses for much of the day, Mondays to Fridays. Main line services were diverted to run via Stourbridge, freight to go via the Camp Hill line.

Track lowering work commenced on 1 October 1990. Of the 63 bridges along the 33 mile route, 25 had an insufficient clearance for electrification and all had to have their parapets raised with the addition of 'unclimable' steeple copings. Station alterations included the provision of longer platforms at Shenstone, Blake Street, Butlers Lane, Four Oaks, and Sutton Coldfield; others having to be raised; Alvechurch station being moved nearer the village, and Redditch station being rebuilt yet again. Permanent way work at 14 locations, from Shenstone south to Lifford West Junction, mainly involving track lowering, reballasting and rationalization, was undertaken between 6 January and 1 December 1991.

The replacement of trains by buses on week nights began on 4 February 1991, and on 17 February, work began on the excavation and concreting of overhead mast bases at Four Oaks. Permanent way work on the section north of New Street was sufficiently advanced by 18 May 1991 for weekend trains to be reintroduced, and the first 47 of the 1,738 catenary masts required by project were erected just north of Erdington on 20 May that year. The whole route was to be electrified, including holding sidings at Lichfield and Longbridge, but only the slow lines on the quadruple section between Kings Norton and Longbridge.

Extensive resignalling work was also required to give improved headways, all signals to be controlled from a new centre established in a converted Vauxhall Shunt Frame box. The northern section required considerable resignalling work to replace the existing mixture of colour light and semaphore signals north of the boundary of the New Street panel, which were controlled by boxes at Erdington, Four Oaks and Lichfield City. This work had been commissioned before the Cross-City line electrification, and was undertaken as a separate, although related, project. The southern section already had colour light signalling, controlled by Saltley panel, but was equipped with 'Reed' type relays which are not immune to stray field effects produced by energized 25kV overhead. Therefore this had to be replaced with solid state interlocking equipment, all the way back to Saltley; a considerable task, which will delay the energizing, and hence the opening, of the the southern section for six months.

To work the newly electrified line, 17 Class 323 EMUs, part of a larger order for 37 such units, were ordered from Hunslet TPL and fabricated in their works at Kilmarnock. Similar in appearance to the Class 321 'Networker' units, each vehicle will be 23m long, providing an overall seating capacity of 289. Delivery of the first units was expected in June 1992, but a mock-up of part of one of the units went on public display throughout the summer of 1991. An electrified service between New Street and Lichfield is expected to be introduced in November 1992, with that to Redditch commencing in May 1993, before which some peak hour through journeys will continue to be operated by DMUs to maintain commuter connections. The existing service pattern will remain, but electrification will offer an overall point-to-point journey time saving of 16 minutes, a typical run from Sutton Coldfield to New Street being four minutes quicker than at present, one to Redditch eight minutes faster; all with concomitant improvements in comfort and reliability.

The Development of Passenger Services since 1963

The very face of Birmingham has been transformed in the last quarter of a century by the electrification and modernization of the city's railways. These changes are reflected in the way that passenger services, local and InterCity, and freight services and facilities have developed.

1 – Local passenger services

Local passenger services on many of the lines desribed in the previous chapters survived but a few months or years into the period now under consideration. The local service between Dudley Port and Dudley was withdrawn on 6 July 1964, but the majority of those on former LNWR lines in the Birmingham area were all formally withdrawn on 18 January 1965, a Monday; with the last trains actually running on Saturday 16 January. Four lines were closed to passengers, together with their intermediate stations: Coventry-Warwick, including Kenilworth; Walsall-Rugeley and Walsall-Lichfield; Coventry-Nuneaton and Kenilworth-Berkswell. All of the lines remained in situ and in use by freight services and the occasional special or diversion. The Walsall-Lichfield line was a very popular diversion for

Above:
The face of the new electric railway age. An EMU on a local service to Coventry approaches Hampton-in-Arden station on 27 September 1967.
British Rail

Sunday engineering work, but it was closed on 14 January 1984, with, as is the way of these things, its last trains being two football specials, carrying Walsall supporters to a match at Rotherham, on 18 January 1984. Its remaining signal boxes were closed on 16 March that year, and most of the line was lifted, save for a portion between Lichfield and Anglesea tanker sidings. Elsewhere in the area, the surviving North Western lines have retained their local passenger services, although Atherstone, Polesworth and Rugeley stations on the Trent Valley line were unstaffed from 2 October1972.

Of the former Midland lines, the W&W Railway, only used by goods services since 1931, was severed by motorway construction work on 28 September 1964, the section to Willenhall, Stafford Street station being used as a siding for a few years thereafter. Its 'other half', the former W&WMJ line, was also closed to passengers on 18 January 1965, although it remains in use for freight services and the occasional diversion. Local passenger services along the former B&DJ and Whitacre-Nuneaton lines were withdrawn on 4 March 1968, and Saltley, Castle Bromwich, Whitacre, Kingsbury, Shustoke and Stockingford stations were all closed.

Former GWR lines also lost their local passenger services within a year or so of falling into LMR territory. These were withdrawn on two lines in 1964: Swan Village-Dudley (4 May 1964), and Old Hill-Dudley (15 June 1964), with Dudley station itself closing just three weeks later, with the withdrawal of the shuttle service from Dudley Port, noted above. Four years later, the race excursion use of Cheltenham Racecourse station came to and end on 21 March 1968, the whole Cheltenham-Honeybourne line closing on 1 November 1976.

Electrification, and the transfer of former Western Region services to New Street, have wrought many changes to the Birmingham area. Those routes formerly working south of Snow Hill were affected the least, simply being transferred to run out of Moor Street, and, in October 1987, transferred back to a rebuilt Snow Hill. Until 1991, when Sprinters took over most of the duties between there and Leamington Spa and Stratford-on-Avon; they were even worked by the same DMUs that had once run in and out of the old Snow Hill. It was a very different story to the north of the rebuilt station, out towards Wolverhampton, as towns along the former BW&D line lay too remote from the allegedly 'duplicate' Stour Valley route, which, itself, was modernised at a cost. A number of intermediate stations were sacrificed to increase speeds and improve clearances, and accordingly, Ettingshall Road & Bilston was closed to passengers on 15 June 1964, and the freight only Albion station closed that 10 August; freight services also being withdrawn from Monmore Green on 4 October 1965.

Generally, the electric local trains introduced to Wolverhampton, Walsall

Below:
The end of the 1980s saw two major reopenings of latter-day freight-only lines to passenger services in the Birmingham area. The first was that between Coventry and Nuneaton, a line originally opened by the LNWR on 2 September 1850. This reopened to passengers on 12 May 1987, with a single intermediate station at Bedworth. This view was taken at Three-Spires Junction, with the Coventry Loop line, on 30 May 1987 and shows two-car Class 116 DMU (Nos 53828/53059) on the 11.37 Stafford-Coventry service.
Colin Underhill

Left:
The second major reopening of the late 1980s in the Birmingham area was that of the Walsall-Hednesford line. The Railway Development Society had campaigned for years to see this reopened and their goal was achieved on 7 April 1989. This opening day shot shows a special 'Press and Dignitaries' train, formed by Super Sprinter No 156427, at Hednesford.
Brian Morrison

and Coventry on 6 March 1967 have proved a success, with more trains, and greater imagination being shown in their scheduling. From 11 May 1987, the Stour Valley EMU local services were extended to run through New Street to Walsall, and morning and evening rush hour trains began to run through to Birmingham International and Coventry. The line has also been improved through funds made available from the West Midlands County Council's 'Greenline' project. Six former industrial sites between Wolverhampton and Birmingham were landscaped under a £162,000 'face lift' programme, and 12 life-size steel horses, designed by artist Keith Atherton, were unveiled on 13 March 1987 by the running of a special train. Various bridges along the line have also been adorned, the best known of these being the 'musical' one at Tipton.

Similarly, the transfer of the Stourbridge trains to New Street, whilst strongly opposed at the time, has been accepted; local people now appreciating the convenience of the vast range of InterCity connections possible at the latter. The survival and later success of these local routes is due mainly to the influence of the West Midlands Passenger Transport Executive (WMPTE), under whose enthusiastic support the

Right:
Most of the prototype DMU replacements have been tried out in the Birmingham area. Here experimental Class 140 No 140001, with a Leyland National style bus body, is pictured at Henley-in-Arden on 20 July 1981, the first day of three weeks of trials.
T. W. Moore

region has enjoyed an unforeseen increase in local rail commuter traffic in recent years. The outstanding success of this period has to be the Cross-City line, but of equal importance has been the successful promotion of Park-and-Ride facilities, notably at Stourbridge Junction. Certain lines have also been reopened, thanks to sustained pressure and reasoned argument by bodies such as the Railway Development Society. Examples include those between Coventry and Nuneaton, which reopened on 12 May 1987, and Walsall and Hednesford, which reopened on 7 April 1989. Additional stations have also been built, such as Tame Bridge, between Hamstead and Bescot on the Walsall line which opened on 4 June 1990.

The gains of the early 1980s did at one point seem likely to be lost in the early 1990s, as the late delivery of the Class 158 sprinters caused the diversion of earlier types away from the area, and Tyseley's fleet of triple-life expired DMUs to stagger on for a while longer. This was felt particularly on the Stourbridge line, where Class 155 and 156 Sprinters, which inaugurated an 'Express' service to Cardiff on 16 May 1988, were first withdrawn, to serve the Provincial Sector services to East

Above:
Another DMU replacement prototype, this time Class 151 No 151001, at work on the Cross-City line at Kings Norton on 24 April 1985.
British Rail

Left:
Saltley shed closed to steam on 6 March 1967 but its name lives on in that of the MPD there. On 9 September 1986, Class 50 No 50035 *Ark Royal*, in Network SouthEast livery, Class 56 No 56009, a pair of Class 58s, one of which was No 58028, and an unidentified Class 47 were the only occupants.
John Whitehouse

Anglia, and then the service itself was transferred to travel via the Lickey and Bromsgrove. Older stock temporarily returned to the line, much to the displeasure of its many thousands of daily users. But the Cross-City electrification work truly heralds a new era in Birmingham's local rail services, and with the second Cross-City line plans, and the *midland metro*, poised to proceed once funding has been secured; the future looks a lot brighter than many could have hoped even five years ago.

2 – *InterCity passenger services*

Starved of most of its Euston services, the few that remained were rescheduled only to work from Birmingham New Street from 8 September 1963, working ECS from Wolverhampton. Steam was also ousted as electrification work proceeded, with express steam locomotives being banned on BR(LMR) lines south of Crewe from 1 September 1964, followed by a ban on all steam through workings between Crewe and Euston, which was originally scheduled for 1 January 1965, but was postponed until that September due to a lack of diesel replacements.

By late 1965 electrification work had progressed so far that the regular electric locomotive haulage of main line passenger trains from Euston could begin on 22 November 1965, all movements into and out of the station becoming by electric traction from 3 January 1966. The new LMR Timetable, commencing on 18 April 1966, also reinstated two evening fast through services to Euston, which were to be electric hauled south of Coventry; and the electric working of main line trains was further extended to Birm-

Above:
A 'Western' at New Street! Class 52 No 1037 *Western Empress* pulls into Platform No 1 with the 09.05 from Paddington on 23 May 1974. These locomotives were seen regularly at Birmingham until their final withdrawal in 1977.
P. A. Rutter

Left:
With the reopening of the Coventry-Leamington line on 17 May 1977, all sorts of inter-regional services became possible. This magnificent long-view of the line at Old Milverton, shows Class 50 No 50022 *Anson* taking an 11.30 Wolverhampton-Paddington special towards Leamington on 11 April 1981.
Brain Morrison

ingham New Street from 5 December 1966. Full electric working from began on 6 March 1967, and was based upon a strict 15 minute past the hour departure from Euston between 08.15 and 20.15, most of the services continuing alternately to Liverpool and Manchester, with an 11 minute wait at Birmingham New Street. The Birmingham Pullman's mantle was assumed by a short lived morning service styled 'The Executive', which required the compulsory reservation of dining seats at a 7s 6d (37.5p) first-class and 5s (25p) second-class surcharge. Completing the changes brought about on 6 March 1967 was the diversion of the 'West Coast Postal' mail train from the Trent Valley line to run via the Stour Valley line.

From 1 May 1972 major improvements were introduced in the frequency of services on the routes linking London with Birmingham and Bristol. Birmingham New Street became the focus of a revision of cross-country services linking the North and Soutwest England and South Wales. A new half hourly service was introduced between London and Birmingham, with Euston-New Street timings of 90-95min and trains leaving Euston at 10 and 40min past the hour; the former all travelling at least as far as Wolverhampton, the latter all terminating at Birmingham. On 6 May 1974 the culmination of a four year £75 million resignalling and electrification project saw the introduction of all electric train services between Euston and Glasgow. The work had involved the electrification and resignalling of the West Coast main line between Weaver Junction, north of Crewe, and Motherwell, south of Glasgow; plus the construction of new electric locomotives, the Class 87s. From Birmingham to Glasgow and Edinburgh, the previous daily service of one train per day was increased to four per day in each direction, one also being extended south to begin and terminate at Bristol.

Over an hour was taken off the journey time from Birmingham to Glasgow or Edinburgh, which could now be reached in just over four hours. An additional service, styled 'The Clansman', left Euston at 09.35 and arrived at Inverness at 19.45; an up 'Clansman' leaving Inverness at 10.30 and arriving at Euston at 21.04. Also, from the summer of 1974, BR's latest Mk III coaching stock was introduced on the Anglo-Scottish electric services; the 75ft 5in vehicles being capable of sustained speeds up to a maximum of 125mph.

The basic pattern of services established then has been maintained, with additions. A major change came about from 16 May 1977, with the re-routing of some Birmingham-Oxford passenger services via Coventry. This was made possible through use of the former LNWR Coventry-Leamington line, opened in 1844. Its passenger service had been withdrawn in January 1965, but in May 1966 the junction at Leamington Spa North was remodelled to give better connections with the former GWR and LNWR systems, so that freight diverted from the closed Great Central route could use it. But, through the number of passenger trains diverted over the line due to weekend engineering work, and the opening of Birmingham International station in 1976, the idea formed to reopen the line to regular services. This was initially to give wider access to the NEC from

Below:
The mantle of 'Britain's Newest InterCity Station' was worn briefly by Sandwell & Dudley when it opened on 14 May 1984. Basically developed out of the old Oldbury & Bromford Lane station on the Stour Valley line, it is celebrated for a major faux pas that very day when, with the BR Chairman on the platform in readiness, the first train to call there hurtled on past – no-one had told the driver to stop! Also that day, Inter City 125 power car No 43125 heads the 08.13 departure to Manchester into the new station
A. J. Miles

other parts of the railway network, but it broke an invisible barrier which had existed in the minds of timetable planners. Despite 30 years of running a single railway system, railway journeys were still operated as though the GWR, LMS, LNER and Southern railways still existed, and inter-regional services were as though they were 'international'. Quite literally at a stroke, the opening of the Coventry-Leamington line enabled an astonishing range of cross-country services to be developed, and placed Birmingham truly at the heart of the rail network.

Allied to this was a relaxation in the near hysterical fears there had been over the effects of 'under the wire' working of diesels on electrified routes. One result of this was that HSTs first ran in the West Midlands from 17 May 1982, when they entered service on the northeast-southwest 'Heart Line of Britain' route. Two years later, two daily HST workings, to Manchester and Liverpool, began on 14 May 1984, and extensions to the number of north-south through workings, which have brought Exeter, Plymouth and Penzance within direct reach of Birmingham. HSTs also began to run on services from Poole to Birmingham and beyond on 8 July 1991. Cross London services, through Kensington Olympia, began on 12 May 1986; offering a whole new range of direct services linking Birmingham with Gatwick Airport, Clapham Junction and Brighton, to name but a few. The '06s', as these are known, due to their departure from platform No 1 at New Street always being at six minutes past the hour, now also serve Dover and Folkestone, whilst Class 156 Sprinters now link Birmingham with Harwich (Parkeston Quay). There have been technical developments too, such as on 14 December 1987, when the 09.26 Wolverhampton-Euston train became the first public service on the West Coast lines to be worked by a push-pull set, comprising a Class 86 locomotive and a driving trailer converted from HST power car No 43123, and since 1988, Class 90 locomotives and Driving Van Trailers (DVTs) have become a regular fixture on the Euston trains.

On 12 November 1991 BR announced the biggest shake-up in the InterCity service between New Street and Euston in 17 years. This came after months of rumour about the future of InterCity services to Wolverhampton, following an earlier announcement of the end of through working to Shrewsbury from May 1992. Spurred-on by competition from the M40, which offered virtually comparable journeys when the time spent in travelling to, and waiting at, InterCity stations was taken into account; BR announced a virtual doubling of the service from Birmingham

Above:
In preparation for the first working of InterCity 125s through New Street on the northeast-southwest services from 17 May 1982, power cars Nos 43153 and 43156 pass the site of Saltley station on a test run from Derby to Saltley. Well, if you're not carrying any passengers, who needs carriages!
Philip Cotterill

Above right:
Few shots could emphasise the fact that InterCity 125s now run through New Street better than this posed publicity one taken in connection with their launch on the 'Heart Line of Britain' route on 17 May 1982.
British Rail

Right:
Class 90 electrics with DVTs are now an everyday occurrence on the New Street-Euston services. On 14 June 1989, DVT No 82107 was photographed leading the 13.55 Euston-Wolverhampton service propelled by Class 86 No 86261 through Stetchford.
Peter Tandy

New Street and International. In the morning peak, a train will run every 15min and a number of additional trains will be non-stop to Euston from Birmingham International; in the evening peak, the service frequency will be increased to one train every 20min, most being non-stop to Coventry. Addi-

Coca-Cola
2

tional trains will also be provided between the NEC and the International Convention Centre, the latter currently being served by New Street station. Declared as Europe's most intensive InterCity service serving two destinations; three extra sets of Pullman-quality Mk IIIb coaches will offer increased comfort on some of these additional services. It is claimed by BR that this service will provide a seat every two seconds from the Birmingham stations to London between 06.30 and 08.30.

A new InterCity station, called Sandwell & Dudley, was developed on the Stour Valley line out of the existing Oldbury & Bromford Lane station. Adjoining this, until 1974, had been Oldbury Steel Terminal, but the lifting of the tracks there in October 1980 gave an opportunity to develop the site. With the new Metropolitan Boroughs of Dudley and Sandwell both lacking an InterCity station, one was created at Oldbury, opening on 14 May 1984. Sadly, despite excellent car parking facilities, the station has been cursed from the start. On the opening day, the first train failed to stop, leaving everyone, from the waiting BR Chairman down, with red faces! Services to the station have also been rather eccentric, with outward trains calling there in the morning, but their evening returns rushing on through to New Street without a care. The station facilities are also rather Spartan, with lavatories only being built five years after the station opened. Local people feel that the station was a good opportunity badly missed, and refer to it mockingly as 'Dudwell & Sandley'.

Sprinters have also made their mark around Birmingham. Class 150/1s entered service in the West Midlands on 12 May 1986. Based at Etches Park in Derby, they were introduced on services from New Street through Wolverhampton to Shrewsbury and the Cam-

Left:
On a cold morning, 21 January 1985, the first Sprinter many had seen waits at New Street to begin the first of a number of runs along local lines; first call, Stourbridge Junction. It was another year or more before they were seen with any regularity in the area.
British Rail

Below left:
Before Sprinterisation on 16 May 1988, a Class 31 and six coaches, one a downgraded FO, could be relied upon between New Street and East Anglia. The author used to conduct passenger surveys on these trains, and with any luck all of the questionnaires would be completed by Nuneaton, and one could settle back for a pleasant, but not rapid, journey – a lot of the author's earlier book, *Rail Centres: Wolverhampton*, was planned on these! In happier times, an unidentified Class 31 works the 13.15 to Yarmouth on 8 April 1983.
Dr L. A. Nixon

brian Coast. On 16 May 1988, Sprinters were also introduced on the New Street to Coventry and Nottingham, with Class 156s ousting Class 31s locomotive hauled services on the Birmingham-East Anglia service, one of the last 'old fashioned' train journeys left from the city – a sad loss.

The Development of Freight Services and Facilities

For over a century, the various railway companies, and their heirs, who had served Birmingham had developed a vast and intricate network of goods depots and yards in the city, supplying, and supplied, by smaller operations at outlying points, most of which were former stations which had been closed to passengers for years. Then along came the 'Reshaping' report, advocating the concentration of freight into its main classes and the use of containers.

The first moves towards concentration in the Birmingham area came in November 1963, when five domestic coal yards were established at Aston, Monument Lane, Lawley Street, Leamington Spa and Stratford-on-Avon. By the end of 1964, these had assumed the work of no fewer than 168 separate, smaller coal depots and wharfs, and each had an annual through put of 40,000-50,000 tons. In March 1964, the LMR in Birmingham announced that it was to extend its present steel railhead arrangements and develop the existing goods facilities at Aston, Great Bridge and Walsall Street, Wolverhampton for this specialised purpose. Existing railheads, such as that at Moor Lane, Brierley Hill, would also be developed, the latter reopening on 5 September 1965. Similar action was taken with regard to oil, a new Shell Mex & BP oil terminal opening at Rowley Regis on the same date. A whole range of steel services, linking the area with South Wales, Sheffield and the northeast, were developed, the first of these running on 4 October 1965.

Central to BR's freight operations in the West Midlands was to be a remodelled Bescot yard. Work to remodel this had begun in 1962 with the up yard, the revised version of which came into use in May 1963. Attention then turned to the down yard which was remodelled from January 1964, the completed scheme coming into full operation on 18 April 1966, with all north bound freight movements being electric hauled. Bescot acted as a central freight concentration point and allowed other more dispersed yards to be dispensed with. Later, on 15 August that year, the overhead on the whole of the Stafford-Coventry-Rugby section of the Grand Junction line was energized, allowing electric hauled south bound freight workings from Bescot.

Below:
Dudley Freightliner Depot was the first to open in the Birmingham area, coming into full use on 16 July 1967. There, on 20 August 1985, Class 31 No 31147 leaves along the former SS line en route to Lawley Street. With Lawley Street eventually taking over its traffic, the Freightliner Depot at Dudley closed.
Paul D. Shannon

The specialised goods facilities designed to handle container traffic had gained the name 'Freightliner' terminals, the first of which in the Birmingham area was announced for Dudley in August 1966. To occupy the side of the former Castle Goods Yard and the closed passenger station there, work to remodel this began in January 1967 and was completed that 7 April, the depot opening on 16 July 1967; it closed on 26 September 1986. In June 1968, work began to on a new international container depot at Montague Street in Birmingham, adjoining Lawley Street; the eight acre site opening on 20 January 1969. Lawley Street was itself undergoing an extensive modernization scheme to create an Inland Port with Customs facilities for both imports and exports. This had begun in May 1966 and the new depot opened on 29 September 1968, the former depot offices and part of the yard being sold to National Carriers Ltd. It served the city for just over 20 years, closing on 6 February 1987. But back in the late 1960s, the Freightliner business was still growing, and very soon after it opened, the depot at Dudley was exceeding its capacity. And so a new depot was planned for Landor Street in Birmingham, opening in November 1969.

All of this investment in new freight handling facilities meant that most of

Left:
Birmingham gained its own Freightliner terminal on 20 January 1969, when one opened in a revamped yard at Lawley Street. Eighteen years later, on 24 January 1987, Class 58 No 58007 waits to leave this terminal with the 12.25 (SO) to Southampton.
Chris Morrison

the former goods depots and yards were gradually declared redundant. First to go was the former Midland goods station at Camp Hill, which closed on 7 February 1966. The following month, work began to demolish the goods station at Curzon Street, although the offices, in the former frontage and hotel, remained open until 23 September 1968, helping to ensure their survival. Enduring a perilous existence over the ensuing period, they were eventually restored, listed, and taken over as the headquarters of The Princes Trust. Behind these, the tracks serving the parcels depot, which had been developed on the site, were disconnected in February 1989, and lifted by the following month. The surviving buildings from the other Curzon Street station, the former GJ one, were demolished in June 1971. Central Goods closed on 6 March 1967, the line there from Church Road Junction closing on 17 December 1967. Four years later, dying on a withering line, Hockley depot closed on 7 August 1971; the allied yard at Soho & Winson Green closing later that year, on 1 November. The following year, hump shunting ceased at Washwood Heath sidings, on 9 December 1972, Nos 1-23 marshalling and No 2 carriage & wagon sidings there being taken out of use on 18 November 1973. The ex-LNWR goods yard at Soho Pool closed to freight on 6 May 1974 and was converted into a Texaco oil terminal, which in turn closed in 1982; the branch closing in early July that year. But the longest survivor of all was the old Windsor Street Wharf, which did not close until 12 May 1980, its trackwork being lifted that September.

Below left:
Class 45 No 45122 heads a freight bound for the WR on to the Camp Hill line on 28 May 1974, passing Bordesley Junction, and overshadowed by the former GWR Goods Warehouse there.
M. C. Barker

As well as the former goods depots, many of the freight lines in the Birmingham area were dispensed with and removed. The Harborne branch was the first to close, in 1963; traffic to the Cape Hill brewery, the last on the line, ceasing earlier in the year; the last goods trains to use the branch travelling along it on 2 November 1963; locomotive No D2386 working the 09.02 (eight full coal wagons, three for Hagley Road station yard and five for Harborne station yard) and the 09.55 return, with just a single brake van! The line closed completely on 4 November 1963, going out in style as a special six-coach train, hauled by Class 2 locomotive No 46429 (in unlined black) and assisted at the rear by No 46522 (in lined green), traversed it; sadly, the open coaching stock used was too wide to allow the train to enter Harborne station. Very quickly afterwards, the bridge carrying the line over the Birmingham Canal, by the the line's very awkward junction with the Stour Valley line, was removed.

Two months later, on 4 January 1964, locomotive No 46505, in green livery, hauled the last train over the Halesowen-Longbridge line; the splendid Dowery Dell viaduct being dismantled in April 1965. Six months after this, on 6 July 1964, the Wombourn line stations closed to goods, the last day of regular freight services coming 27 February 1965, the line closing five days later, on 1 March. Later in 1964, there had been a great weeding-out of Black Country goods branches; those at Spinner's End and Hayes Lane closing on 10 August 1964, that at Oldbury on 7 September. On the 28th of the same month, the ex-Midland Railway W&W

Below:
To illustrate the types of equipment to be used at the new Freightliner Depots, the first of which in the Midlands was to be at Dudley, BR held an exhibition at Moor Street station during the period 4-13 April 1967. *British Rail*

Left:
The junction made by the Harborne Railway with the Stour Valley line had always been awkward and following the line's closure on 4 November 1963, little time was wasted to sever it and to remove the bridge over the Birmingham Canal; the operation which is recorded here.
British Rail

Right:
Another almost forgotten line which closed to freight was the former GWR branch to Halesowen and Halesowen Basin. Steel traffic sustained the line until October 1969, when it was closed. Three years earlier, on 26 September 1966, a Class 2 2-6-0 No 46442, banks a train out of Haden Hill tunnel en route for Stourbridge Junction.
R. E. B. Siviter

line was severed; the section to Willenhall (Stafford Street) station became worked as a siding.

This trend was continued in 1965, the Corngreaves Goods branch closing on 12 April and the Walsall Wood branch closing to traffic on 2 August. The latter was made into siding for BICC Co, but closed permanently on 9 February 1969. Stourbridge Town Goods branch closed to regular traffic on 5 July 1965, followed by the yard there on 20 September; a last train working along it 10 days later; but the line was not officially closed until 22 October 1967. Closure came to the former GWR Kingswinford branch, north of Shut End, on 1 April 1968, line reverting to more or less how it had been upon its opening in November 1858. Sustained by some steel traffic from the adjacent firm of Walter Somers Ltd, specialists in steel tubes, this was insufficient to prevent closure of the goods branches to Halesowen and Halesowen Basin on 1 October 1969; both being taken out of use 10 days later. All that remained of the former Midland Railway line between Whitacre and Hampton Junction was severed 300yd from its start, on 12 December 1970, the remaining stub being retained as a siding. Finally, almost 20 years later, the Kingsbury branch closed to freight in March 1989.

Allied to the closure of former goods depots and lines, was that of the many former passenger stations which had remained open to feed goods and parcels to the great depots and yards in Birmingham. These were closed in great swathes, starting in 1964. The year saw the closure of: Hampton (4 January); Hunnington (6 January);

Left:
The 'LMS' maintained a presence at the new Birmingham New Street for a few years, station shunter No 08601 being decked-out in pseudo-LMS livery during the mid-1980s. It is seen here at Tyseley on 29 November 1986. *Robert C. Jones*

Right:
With more and more traffic diverted to the roads, Dudley Freightliner Terminal became surplus to requirements and on 26 September 1986, No 58030 had the dubious honour of drawing the last load out of the yard there, forming the 18.50 to Glasgow. Note the wreath on the front of the locomotive. *Brain Robbins*

Coleshill, Lifford (ex-B&G line) and Rubery (all on 6 July); Aldridge, Short Heath (Clark's Lane) and Sutton Park (all on 7 December). 1965 brought closure to: Penns for Walmley (1 February); Hazelwell and Whitacre (1 March); Bromford Bridge (28 June); Wednesfield (4 October) and Willenhall (Stafford Street) (1 November). Finally, King's Heath closed on 2 May 1966, and Redditch on 8 September 1968.

In a little over five years, Birmingham's freight handling facilities had been completely overhauled, but these transformations were, in hindsight, only a stop-gap measure. The economic recession of recent years has found BR's freight business struggling to survive. In Birmingham, many of the modernised depots and yards have closed, but there are plans to further adapt those that remain to meet the challenges of the 1990s, which offers the prospect of a direct rail connection to Europe.

6: Miscellaneous Railway Activity

Away from its main lines and busy stations, Birmingham also nurtured a great deal of industrial activity which served or relied upon the railways. It was the home of many of the country's biggest carriage and wagon builders, and numerous working days were spent in providing those often overlooked essentials upon which railway services depend. The city's rail system is also far from static, and extensive additions are planned under the proposals for the *midland metro*.

Railway Related Industries

Birmingham's entrepreneurs were a perspicacious lot, quick to identify new markets for their skills. The coming of the railways presented just such an opening, and within a few years of the GJ's arrival in the town, a number of local manufacturers had either added railway products to their catalogues, or become established specifically to serve the needs of this new industry.

The rise of these manufacturers is charted in local trade directories. Whilst some Birmingham firms catered for the needs of railway builders and operators from the early 1830s onwards, it is not until 1846 that the heading 'Railway . . . ' is used to distinguish them from other engineering and manufacturing concerns. That year entries are given for two 'Railway Spike Makers' and two 'Railway Whistle Makers', plus three of the carriage builders whose story is told below. The inventiveness of Birmingham's manufacturers to meet the needs of the railways probably reached its zenith in the 1860s. An 1867 directory describes the greatest variety of railway related products of all. These comprise, Railway: Fastening Manufacturers (2); Ironmongers (2); Material Manufacturers (1); Plant Manufacturers (2); Spring Manufacturers (1); Stores Contractors (4); Wheel & Axle Makers (3) and Wrench Manufacturers (1); plus no fewer than four Signal Makers: Henry Baynton in Broad Street; Gray, Martinego & Co. of 40 Newhall Street; Arthur Linley & Co. at 132-133 Lionel Street, and Joseph Ratcliffe & Sons in New Church Street.

With increasing standardisation, railway companies began to make more and more of their own rolling stock and equipment, driving many of Birmingham's manufacturers to diversify away from the production of such items. This trend is marked throughout the 1870s and 1880s; a directory of 1886 listing only Railway: Grease Manufacturers (2); Switch & Crossing Makers (2); Tyre Makers (2), and Wrench Manufacturers (2); whilst an 1890 directory could only find a Carriage Rug Manufacturers and a Chair Maker to list under 'Railway . . .'.

Carriage and Wagon Builders

A somewhat more enduring facet of railway manufacturing, which has been a part of the local economy for almost as long as railways have served Birmingham, is that of carriage and wagon building, which was, at various times, represented there by seven notable companies.

Fox, Henderson & Co

Our 1846 directory lists three firms engaged in this trade: Bassano & Fisher in Liverpool Street, Joseph Wright (of whom more presently), at Saltley, and Fox, Henderson & Co. The latter, it may be recalled, designed and erected the roof of New Street station, but were also in the railway carriage building business from the late 1830s. Established c.1832, the company built its 'London Works' on the Dudley Road in Smethwick. These were visited by Samuel Sidney for his *Rides on Railways* volume, published in 1851, which has preserved the following description: 'The shops, which are of large dimensions, are built in a quadrangle, enclosing a large area, which is employed as a yard for material or finished goods. . . . The first place into which the stranger is shown is called the Truck shop, and will accommodate three hundred carriage builders and carpenters. Adjoining it is the Boiler Makers' shop, or, more properly, a shop for workers in plate-iron, for boilers are not made in the establishment, but iron doors, navy casks, and wrought iron railway carriages are produced in this department. These shops form one side of the quadrangle. The forges, which are very numerous, occupy the first department of another side of the range of buildings. . . . The Mechanical Engineering shops join the forges. . . . Here the switches used for conducting trains from one line to another are made, as well as all kinds of machine work. Connected with this is the Turntable shop. . . . The Wheel shop, which is next visited, is chiefly used for the manufacture of railway carriage wheels, of which, as must be well known, there are many varieties. The other two sides of the quadrangle are occupied by saw-pits, painters' shops, stores, offices, and all the conveniences required for carrying on a business which frequently gives employment to eleven or twelve hundred men. . . . Strangers, if introduced, are permitted to see the works'.

Joseph Wright & Sons

Fox, Henderson & Co had gone out of business by 1860, and in the same period, other rolling stock manufacturers, such as Isaac Marshall & Co in Bordesley, and William Middleton, of the Vulcan Ironfoundry in Bridge Street West, Smethwick, had also come and gone. Far more lasting proved to be the Saltley Works of Joseph Wright & Sons. Wright was an established London coachbuilder, who had accrued a considerable fortune through contracts for the Royal Mails and by being the owner of most of the stage coaches

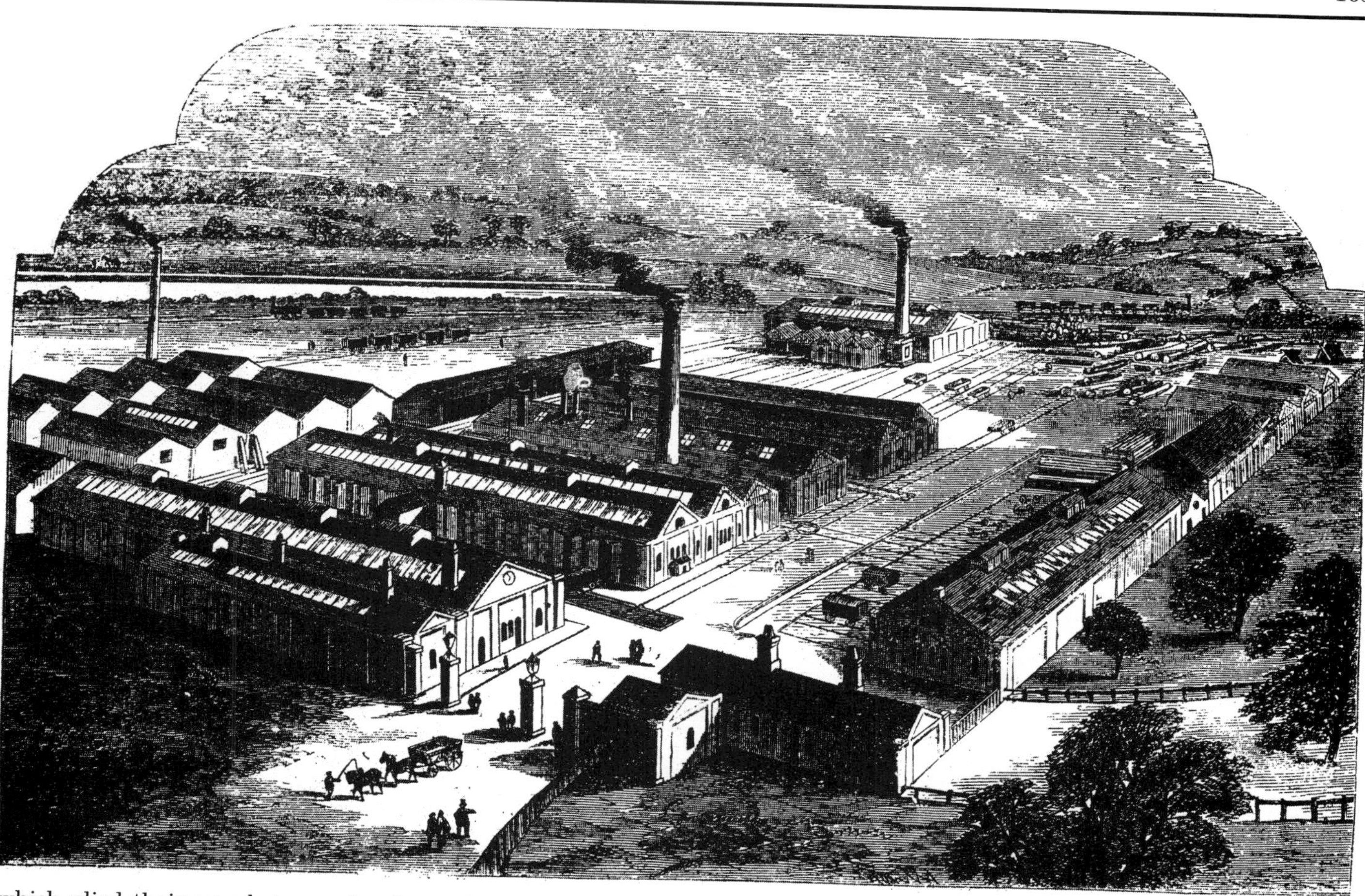

Above:
The Carriage Works of Mr Joseph Wright, Saltley, near Birmingham, an illustration from *Measom's Guide to the GWR* published in 1860. This shows Wright's works as it was when the company's founder had just died in 1859. There is plenty of land available for extensions to the premises and stocks of timber are much in evidence. Over to the right is what appears to be the wagon shops, with completed wagons and trucks on a series of short tracks served by a traverser.
Author's Collection

which plied their way between London and Birmingham. A proponent of railways, he saw the hastening demise of the stage coach as an opportunity to diversify, and began to manufacture railway carriages c1841. Being a substantially larger product than a stage coach, and in great demand, Wright's London premises were soon deemed too small, and so he sought somewhere else to start afresh. He must have been very familiar with Birmingham from his coaching business, and the fact that it was served by no fewer than four railway companies, plus its available, highly skilled, workforce, made Birmingham an attractive prospect.

In May 1845, Wright leased six acres of land at Saltley, building a works which included 'workshops, offices, a wharf and other buildings', and was equipped with 'engines, boilers and the newest and most expeditious mechanical appliances'. The company was restyled 'Joseph Wright & Sons, Railway Carriage & Wagon Builders & Contractors', and began operation in 1846. By the following year, Henry Wright, Joseph's son, had leased a further 50 acres of adjoining land on to which new shops were constantly being erected. By 1853, so much production had been transferred to these newer premises that the 'Saltley Old Works', as it was already being termed, was let to the LNWR, who used it for the building and repair of their own rolling stock until 1870. In 1858, the company began to lease railway wagons, having no fewer than 1,300 of these at work by the end of that year. Joseph Wright died in 1859, the business being carried on by his other son, also named Joseph, until 1862.

Brown, Marshalls & Co

Joseph Wright's example was followed by a local firm of coachbuilders, Brown, Marshalls & Co, who had small premises at 115-116 New Canal Street, just off Curzon Street, in Birmingham. They are first listed as railway carriage and wagon builders in a local directory for 1852, and the following year they opened new premises, the Britannia Works, in Arden Road, Adderley Park, by the former L&B main line. The business was converted into a limited liability company on 17 June 1870, coming to specialise in luxurious carriages, such as the P&O Express Dining Cars they built for the Compagnie Internationale des Wagons Lits in 1892. Ten years later the firm became part of the Metropolitan Amalgamated Railway Carriage & Wagon Co Ltd, and production was transferred to Saltley in 1908, Britannia Works being sold to the Wolseley Motor Co Ltd, whose massive Adderley Park works adjoined them, in 1911.

Oldbury Railway Carriage & Wagon Co Ltd

By the early 1850s, Birmingham's reputation as a carriage and wagon building centre was such that established companies began to relocate there, to take advantage of a skilled workforce and the town's good name. Messrs Johnson & Kinder had built a carriage works by the Midland Railway at Bromsgrove around 1850, but moved to a new site in Broadwell Road, Oldbury, adjoining the Stour Valley line, and Oldbury & Bromford Lane station, in 1856. The company's name was changed to the Oldbury Railway Carriage & Wagon Co Ltd to fit in with this move. It was an ideal site, with a pit-shaft producing coal only five yards from the shops, and over 30 rolling mills within a two mile radius.

A visitor to the works in 1890 observed that it covered: 'an area of fully ten acres. This large space is crowded with workshops, dealing with every department of the industry, in iron, steel, and woodwork; and a vast amount of improved modern machinery is in use, power for the same being supplied by numerous steam engines, located in various parts of the premises. . . . This company have turned out some of the best railway carriage work ever done in England . . . and improved tramway cars also form a feature in which splendid work is being done upon an ever increasing scale. Ballast wagons and trucks adapted for carrying sheep or cattle are likewise among the notable specialties of the concern. . . (which gives) employment to between 700 and 800'. In 1902 the Oldbury Railway Carriage & Wagon Co Ltd was amalgamated into the Metropolitan Amalgamated Railway Carriage & Wagon Co Ltd. Production remained at the Oldbury works until 1932.

Midland Railway Carriage & Wagon Co Ltd

Companies became involved with carriage and wagon building through various routes. The Midland Railway Carriage & Wagon Co Ltd was formed in 1853 to buy railway wagons and let them out on hire to private owners. This enterprise prospered, and in 1864 the company decided to commence the manufacture of its own rolling stock. They bought the vacant 'Midland Works', an appropriately named former railway carriage manufactory situated in Landor Street, Birmingham, the premises of William Alexander Adams since c1851. By 1906, demand for heavier kinds of rolling stock, which Adams' cramped land-locked site was not designed to build, had soared, and so the company purchased the freehold on a 51 acre site in Common Lane, Washwood Heath, alongside the Midland Railway's main B&DJ line. Between 1909 and 1912, a modern carriage works was erected on this site, enabling the Landor Street premises to be closed and disposed of.

In 1919, Cammell Laird & Co Ltd began to manufacture railway rolling stock at the National Ordnance Factory in Nottingham, also acquiring a controlling interest in the Midland Railway Carriage & Wagon Co Ltd that year.

Birmingham Railway Carriage & Wagon Co Ltd

Railway wagon hire was also the means of entry into carriage and wagon building for the Birmingham Railway Carriage & Wagon Co Ltd (BRCW). Established in 1854 as the Birmingham Wagon Co Ltd, by a group of local businessmen, its objects were to finance collieries, coal merchants and other traders to enable them to possess their own railway wagons, either on hire or purchase; to provide the wagons and to maintain them in repair. Construction and maintenance work was sub-contracted to Brown, Marshalls & Co, at Saltley, and the business operated as stated for nine years, until they decided to enter into the manufacture of their own rolling stock. A 10 acre site was bought in Middlemore Road, Smethwick, alongside the GWR's BW&D line, where a new works was erected. In 1876, the company began to build passenger carriages, changing its name accordingly to the familiar BRCW.

New products were identified, tramcars being added to the range c1878, and in 1902 the company was the first to manufacture all steel passenger coaches, under an order from the Central London Railway, later part of the Underground Group. By the end of World War 2, the company's works had grown to cover 60 acres and it employed almost 3,000 people. More and more of its production was for overseas railways, and in the early 1950s the company began to manufacture first railcars, and then diesel locomotives. By the end of the decade, they had secured large orders from the British Transport Commission, building the whole of the Class 104 DMUs; Class 26 locomotives (D5300-D5346); Class 118 DMUs; Class 33 locomotives (D6500-D6597); Class 110 DMUs, and Class 27 locomotives (D5347-D5415), between 1957 and 1962.

The locomotives had been built in collaboration with Sulzer Bros, and one further joint venture with that company, plus AEI, proved to be the BRCW's downfall. This was the Type 4 (later Class 47) diesel-electric prototype locomotive *Lion*. Handed over to British Railways for trials in May 1962, a succession of mechanical and electrical failures saw it limping around the rail network during 1963, and shortly after returning to Smethwick, following a main generator flash over near Huntingdon on 20 January 1964, the BRCW's bankers forced the closure of the company's railway building operations.

Metropolitan Railway Carriage & Wagon Co Ltd

Joseph Wright's former company was reformed as the Metropolitan Railway Carriage & Wagon Co Ltd in 1862. This regained possession of Wright's Old Works from the LNWR, upon the termination of their lease in 1870, and the company developed steadily on both parts of the site. By 1896, it has outgrown its original Articles of Association, and so a new company was formed bearing the same name. In 1902, this much expanded business began the first moves towards the consolidation of the British rolling stock industry, by forming the Metropolitan Amalgamated Railway Carriage & Wagon Co Ltd. Two local firms: Brown, Marshall's & Co Ltd and the Oldbury Railway Carriage & Wagon Co Ltd were taken over, together with the Patent Shaft & Axletree Co Ltd, of Wednesbury, which had been manufacturing its eponymous product since 1835. Production was gradually concentrated at Saltley, older works being closed and disposed of.

Right:
During the 1950s the BRCW built-up a considerable export trade. This 3ft 6in gauge Special Saloon was built for Nigerian Railways and is seen in the yard of the works at Smethwick. *Modern Transport/IAL*

Below right:
The BRCW's final fling was the Type 4 prototype D0260 *Lion*, developed jointly with AEI and Sulzer Bros. This underwent extensive testing on the East Coast main line in 1963, and is seen here at Sandal with the up Yorkshire Pullman. Electrical and Mechanical failures dogged *Lion*, and even though the BRCW's contribution, the body and bogies, performed well, this did not save the company, which ceased carriage building early in 1964. *Eric Treacy*

The scene at Saltley was described by members of the University of Birmingham Engineering Society, who visited the works on 3 May 1911: 'The Smithy consists of three bays, the first of which contains two rows of steam hammers used for forging various parts of the under frames of the carriages. In the second bay are the smiths' hearths and in the third the stamps. . . . The Press Shop is equipped with hydraulic presses from 50 to 500 tons. . . these are mainly used for pressing brackets. . . . The Assembling Shop is divided into three bays, each served by a 10-ton travelling crane, and here the under frames and bogies are put together. . . . The Foundry (where) the axle boxes and number plates are cast. The larger castings are not made in the works, but are obtained from other firms. . . . Before leaving this shop the axle boxes and bearings are fixed on to a dummy axle and tested. . . . The Carpenter's Shop (has) a large Ransome's horizontal log band saw, which travels at the rate of 7,000 feet per minute. The Painting and Erecting Shop (is where) the upper parts of the carriages are made and put together. . . . There was some stock for the London and Brighton new electric service. . . . The Power House contains four Bellis engines each driving a 250kw dc generator and running at 375rpm'.

In 1919 Vickers Ltd acquired the shares of the Metropolitan Amalgamated Railway Carriage & Wagon Co Ltd, and in 1929 they merged their rolling stock interests with those of Cammell Laird & Co Ltd to form the Metropolitan-Cammell Carriage & Wagon Co Ltd, with its head office at Saltley. This name was abbreviated to Metropolitan Cammell Ltd (Metro-Camm) in 1964, and in 1967 the firm moved its head office to the former Midland Railway Carriage & Wagon Co Ltd site at Washwood Heath. Fitful orders from British Rail, and declining demand for tube stock from London

NIGERIAN RAILWAY
SPECIAL SALOON FOR USE OF
H.E. THE GOVERNOR,
NORTHERN REGION.
3'-6" GAUGE REQ.N No 3993/1
BUILDERS
THE BIRMINGHAM RAILWAY
CARRIAGE & WAGON Co. LTD.
SMETHWICK, ENGLAND.

1E08

Left:
Cadbury's works at Bournville once had an extensive private railway system with five miles of track. In this view, taken about 1955, saddle tank locomotive No 10 is seen shunting in waterside sidings.
R. S. Carpenter Collection

Transport, saw Metro-Camm diversify away from railway contracting in the 1970s. Ventures into both bus (Metrobus) and taxi (Metrocab) manufacture helped to buoy the company, which was taken over by GEC on 26 May 1989, and survives in production, albeit with a much reduced works and workforce.

Industrial Lines

In addition to the myriad of lines built by the various railway companies, which contributed to Birmingham's rail network; a number of large companies and concerns built-up substantial internal rail systems on both standard and narrow gauges. A list of those in operation in 1947 is presented in Appendix 4.

By far the greatest track mileage of industrial lines in the Birmingham area was owned and operated by the City Corporation's Electricity, Gas and Water Departments. The Electricity undertaking worked up to 10 locomotives within its two power stations at Nechells and Hams Hall; the latter had the greater complement, plus a 2ft 6in gauge system operated by four petrol driven locomotives. Four gasworks, at Nechells, Saltley, Swan Village and Windsor Street, required a fleet of about 30 locomotives, plus another three at a Wagon Repair Works in Washwood Heath. Here, a fleet of 1,750 trucks was maintained, all of which were necessary as, in cold spells, around 21,000 tons of coal were used by these works each week; and annually, around 1,000,000 tons were required. Birmingham's Water Department also had a standard gauge rail system at Frankley Reservoir. Built to store water received via the Corporation's Elan Aqueduct (built between 1893 and 1906), this required a railway to supply coal to the pumping station there; the line being a sinuous, mile long, branch leading off the Halesowen Railway at Hollyhill Farm, and following the line of the aqueduct as it approached the reservoir.

Of the industrial concerns having internal rail systems, possibly the best known and most extensive were those at the Austin Motor Co at Longbridge, and Cadbury's works at Bournville. The latter branched of the West Suburban line in between Selly Oak and Bournville stations, and described a large loop around the works site. Together with extensive sidings and a canal interchange, the Cadbury system totalled five miles of track, a fleet of nine locomotives supplying coal to the works' power station, and moving raw materials and finished confectionery in and out of the 82 acre site.

Austin's rail system was connected to the Halesowen Railway, and, by virtue of this, also to the Midland Railway's main line at Longbridge. Developed to serve the works' power station, and for internal transport; its role altered with changes in the structure of the British motor industry. Greater standardisation meant an increased sharing of facilities and components, giving 'The Austin's' main line connection greater importance, as body panels and other components were brought in from outlying plants in the British Motor Corporation/British Leyland/Austin Rover/Rover Group empire. Longbridge Works also had its own private station, as noted in Chapter 3, and the workmen's trains, plus the traffic noted above, have served to keep at least this part of the former Halesowen Railway open. All of the tracks within the works were bought from British Rail on 6 March 1968, although the line follows a slightly different course at its present northwestern extremity. Once, a fleet of nine industrial steam locomotives busied themselves around the works system, but now this consists of a few diesels. British Rail locomotives are allowed into the works, to bring in consignments of components or to take out Cartic transporters full of finished vehicles; but all marshalling of loads received or for despatch is done by the company's own locomotives.

Below:
'The Austin' works at Longbridge on 4 June 1966, with Kitson-built 0-6-0ST No 1 *Austin* shunting works' wagons. Ahead is the North Works, the railway passing beneath the Bristol Road South. To the left is Longbridge East signal box, with one platform, formerly used by the workmen's services, visible below the main station building, which was by this time only open for parcels. *R. E. B. Siviter*

Left:
A view inside the shops at Metro-Cammell when the company was producing a series of railcars for Jamaican Railways. *Metropolitan-Cammell Carriage & Wagon Co Ltd*

The *midland metro*

Rapid transit schemes of one form or another have been proposed to solve Birmingham's transport problems over the last 25 years or so, but took more positive steps with the formation of the WMPTA. Upon the abolition of the West Midlands County Council (WMCC) in 1986, the the latter became the joint responsibility of the seven District Councils served by its Executive (Birmingham, Coventry, Dudley, Sandwell, Solihull, Walsall and Wolverhampton). Determined to launch a rapid transit scheme, the PTA sought these Council's views on the identification of possible transport cor-

ridors which could be developed for use by a rapid transit system. From this exercise it emerged that one system could be developed to serve the Black Country and to link this with Birmingham, whilst Coventry was probably better served by a similar but isolated system.

Fleshing out these ideas produced the *midland metro* project, taking a name with optimistic overtones of the country's only successfully completed rapid transit scheme to date in Tyne & Wear. It brought little else other than lessons learned through bitter experience from earlier proposals, but had the benefit of dedicated and enthusiastic support from local politicians. The timing was right. The *midland metro* was not the only rapid transit scheme under consideration in the country at the time, and the Docklands Light Railway was open, proving the powerful effect one such system could have upon the regeneration of a run down area; and one in the heart of the nation's capital to boot. Promotion of the project began on 28 August 1987 and it was given its official launch on 10 September 1987.

The initial scheme

In planning the *midland metro* its engineers visited a number of the newly installed rapid transit schemes in Europe. They found those in Nantes and Grenoble in France to be operating in ways closest to how they envisaged the *midland metro* would function, and used technical information gathered from these systems in the detailed planning of its initial scheme.

The metro's first phase consists of three proposed lines serving the Black Country and the NEC. Estimates put the cost of these at around £200 million, of which it is hoped that up to a half can be obtained through the European Regional Development Fund; that a quarter will come in the form of a Government grant and that the balance will be raised through private sector funding, loans and investments. Line 1 will link Birmingham and Wolverhampton, serving West Bromwich, Wednesbury and Bilston en route. Line 2 will link Birmingham at Five Ways with the NEC, also serving intermediate industrial and housing developments; Line 3 linking Wolverhampton with Dudley by way of Walsall, also serving Wednesfield, Willenhall and Darlaston en route. These lines will rely upon proven technology and will employ lightweight vehicles operating, for the most part, on segregated track with their own right of way. Some of this will parallel existing roads, occupying the central strip on dual carriageways or on segregated portions of existing streets. But the initial lines will make great use of abandoned railway formations, many of which were safeguarded by the former WMCC under the terms of its Structure Plan.

Vehicles and operation

Designs for the metro's vehicles have still to be finalised, but the artists impressions and models used to promote it seem to combine features from those used in Nantes and Grenoble, adorned with the scheme's distinctive livery of white with green and blue lining. The technical parameters adopted by the project's engineers for the vehicles are: Length: 28-30m; Width: 2.65m; Seating capacity: 60-75; Standing capacity: 120-180; Total capacity: 180-255; Floor to platform height (max.): 35cm; No of doors/side: 4 (1.5m wide); Weight: 36-38 tonnes; Average acceleration: 1.2m/sec., and Maximum speed: 80km/h. The metro's lines will be constructed to the following standards: Gauge: 1.435m (Standard gauge); Maximum gradient: 6-8 %; Power supply: 750V dc. The metro will have stops spaced at about every 500-700m; each being unstaffed, but equipped with route maps, second-by-second updated service information and automatic ticket machines; the units operating a minimum service frequency of one every 10min, becoming more frequent at peak times.

Plans and progress

Following a lengthy public consultation period, lasting almost a year, WMPTE prepared their first Parliamentary Bill for powers to construct Line 1 of the initial scheme. This was published on 21 November 1988 and submitted to Parliament on 30 November 1988; describing in minute detail the 11 phases of work involved in constructing this line, including the building of a depot at Wednesbury to house and maintain the metro vehicles. The route begins at the rebuilt Snow Hill station and runs along the disused trackbed of the former BW&D line as far as the Monmore Green in Wolverhampton, where it will rise to road level and continue along Bilston Road before terminating in Market Street, by Sainsbury's. This gives a total length of 21km, of which the street running section forms about 1.8km. There will be 27 stops, many of which will offer bus or rail interchange facilities and/or park and ride provision to the estimated 150,000 people who will be served by it.

The Bill for Line 1 had an easier than expected passage through Parliament during 1989, passing all three readings and finally gaining the Royal Assent on 16 November 1989. Now, as the engineers working on the line put it: 'all we have to do is raise the money!', but there is cautious optimism about the prospect of doing this. Bill No 2 was submitted to Parliament in November 1989. This relates to Lines 2 and 3, the remainder of the initial scheme. Similar public consultation exercises to that engaged in for Line 1 were conducted for these lines, but this time public opposition was encountered to the latter, but once again these initial fears have been overcome.

Curiously, whilst Line 3 has come in for the most public opposition, it is Line 2 which presents the most engineering difficulties. At its city end, the portion from Five Ways to beyond New Street will run underground, with a consequent increase in construction time and cost (an estimated £30 million). Once out of this tunnel, Line 2 differs from the other two lines in the initial scheme by not having an abandoned rail formation to take advantage of. As a result it will wend its way out towards the NEC by means of an ingenious combination of paralleling existing railway lines and roads, plus new rights of way, which will require the construction of embankments and elevated portions of the line.

The eventual network

At its launch in 1987 the *midland metro* was announced as a complete network to serve the West Midlands, the whole scheme being estimated to cost some £800 million and to take upwards of 25 years to complete. The majority of the detailed planning to date has concentrated upon the first three lines and no definite plans have been formulated regarding the remaining routes, although there has been some speculation. An isolated system in Coventry has already been mentioned, but this may be supplemented by additional lines radiating from the centre of Birmingham. The Black Country Councils have shown a keen interest in securing a greater penetration of their areas by the metro, including a line to link Dudley, and its major tourist attractions of the Zoo, Black Country Museum and proposed Black Country World, with West Bromwich and, en route, InterCity rail travellers at Sandwell & Dudley station. In addition, Dudley Council, whose area was poorly served by the initial metro scheme, has pressed for extensions to the network as far as Stourbridge and Halesowen.

Prospects

Five years of planning and public relations have secured the *midland metro* project a high public profile, but as yet there is nothing to show for it. The flaming torch has also been snatched from the project's hands by the Manchester Metrolink scheme, which will have recognisable 'tram-like' vehicles running in that city's streets later this year. Funding is undoubtedly the problem, but some are beginning to ask why, if one major British city can secure this, then why not another; especially the country's second city? They fear that the *midland metro* project is in danger of becoming just another transport white elephant, and worry that the next tram may already have gone. Let us hope not.

Appendices

Appendix 1: Resolution of the South Staffordshire Ironmasters regarding the formation of a rail road between Birmingham and Liverpool and Manchester

Wolverhampton, April 7, 1824

We the undersigned propose to subscribe for the number of shares attached to our respective names at £100 each, for the purpose of forming and carrying into effect a railroad from Birmingham and the Staffordshire and Shropshire Ironworks to Liverpool and Manchester for the conveyance of iron and other goods to and from the above mentioned places.

W. & J. S. Sparrow & Co	Wolverhampton	20
M. Grazebrook Iron	Stourbridge	10
J. Bagnall & Sons	West Bromwich	10
Francis Finch	West Bromwich	5
Henry Hunt	West Bromwich	20
John Bradley & Co	Stourbridge	50
John Walker	West Bromwich	10
John Barker for George Jones		10
Phillip Williams & Son	Wednesbury Oak	20
Caponfield Furnace Co		10
Thomas Attwood		10
George Attwood		10
George Jackson		10
Icorns & Son	Liverpool	20
T. G. Bunt	Brades	10
J. W. Umith	Birmingham	10
John Phillips	Birmingham	10
William Orme Foster	Stourbridge	5
R .Sparrow	Birmingham	10
Henry Chuter	London	10
Thomas Webb		10
Zepheniah Parker		10
W. Aston & Co		15
Thomas Millington	Brades	2

Appendix 2: Weekday train departures from Birmingham New Street, October 1938, 17.00 to 18.00

Platform	*Time*	*Destination*
6	17.00	Local stations to Aschurch, via Redditch and Alcester
2	17.00	Restaurant Car service to Euston, via Northampton
4	17.00	Local stations to Derby
2 (Bay)	17.04	Local stations to Stafford, Crewe and Liverpool
1	17.05	Local stations to Lichfield Trent Valley
1 (Bay)	17.10	Berkswell, Kenilworth, Warwick, Leamington
6 (Bay)	17.12	Five Ways, Selly Oak, Bournville, King's Norton
5	17.15	Local stations to Leicester
1	17.15	Local stations to Rugby
2	17.20	Local stations to Four Oaks
5	17.20	Local stations to Redditch
2	17.23	Stour Valley line local service to Wolverhampton
6	17.26	Local stations to Aschurch, via Worcester and Great Malvern
3	17.30	Lichfield (City & Trent Valley), via Walsall and Rugeley
4	17.35	Local stations to Walsall, via Castle Bromwich and Aldridge
2	17.36	All stations to Perry Barr, via the Soho Loop line
6	17.40	Restaurant Car service to Bristol (Temple Meads)
2	17.40	Local stations to Four Oaks
5	17.42	Local stations to King's Norton, via the Camp Hill line
1 (Bay)	17.45	Local stations to Coventry, Kenilworth, Warwick, Leamington
5	17.46	Local to Gloucester, via Bromsgrove, Worcester and Aschurch
4	17.50	Manchester (Central), via Derby, Nottingham and Buxton
3	17.50	Restaurant Car to Manchester (London Road) and on to Liverpool
2	17.50	Local stations to Walsall, via Aston and Perry Barr
2	17.57	Stour Valley line local to Dudley via Dudley Port

Appendix 3: Trains working into Curzon Street (Goods) 10 October 1935

Departure from:	*Time due:*	*Traffic brought:*
Camden	00.13	London, Boxmoor, Northampton, Aston, South of Thames stations
Liverpool	00.21	Meat and fruit
Liverpool	00.40	Liverpool fruit and sheds
Birkenhead	01.05	Birkenhead, London roads, Chester, Holyhead
Camden	01.13	Londons, south of Thames traffic, Bedfordshire vegetable traffic, Aylesbury butter
Warrington	01.48	Warrington, Prescot, L&Y traffic
Bushbury	02.42	Wolverhampton, Albion, Ettingshall Road, Spon Lane, Soho, Tipton and Bloomfield
Peterborough	03.26	Lincolnshire vegetable traffic via Peterborough and London traffic
Liverpool	04.20	Stafford and Liverpool
Bescot	04.35	Coal
Midland	04.45	Redditch, Evesham, Bristol and Gloucester
Manchester	04.57	Manchester late wagons, odd norths
Bescot	05.43	Coal and later Norths and Rugeley
Coventry	05.50	Londons, south of Thames wagons
Peterborough	06.35	Kings Cross, Farringdon Street (vegetable traffic ex GN stations via Peterborough), Leicester
Burton	07.02	Nottingham, Derby, Doncaster, Derby Mid., Hull L&NE, Sheffield (GN vegetable traffic via Burton)

Aston	07.28	Manchester Docks Traffic and odd Norths
Midland	10.40	Bristol, Bath and odd wagons ex Midland Co.
Bescot	11.05	Kidderminster, Worcester, Cradley, Lye, Stourbridge
Bescot	15.10	Hereford, odd North traffic, Southam Road cement
Lichfield	15.25	Shenstone, Blake Street, Sutton Coldfield
Vauxhall	17.41	Empties
Bescot	17.41	Coal and odd North wagons
Midland	18.55	Midland traffic
Midland	18.55	Midland traffic
Aston	20.53	Tranship loads
Midland	22.15	Midland traffic
Bescot	23.31	Dudley, Wednesbury, Walsall, Darlaston, late wagons ex North

Appendix 4: Industrial railway systems in the Birmingham area, 1947

Standard Gauge Systems
Adams & Benson Ltd, West Bromwich
Albright & Wilson Ltd, Oldbury
Austin Motor Company, Longbridge
Birmingham Chamber of Commerce, Castle Bromwich
Birmingham Railway Carriage & Wagon Co, Smethwick
Birmingham Small Arms (BSA) Co Ltd, Small Heath
Birmingham Tame & Rea District Drainage Board, Washwood Heath
British Cyanides Ltd, Oldbury
British Thompson Houston Co Ltd, Rowley Regis
Cadbury Bros Ltd, Bournville
City of Birmingham Electric Supply Department, Hams Hall Power Station
City of Birmingham Electric Supply Department, Nechells Power Station
City of Birmingham Gas Department, Nechells Works
City of Birmingham Gas Department, Saltley Works
City of Birmingham Gas Department, Swan Village Works
City of Birmingham Gas Department, Wagon Repair Works, Washwood Heath
City of Birmingham Gas Department, Windsor Street Works
City of Birmingham Water Department, Frankley Reservoir
County Borough of Smethwick Gas Department, Soho
Darlaston Steel & Iron Co Ltd
Dunlop Tyre & Rubber Co, Fort Dunlop
F. H. Lloyd & Co, James Bridge Works, Darlaston
ICI (Metals) Ltd, Witton
John Wilson, Contractor, Birmingham
Metropolitan-Cammell Carriage, Wagon & Finance Co, Oldbury
Metropolitan-Cammell Carriage, Wagon & Finance Co, Saltley
Midland Tar Distillers Ltd, Oldbury Works
Mitchells & Butlers Ltd, Smethwick
Patent Shaft & Axletree Co, Ltd, Wednesbury
Rubery Owen Co. Ltd, Victoria Iron Works, Darlaston
Sandwell Colliery Co, West Bromwich
South Staffs Mond Gas Co, Dudley Port
Wolseley Motors Ltd, Adderley Park Works
Wolseley Motors Ltd. Washwood Heath Works

Narrow Gauge Systems (2ft 6in)
City of Birmingham Electric Supply Department, Hams Hall Power Station

Narrow Gauge Systems (2ft)
Birmingham Tame & Rea District Drainage Board, Minworth
D. McKenzie & Co. Shakespeare Drive, Shirley
Midland Macadams Ltd, Blue Rock Quarry, Oldbury
Midland Rolling & Haulage Co, South Yardley

Appendix 5: Birmingham locomotive shed allocations, 1933; 1950 & 1965

The following lists show the steam locomotive allocations at three sheds in the Birmingham area: Monument Lane, built by the LNWR; Saltley, built by the Midland Railway, and Tyseley, built by the GWR. Allocations are given for March-May 1933, when many pre-Grouping locomotive classes were still in use; July 1950 and March 1965. The information for these lists was gleaned from a variety of sources, including the *Railway Observer*, the *Journal of the Stephenson Locomotive Society*, and various works published by Ian Allan Ltd.

Monument Lane Shed (ex-LNWR)

March 1933 (Code 10M)

1128	1129	1160	1170	1172	1173	1174	1777	1818	3005	3006
3007	3008	3009	3010	5338	5339	5340	5706	5707	5708	5709
5710	5711	5715	6648	6671	6672	6820	6821	6822	6823	6923
6924	6925	6926	6927	6928	6956	6957	6958	6985	7310	7399
7591	7594	7811	8094	8095	8099	8265	8296	8299	8561	8562
8564	8565	8566	16450	16451						

July 1950 (Code 3E)

41111	41116	41151	41172	42262	42264
42267	42489	42263	42265	42469	42579
43231	44057	44361	44506	44514	44592
44829	45015	45390	45418	46900	46912
46922					

Monument Lane (Code 21E) shed ceased steam working on 16 February1962

Saltley Shed (ex-Midland Railway)

May 1933 (Code 3)

2	18	19	276	368	369	396	397	439	486	505
507	508	509	510	511	512	513	517	668	710	711
712	713	715	716	745	1348	1361	1430	1699	1700	1727
1773	1781	1871	1879	2014	2015	2016	2023	2024	2025	2026
2027	2028	2029	2030	2031	2032	2033	2035	2036	2037	2038
2039	2630	2729	2818	2819	2834	2844	2928	2978	3063	3074
3116	3117	3203	3210	3223	3224	3277	3316	3336	3339	3356
3425	3431	3432	3435	3490	3491	3492	3516	3517	3518	3519
3520	3521	3522	3525	3526	3527	3529	3530	3531	3533	3535
3536	3540	3542	3543	3544	3551	3568	3570	3594	3615	3624
3627	3640	3644	3667	3673	3674	3675	3677	3680	3681	3683
3684	3686	3687	3688	3689	3690	3691	3693	3695	3696	3698
3699	3822	3869	3870	3871	3874	3908	3911	3912	3913	3924
3925	3926	3928	3939	4092	4125	4126	4133	4269	4270	4405
4406	4523	4524	4525	7113	7114	12105		12107		13059
13060		13061		13063		13064		13139		13195
13196		13197		13198		13199		13200		16720
16721		16722								

July 1950 (Code 21A)

40097	40115	40117	40171	40175	40486
40511	40928	41035	41046	41699	41856
41879	42141	42326	42337	42754	42758
42764	42790	42818	42822	42824	42825
42826	42827	42829	42857	42890	42900
42903	43011	43014	43043	43044	43048
43201	43210	43214	43223	43225	43246
43257	43284	43321	43336	43339	43374
43433	43435	43441	43443	43484	43490
43491	43507	43531	43540	43544	43594
43620	43621	43624	43627	43644	43673
43674	43680	43684	43690	43698	43759
43762	43791	43800	43812	43843	43845
43855	43869	43879	43891	43911	43912
43939	43940	43941	43946	43949	43951

43968	43986	44010	44023	44026	44049
44084	44088	44092	44108	44112	44137
44145	44150	44165	44176	44179	44184
44185	44187	44190	44200	44203	44213
44224	44248	44263	44289	44317	44362
44406	44413	44418	44427	44475	44515
44516	44520	44524	44525	44538	44545
44567	44571	44580	44591	44659	44660
44661	44666	44717	44804	44805	44810
44813	44814	44842	44919	44920	44966
45186	45265	45268	45269	45273	45447
47276	47301	47313	47638	48027	48317
48336	48339	48351	48388	48401	48417
48420	48424	48669	48687	48700	48763
58167	58230	58231	58261	58271	

March 1965 (Code 2E)

44663	44666	44775	44776	44777	44829
44843	44859	44944	44945	44965	44966
44981	45052	45058	45264	45280	45369
45447	46443	46448	46454	46526	48085
48109	48133	48220	48339	48351	48629
48646	48669	76038	76043	76048	76052
92029	92125	92135	92136	92137	92138
92139	92150	92151	92152	92155	92164

Saltley shed officially closed to steam on 6 March 1967

Tyseley Shed (GWR)

March 1933 (Code TYS)

564	656	766	767	1080	1529	1540	1549	1554	1742	1763
1788	1803	1812	1950	1955	2036	2052	2071	2078	2092	2145
2392	2439	2460	2602	2612	2618	2621	2662	2712	2714	2717
2813	2814	2834	2837	2874	2875	2878	2941	3001	3274	3281
3327	3359	3360	3369	3373	3374	3381	3403	3417	3423	3450
4314	4333	4334	4362	4372	4386	4501	4579	4580	5100	5102
5103	5104	5109	5111	5136	5142	5143	5145	5146	5149	5151
5162	5164	5165	5170	5171	5173	5174	5176	5177	5178	5181
5317	5348	5724	5725	5726	5742	6339	6374	6723	6745	6746
6747	7301	7309	7320	7714	7758	7797	8726			

July 1950 (Code 84E)

2203	2238	2257	2296	2848	2849	2867	3016	3101	3151	3180
3624	3625	3650	3653	3657	3658	3660	3664	3673	3689	3693
3743	3751	3769	3837	4101	4106	4107	4110	4111	4116	4147
4157	4159	4165	4166	4170	4172	4605	4648	4683	4924	4959
4964	4980	5102	5106	5152	5156	5164	5166	5171	5175	5177
5182	5187	5188	5190	5198	5333	5346	5369	5370	5700	5712
5736	5738	5745	5790	5907	5909	5916	5927	5950	5993	5997
6336	6611	6630	6843	6847	6853	6858	6866	6904	6942	6971
7317	7438	7713	7735	7758	7800	8180	8410	8415	8452	8700
8784	9008	9010	9608	9610	9614	9635	9680	9682	9724	9733
9748	9753	9793	9798							

March 1965 (Code 2A)

3625	4111	4125	4155	4158	4178	4635	5606	5658	5684	5988
6633										
6667	6668	6681	6853	6861	6866	6879	6922	6926	6930	6964
7908										
7915	7929	8109	9753	9774						

48415	48474	92001	92118	92212	92217
92002	92204	92215	92223		

Tyseley shed officially closed to steam on 7 November 1966

Overleaf:
The down 'Clansman' departs Birmingham New Street behind Class 87 No 87008 *City of Liverpool* on 18 March 1987. *Brian Morrison*

TOWN COUNTRY
Inter-City

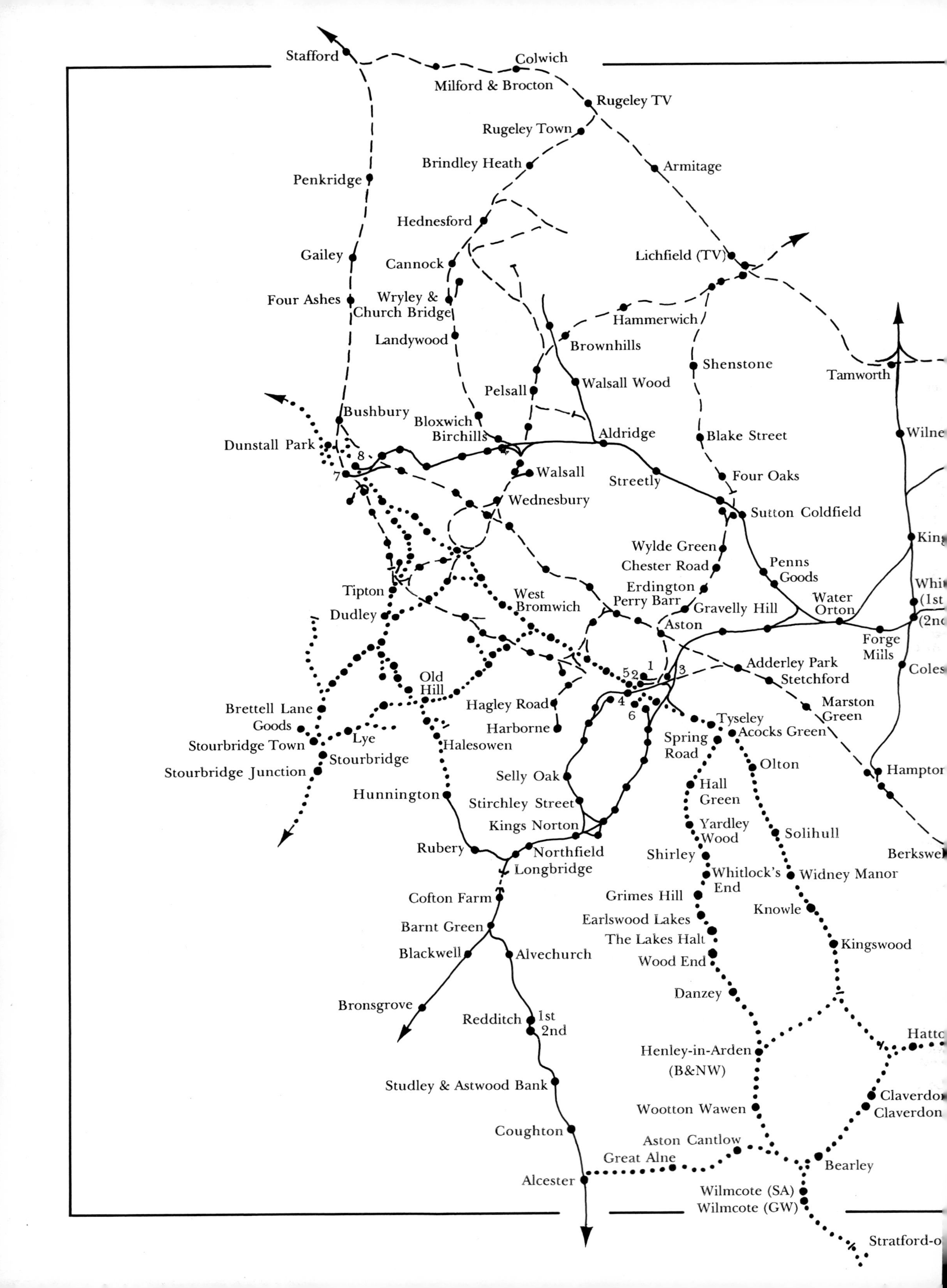
Stafford
Colwich
Milford & Brocton
Rugeley TV
Rugeley Town
Brindley Heath
Armitage
Penkridge
Hednesford
Gailey
Cannock
Lichfield (TV)
Four Ashes
Wryley & Church Bridge
Hammerwich
Landywood
Brownhills
Shenstone
Tamworth
Walsall Wood
Pelsall
Bushbury
Bloxwich
Birchills
Aldridge
Blake Street
Wilne
Dunstall Park
Walsall
Streetly
Four Oaks
Wednesbury
Sutton Coldfield
Wylde Green
Chester Road
Penns Goods
Erdington
Perry Barr
Water Orton
Tipton
West Bromwich
Gravelly Hill
Dudley
Aston
Forge Mills
Adderley Park
Stetchford
Old Hill
Brettell Lane Goods
Hagley Road
Marston Green
Tyseley
Acocks Green
Stourbridge Town
Lye
Harborne
Spring Road
Stourbridge
Halesowen
Stourbridge Junction
Olton
Selly Oak
Hall Green
Hunnington
Stirchley Street
Kings Norton
Yardley Wood
Solihull
Rubery
Northfield
Shirley
Longbridge
Whitlock's End
Widney Manor
Cofton Farm
Grimes Hill
Knowle
Earlswood Lakes
Barnt Green
The Lakes Halt
Kingswood
Blackwell
Alvechurch
Wood End
Danzey
Bronsgrove
Redditch
1st
2nd
Henley-in-Arden (B&NW)
Studley & Astwood Bank
Wootton Wawen
Coughton
Aston Cantlow
Great Alne
Bearley
Alcester
Wilmcote (SA)
Wilmcote (GW)
Hampton
Berkswel
Coles
Hatto
Claverdo
Claverdon
Stratford-o